The French Experience from Republic to Monarchy,
1792–1824

The French Experience from Republic to Monarchy, 1792–1824

New Dawns in Politics, Knowledge and Culture

Edited by

Máire F. Cross
Senior Lecturer in French Studies
University of Sheffield

and

David Williams
Professor of French
University of Sheffield

First published 2000 by
PALGRAVE
Houndmills, Basingstoke, Hampshire RG21 6XS and
175 Fifth Avenue, New York, N.Y. 10010
Companies and representatives throughout the world

PALGRAVE is the new global academic imprint of
St. Martin's Press LLC Scholarly and Reference Division and
Palgrave Publishers Ltd (formerly Macmillan Press Ltd).

ISBN 0–333–77265–2

This book is printed on paper suitable for recycling and
made from fully managed and sustained forest sources.

A catalogue record for this book is available
from the British Library.

Library of Congress Cataloging-in-Publication Data
The French experience from republic to monarchy, 1792–1824 : new dawns
in politics, knowledge and culture / edited by Máire F. Cross and David
Williams.
        p. cm.
Includes bibliographical references and index.
Papers presented at a conference held at the University of Sheffield,
March 1999.
ISBN 0–333–77265–2 (cloth)
    1. France—Civilization—1789–1830—Congresses. 2. France—History—
–First Republic, 1792–1804—Congresses. 3. France—History—
–Restoration, 1814–1830—Congresses. I. Cross, Máire. II. Williams,
David, 1938–
DC33.5 .F72 2000
944.06—dc21
                                                            00–040455

10 9   8   7   6   5   4   3   2   1
09 08 07 06 05 04 03 02 01 00

Printed in Great Britain by Antony Rowe Ltd, Chippenham, Wiltshire

Contents

List of Tables

Acknowledgements

This volume is the result of the successful two-day conference which took place in Sheffield University in March 1999. The idea of exploring the period 1792-1824 arose from research collaboration between two colleagues in the French department of the University of Sheffield, Professor David Williams and Dr Máire Cross. Financial support for the conference was generously given by the cultural service of the French Embassy, the Association of Modern and Contemporary France, the company SDL of Sheffield and their own French department. Colin Lawson's illustrated paper and his lunchtime recital with players Jonathan Gooing (fortepiano) and Ingrid Pearson (clarinet) from Sheffield's music department on period instruments embellished the proceedings. Lynda Laskey was the great behind-the-scenes conference organiser, and Conrad Smith did a sterling job in the final preparation of the manuscript for the press. To all of the above, the editors would like to express their heartfelt gratitude.

Notes on the Contributors

David Andress is Senior Lecturer in Modern European History at the University of Portsmouth. He received his DPhil from the University of York in 1995, and since then has published a number of articles on politics and popular culture in Paris during the French Revolution, together with his first book, *French Society in Revolution, 1789–1799* (1999). His second book, *Firing on the People: Popular Politics, Revolutionary Culture and the Champ de Mars Massacre*, will be published shortly.

Ian H. Birchall was formerly a Senior Lecturer in French at Middlesex University, and is now an independent writer specialising in the history of socialism. He is the author of *The Spectre of Babeuf* (1997), and various articles on Babeuf, including two in the *British Journal for Eighteenth-Century Studies*; he has also contributed an article in the forthcoming publication of the proceedings of the 1997 Babeuf bicentenary conference. He has published translations of Alfred Rosmer and Victor Serge, and is currently completing a book on Sartre and the French anti-Stalinist Left.

Patrice Bret obtained his History doctorate in *sciences politiques,* and is a research fellow jointly at the *Centre de recherche en histoire des sciences et des techniques de la Cité des sciences et de l'industrie* and the *Centre national de la recherche scientifique* (CRHST / CSI; CNRS). A member of the editorial board of *Annales historiques de la Révolution française,* he is currently working on the history of public institutions and networks in relation to technical and scientific practices, and on the history of public policies on inventions and military research.

Laurence Brockliss is currently Fellow and Tutor in Modern History at Magdalen College, Oxford. His primary research interest is in the history of education, science and medicine in early modern France. His publications include *French Higher Education in the Seventeenth and Eighteenth Centuries: a Cultural History* (1987) and, with Colin Jones, *The Medical World of Early Modern France* (1997). He is at present writing a study of the Enlightenment in Provence based around the life of the physician, natural historian and antiquarian, Esprit Calvet of Avignon (1728–1810).

Jean-Claude Caron, *maître de conférence* in Contemporary History at the Université de Besançon, works on the nineteenth-century social and political history of France, and in particular on the history of youth and education. His publications include *Générations romantiques. Les Etudiants de Paris et le quartier latin (1814–1851)* (1991), *A l'école de la violence. Châtiments et sévices dans l'institution scolaire au XIXe siècle* (1999); and an article in *l'Histoire des jeunes en Occident,* ed. G. Levi et J.-C. Schmitt (1996).

Barbara T. Cooper is Professor in the Department of Languages, Literatures and Culture in the University of New Hampshire. Her primary areas of research include French drama of the Restoration and Romantic periods and the works of Alexandre Dumas *père.* Among her recent publications are *French Dramatists, 1789–1914,* volume 192 of *Dictionary of Literary Biography* (1998) of which she is editor; 'Ancelot's Louis IX and the Definition of National Identity in Restoration France', in Norman Buford (ed.), *French Literature Series* (1999); 'Comment peut-on parler caraïbe ? Innovations et traditions linguistiques dans *Christophe Colomb,* de Pixérécourt', in Graham Falconer, Andrew Oliver and Dorothy Speirs (eds), *Langues du XIXe siècle* (1998); 'Tavernes et auberges : Elément du spectacle romantique dans Kean et d'autres pièces de Dumas, Hugo et Musset' in Georges Zaragoza (ed.), *Dramaturgies romantiques* (forthcoming).

Malcolm Crook is Professor of French History at Keele University. He has published extensively on the French Revolution, and his most recent book is entitled *Napoleon Comes to Power: Democracy and Dictatorship in Revolutionary France, 1795–1804* (1998). He is currently working on the development of electoral culture in nineteenth-century France.

Máire F. Cross is a Senior Lecturer in the French Department at the University of Sheffield. A member of the editorial board of *Modern and Contemporary France,* she has numerous articles on the politics of nineteenth and twentieth-century feminism, as well as a book, co-authored with Felicia Gordon, *Early French Feminisms: a Passion for Liberty* (1996). She jointly edited, with Sheila Perry, the proceedings of the 1995 ASMCF conference, *Voices of France: Social, Political and Cultural Identity* (1997) and *Population and Social Policy in France* (1997). Recent publications on Flora Tristan include 'L'itinéraire d'une femme engagée dans la cité, Flora Tristan. Un exemple à éviter ?' in Alain Corbin, Jacqueline Lalouette, Michèle Riot-Sarcey (eds), *Femmes dans la cité 1815–1871* (1998), and

'Flora Tristan's Socialist Propaganda in Provincial France 1843–44', in Bertrand Taithe and Tim Thornton (eds), *Propaganda, Political Rhetoric and Identity 1300–2000*, (1999). She is currently working on the socialist campaign of Flora Tristan.

Denise Z. Davidson is an Assistant Professor of History at Georgia State University in Atlanta. Her research has focused on cultural practices, urban life, gender and class in early nineteenth-century France. She is currently working on a book based on her PhD thesis, *Constructing Order in Post-Revolutionary France: Women's Identity and Cultural Practices 1800–1830*.

Joël Felix is a Lecturer in the Department of French at the University of Reading, and was formerly a research officer for the French Ministry of Finance from 1989 to 1997. He continued to develop his research interest, begun when a student at the EHESS in Paris, on the nobility of Paris and the Ile de France, 1787–1848. His main research interest is in public finance questions and the involvement of the nobility in business. He has published the following books: *Les Magistrats du parlement de Paris 1771–1790* (1990); with Edna Lemay, *Dictionnaire des Constituants*, 2 vols (1991); *Finances et politique au Siècle des Lumières: le ministère L'Averdy 1763–1768* (forthcoming).

Felicia Gordon currently holds a Leverhulme Emeritus Fellowship. She has researched and published extensively on literary criticism, philosophy, literature, and women's and feminist history. Her recent publications include *Early French Feminisms, 1830–1940: a Passion for Liberty*, with Máire Cross (1996); 'Les Femmes et l'ambition', in *Madeleine Pelletier (1874–1939): Logique et infortunes d'un combat pour l'égalité*, ed. Christine Bard (1992); 'A Parodic Strategy' – Sartre's *Les Mots*', *Nottingham French Studies*, 23 (1984), 51–68, reprinted in *Sartre*, ed. Christina Howells (1995); 'Legitimation and Irony in Tolstoy and Fontane', in *Scarlet Letters: Fictions of Adultery from Antiquity to the 1990s*, ed. Nicholas White and Naomi Segal (1997). Her current project is a book on the life and feminist writing of Marie Madeleine Jodin.

Colin Lawson has an international profile as a performer on historical clarinets, and holds the Chair of Performance Studies at Goldsmiths College in the University of London. His publications include Cambridge monographs on the Mozart Clarinet Concerto and Brahms's Clarinet Quintet, and he is editor of *The Cambridge Companion to the Clarinet*.

He is co-editor of a new series of Cambridge Handbooks to the Historical Performance of Music and co-author of *The Historical Performance of Music: an Introduction*. His book *The Early Clarinet: a Practical Guide* will be published shortly.

Munro Price is Senior Lecturer in the Department of European Studies at the University of Bradford. He is the author of *Preserving the Monarchy: the comte de Vergennes, 1774–1787* (1995) and (with John Hardman) *Louis XVI and the comte de Vergennes: Correspondence, 1774–1787* (1998), as well as several articles on late eighteenth-century French politics. In 1998 he was awarded a Leverhulme Research Fellowship to work on his next book, a study of the French Monarchy and the Revolution.

David Williams is Professor of French at the University of Sheffield. He is the author of numerous books and articles on eighteenth-century France, and has particular interests in Voltaire and Condorcet. He is a former President of the British Society for Eighteenth-Century Studies, and is a member of the executive of the Voltaire Foundation, and of the editorial board of the Voltaire Complete Works. His recent publications include *Voltaire: Political Writings* (1994) and *The Enlightenment* (1999). Following the award of an AHRB research fellowship, he is currently writing a book on Condorcet's political thought.

David Wisner is currently Associate Professor in History, and Chair of the Department of History and International Relations at The American College of Thessaloniki, Thessaloniki, Greece. His research to date has focused on the French Enlightenment, the cultural, intellectual and political origins of the French Revolution, and the cultural and institutional legacy of the Revolution in post-Revolutionary France. He has published a monograph in *Studies on Voltaire and the Eighteenth Century*, in addition to numerous articles in journals including *French History*, the *Journal of the History of Collections*, *Annales historiques de la Révolution française*, and the *Journal of the History of Ideas*. He has most recently completed a book-length manuscript on French neo-classicism.

Part I

1
New Dawns in the Making of Modern France: the Consequences of Revolutionary Change

Máire Cross and David Williams

'...the Revolution in France is the great ingredient in the cauldron'.[1]

English intellectual visitors to Paris in the early 1790s such as the poet, William Wordsworth and Mary Wollstonecraft, author of *A Vindication of the Rights of Woman*, were eager to witness for themselves and express their enthusiasm for the dawning of a new political era in France.[2] Their joy turned to shock at the violence of the public executions by guillotine and the massacres for which they were unprepared.

The fascination with the events of the Revolution itself as a dramatic process of change remains to this day. As this twentieth century closes and the focus is on wondering what the future millennium will hold for societal changes, historians are also affected by the *fin de siècle* bug. As they devise new ways of assessing the past there is a temptation to look at other turns of centuries as important markers in identifiable processes with starting and finishing moments. While the idea for this volume began along similar lines the editors have found that considerable emphasis is to be placed on the interpretation of the end of the eighteenth and beginning of the nineteenth centuries as one with several starting moments. New dawns of opportunity to break with the past occurred rather more frequently than many would have wished with political instability continuing after the establishment of the First Republic in 1792. It goes without saying that the end of the eighteenth and beginning of the nineteenth centuries are blurred by the momentous events of the French Revolution. So momentous was it that its completion is still in question. However, that debate is not the concern of this volume. Our prime concern was to attempt to bridge the gulf which separates studies of both centuries. Traditionally there are those who study the Enlightenment period and rarely venture beyond the fall of the monarchy in 1792, or Year I of the revolutionary calendar. It is equally conventional for nineteenth-century historians to take the period 1789 to 1914 as a block beginning either with this new era as a new dawn or with the restoration of 1815.[3] The editors wished to explore ways of crossing the great historiographical divide of 'before' and 'after' 1789 in order to make connections between their own research interests, and provide an overview of the period.

Why 1792? The strength of feeling about the achievement of, or the necessity of, further revolution was rife almost before it was under way and still arouses controversy.[4] Taking the implementation of the new state apparatus of the First Republic as the first new dawn set the pace for our project and facilitated the exploration of the ways in which the revolutionary principles of freedom from court patronage and equality of opportunity in public life were implemented in practice. What were the windows of opportunity for those on the lookout for new freedoms as in the case of thinkers like Jodin and Babeuf, for instance? How did individuals adapt to the ever-changing political landscape in order to benefit from, or become trusty servants of, the new regimes? Artists, scientists, inventors all needed state patronage in order to survive but how were they to know what form this new patronage would take if the very new structures kept being altered by the next new dawn heralding the next type of political regime, and with it new political masters? It was vital to be able to successfully network if one wanted to succeed well, or even just survive. How did scientists and educationalists lobby the new masters without losing their jobs or their heads? Equally, how did the State create its legitimacy in the new structures it sought to impose in the fields of science, education and culture? How did new values shape new institutions of education and research to reflect the promise of a new dawn?

New dawns start off well or badly according to one's viewpoint. For those wishing to see the destruction of the old oppressive order the dawn could not break quickly enough. During the First Republic (1792–99), the Directory (1795–99), the Consulate (1799–1804), the Empire (1804–14), the Hundred Days (1815), and the Restoration of the Bourbon Monarchy of Louis XVIII (1815–24) the actors were highly desirous of making an impact on a new society in order either to turn back the clock or to advance in the name of progress.

This book is not about controversial interpretations nor about the political institutional changes from Republic to Monarchy, which for long held pride of place in the great historical narratives of previous generations. Yet these political institutions must not be ignored. They are the familiar framework into which the chapters slot. Little is mentioned directly of the old values of the *ancien régime*, yet they are present by implication: the actress Jodin's life and values provide a succinct critique. Likewise, the attempt of the oldest political survivor, the Bishop of Pamiers, to recommend a reformed constitutional monarchy remind us of the shortcomings of the reign of Louis XVIII, restored by European powers anxious to be rid of the troublesome Revolution. Mockery of old Pamiers' outdated appearance underscores values of the monarchy in its crepuscular state. However, many of the *ancien régime*'s noble families, customs and practices had survived only to re-emerge in new guises in successive regimes. We learn much about the mentality and values of the First Republic through the functioning of the Ministry of the Interior struggling to take over and fill the space left by the patronage system of the old order. It is not hard to distinguish Napoleon's authority over sectors like education. He channelled the revolutionary momentum via an increasingly centralised state to re-legitimise it into his own dawn from Consul to Emperor. His shadow lurks in the background of university institutions and electoral systems.

The authors of the chapters which follow explain how changes occurred according to opportunities in specific areas. Each has individual significance, but considered collectively they crystallise the spirit of the age, one of a culture of transition and movement. Looking at history 'from below' has the advantage of going behind the political scenes to get a closer look at how the ways of change affected different classes and groupings. Important though it is the social question has not featured in this volume. Rather these chapters fit into the more recent phenomenon of cultural history interested largely in the transmission of values through representations of 'mentalities, sensibilities and emotions'.[5] Through the cultural history approach these chapters indicate clearly that there were many more new dawns beyond political events which have not yet been fully explored. It is a period of contradictions. Many feared that the revolutionaries had gone much too far when the execution of the King and Queen sealed the founding of the First Republic. The shaky start is reflected in the turmoil of the development of new state functions which took over from the role of the *ancien régime* court in patronage and control of knowledge. How individuals and values of the old world adapted to new opportunities has yet to be fully appreciated. The actress's challenge to the old regime went virtually unnoticed until the development of feminist history in the closing years of the twentieth century. By contrast the off-stage historical part of the royal personage of King Louis XVIII in this volume is symbolic of his distant influence on the shaping of modern France. The best and worst service

Louis XVIII rendered to France in 1824 was his death in office, the first sign of a 'normal' end of an era as it was the first time a reigning monarch had died in his bed since the death of Louis XV in 1774.

The succession of Charles X was a further dawning of conservative hopes for institutional stability, and was to be a tough test for a rescued monarchical regime. The French Revolutionary period had caused such an upheaval to the institutions of France that further revolutions were not far off. Moreover, its impact beyond 1824 is still being assessed. True, the main political events have been recorded for posterity but the more discreet areas of change in culture, science, education and their relation to new political practices have yet to be assessed. Many combinations of Revolution to Republic or Monarchy to Republic exist in studies of the period.[6] By choosing the more unusual linear development from Republic to Monarchy this collection shows how the creative forces of knowledge, begun during the Enlightenment, become part of the new value system of French society in the nineteenth century, a period equally rich in cultural expression and political upheaval. Rather than limit the scope of the book to one discipline of education, culture or science the editors have assembled the work of specialists in several quite different fields where collaboration is not usual. They show that there is a common thread running throughout, namely the politics of dismantling the old regime, building a new one and maintaining or discarding new values, and that this process paralleled the retention or rejection of institutions according to their political usefulness. For clinical practices, musical performances and scientific research, the period should have been a glorious dawn, given the rapidity of technological advance. France was after all the cultural leader of Europe in 1800.

Cultural expression diversified considerably during the nineteenth century. Many promising developments did not come to fruition as quickly as one might have anticipated in 1824. These chapters show that against a background of political changes from 1792 to 1824, which in themselves provided many new opportunities, the growth of new state structures was a function of the successful bedding-down of new values and practices. Modern France developed almost in spite of the changing political landscape and the stringency of Napoleonic wars. Equally important in the making of modern France was a laborious process of transformation in all fields of knowledge, caused by the transmission of values and the development of modern political processes, but whose significance has only become apparent 120 years after the slow dawning of the Third Republic which finally laid to rest the era of monarchy and bonapartism.

Part I of this collection illuminates from different angles relatively unexplored corners of this new political landscape that was emerging in France as the eighteenth century turned into the nineteenth. Some of the contributions in this part of the volume are concentrated chronologically on the Revolution itself and its immediate aftermath, but others will take the reader forward to the Napoleonic era and the Restoration.

In her study of the career and writings of Marie Madeleine Jodin, Felicia Gordon rehabilitates the work of one of the earliest feminists of the Revolution whose call for the elimination of prostitution, the establishment of a female legislature, the right to divorce, welfare provision for poor women, and numerous other proposals relating to the improvement of women's lives anticipates the work of Olympe de Gouges and Mary Wollstonecraft. Jodin's defence of women's rights to citizenship and honourable status (even for actresses) exposed a glaring omission in the reformist programme of 1789 with its promise of a new dawn for only one-half of the human race. The explosive issue of representation in the Revolution is continued by David Andress in his study of the links between political debate and the politicised theatre of the Terror years. Andress relocates the evolving concepts of 'the people', of popular sovereignty, of the legitimacy of political action, and other key components of the politics of the Revolution within the context of the period's melodrama. We see here how the Revolutionaries thought and operated within the conventions of a melodramatic plot and discourse, and how the subsequent theatricalisation of the horrors of the Terror by the Thermidorians ensured that the public stage of the Revolution merged with that of melodrama in ways that anticipate the politics of the next century.

In 'When the Revolution Had to Stop', Ian Birchall sees the upheavals of Thermidor, not as the sunset of the Revolution, but rather as one of the most significant of the period's many new dawns. Gracchus Babeuf, and the whole phenomenon of *babouvisme* in the years 1796–97 occupy a central position in the debate on the nature and timing of the end of the Revolution, and Birchall takes the force and originality of the challenge presented by Babeuf as a sign of the birth pangs of a modernity that was to usher in two centuries of Revolutionary socialism. The Revolution was by no means over in 1797. In some ways it had barely started.

The electoral experiment was continued in Bonapartist France, and Malcolm Crook, in his study of elections and plebiscites under Napoleon, highlights the ways in which Napoleonic electoral practices represent a bridge rather than a chasm between the electoral culture of the

Revolution and that of the Restoration. Close analysis of participation rates in the election of representatives to electoral assemblies, the use of plebiscites to test public opinion, and the mechanics of voting procedures all testify to the preservation of the Revolutionary heritage, and the onward transmission of the democratic ideals of 1792 to the post-Napoleonic era.

Continuity between the *ancien régime*, the Revolution, the Consulate, the Empire and the Restoration is also well demonstrated in Munro Price's examination of the life and ideas of the unjustly neglected Bishop of Pamiers, whose links with the royal family before and after the death of Louis XVI ensured that he remained informally at the centre of French political life in those key decades of transition from the fall of autocracy to the restoration of the Bourbons. As a witness to, and an active participant in, five decades of tumultuous change, the Bishop's testimony, recorded in a number of treatises and pamphlets (one of which was recently discovered by Price in the Bibliothèque de Port-Royal), offers many insights into the process of revolution and counter-revolution, as well as into the conditions in which the green shoots of constitutional monarchy could take root.

The creation and successful management of a new political reality required the mobilisation of artists as well as scientists, and in the last article in this part of the volume David Wisner looks at painters and the range of public patronage of art under the First Republic, and at the role of the Ministry of the Interior under the Directory. With the collapse of the pre-1789 world of court patrons, Wisner draws our attention to the work of artists like Lafitte, Perrin, Belle, Le Barbier and David, and his analysis of republican modes of patronage illuminates the factors that facilitated a growing centralisation of artistic endeavour under Napoleon. This would usher in, well before the Restoration, the revival of a court system of patronage generating in turn a new dawn of state control and intervention that links up with what Patrice Bret has to say about the State in the scientific context.

The overarching themes of Part II, many interlocking with those of Part I, relate to new developments in cultural and scientific fields, education, medicine, music and art, but the chronological focus is now on the post-Consulate years and the Restoration. Jean-Claude Caron considers the historical circumstances in which French universities and their relationship to the State evolved from the archaic structures of the *ancien régime*, and concentrates in particular on the emergence of a centralised authority for the organisation of university teaching in the post-Revolutionary period. Here we are shown how a reformed structure of higher education and new requirements and priorities for the training of professionals in various fields reflect the post-1789 upheavals in the socio-political order, and epitomise the transition from an Age of Revolution to an Age of Evolution. The themes of innovation and reform in the universities is taken up again by Laurence Brockliss in the more specialised context of revolutionary medicine and the training of doctors at the new Paris Medical School established by Fourcroy in Year III of the Revolution. A new era in medical education dawns here in which the training of physicians and surgeons would be integrated, and doctors given a more hands-on, practical education with a radically changed programme of clinical instruction that would see the transformation of the lecture room into the lecture theatre (a process of theatricalisation that links up interestingly with themes in other essays). From 1794 to the 1840s French medical teaching, research and clinical practice would be the envy of Europe, and its benefits to society at large seen as tangible evidence of the enduring achievements of the Revolution.

As with the Paris Medical School so with the Paris Conservatoire. In his study of Lefèvre's *Méthode de clarinette* of 1802, Colin Lawson traces the revival of orchestral performance in the aftermath of the Revolution, and the development in the early nineteenth century of France's first modern institution for music education. Music education outstripped in many ways the quality of French music itself at this time, but the contribution of the Paris Conservatoire to pedagogical and technical practice in the post-Revolutionary period, and particularly with regard to Lefèvre's achievements in the teaching of clarinet performance technique, had a European-wide impact. We can see in this essay how music, no less than politics, science, literature and education, lay at the heart of the cultural reorientation that characterised the emergence of modernity in the 1792–1824 period. Education in a broader cultural sense is also explored from the standpoint of women's literature and the intellectual history of post-Revolutionary female and female-directed discourse in Denise Davidson's study of what the women of this period were actually reading. The place of popular literature in the education of women, its format, and the sheer volume of publications that came from the pens of women themselves for the benefit of other women in a culture of prescriptive moralism, invite a reassessment of the importance of this neglected current of writing as a key component in the construction of the new moral order.

The management of knowledge in the interests of the state in the context of war and the demands that a war situation makes on the scientist as a public servant are closely analysed by Patrice Bret in his study of the mobilisation of scientists and military engineers in the face of external threats to national security. Bret demonstrates how science and politics in the 1790s and subsequently were drawing together in networks whose scientist-members had access to the highest levels of government. Scientists in this period often controlled key government committees with responsibility for the formulation of policies on weapons research programmes and military policy. In the reorganisation of science teaching and research after the Revolution, and particularly under the Consulate and the Empire, Bret locates the dawning of our own world of state-driven and state-controlled scientific research, with all of its problems and ambiguities. New dawns are not necessarily all that rosy. The phenomenon of the survival of the nobility in the increasingly urbanised and bourgeois society of the Empire and the Restoration, and the contributions of a surviving aristocratic *élite* to the technological revolutions of the Empire and the Restoration are explored by Joël Felix in an essay that complements usefully Bret's study of scientists in a more professionalised context. The somewhat paradoxical involvement of a formerly discredited and proscribed nobility in the economic and technical modernisation of the France of the new century must be one of the more ironic features of Revolution's legacy. Felix's study of the statistics of inventions and the taking out of patents as indicators of national regeneration sheds much-needed light on the distinct figure of the noble scientist and inventor as a key entrepreneurial player in the industrial revolution that marked France's final emergence from its feudal past.

The volume concludes with an essay by Barbara Cooper that returns us to the world of politics and theatre with an analysis of the preamble to the constitutional charter granted by Louis XVIII in 1814 and a one-act prologue written for the reopening of the *Théâtre de la Porte Saint-Martin* in 1814. A comparison of the two texts reveals significant alignments (and even more significant points of diversion) between the two forms of inaugural discourse. Both address the question of legitimising restoration, but while the first sought vainly to revive a political institution in the light of *ancien régime* disregard for the lessons of the Revolution concerning popular consent, the second sought to revive a cultural institution in which art in 1814, unlike politics, was ready to embrace the new realities of market forces. The dual image generated by these 'inaugural acts' of a sun setting on France's past overlaid with a sun rising on France's future in those crucial, but still neglected, years between the execution of Louis XVI and the enthronement of Charles X brings the volume to what we think is a fitting conclusion.

Notes

1   Edmund Burke, 'Reflections on the Revolution in France, and on the Proceedings in Certain Societies in London Relative to That Event: in a letter intended to have been sent to a gentleman in Paris' cited in David Williams *The Enlightenment* (Cambridge, Cambridge University Press, 1999), p. 511.

2   See Richard Holmes, *Footsteps. Adventures of a Romantic Biographer*, Flamingo, London, 1985, pp. 73–132.

3   See Jean El Gammal, 'Miroirs du XIXe siècle: représentation et rétrospection' in a special issue of the *Revue d'Histoire du XIXe siècle*, 'Repenser le XIXe siècle' sous la direction de Jean-Claude Caron, Alain Corbin, Michèle Riot-Sarcey, Rosemonde Sanson, no. 13–1996/2, p. 14.

4   David Andress, *French Society in Revolution 1789–99* (Manchester University Press, 1999), pp. 2–5.

5   Martin Alexander (ed.), *French History since Napoleon* (London, Arnold, 1999), p. 7. On 'history from below', see *The Darnton Debate. Books and Revolution in the Eighteenth Century* (Oxford, The Voltaire Foundation, 1998).

6   See for instance Jacques Droz, *De la restauration à la révolution 1815–1848*, Paris, Armand Colin, 1967; Alfred Cobban, *A History of Modern France*, 3 vols. Vol. 1, Old Regime and Revolution 1715–1799, vol. 2, From the First Empire to the Second Empire 1799–1871, vol. 3, France of the Republics 1871–1962, Penguin, Harmondsworth, 1965; A. Jardin and A.-J. Tudesq, *La France des notables 1815–1848*, Nouvelle histoire de la France contemporaine, Paris, Seuil, 1973; M. Vovelle, *La chute de la monarchie (1787–1792)*, Nouvelle histoire de la France contemporaine, Paris, Seuil, 1973; M. Bouloiseau *La république jacobine (10 août 1792–99 thermidor an II)*, Nouvelle histoire de la France contemporaine, Paris, Seuil, 1973.

2
The Gendered Citizen: Marie Madeleine Jodin (1741–90)

Felicia Gordon

In 1790 a treatise entitled '*Vues législatives pour les femmes*' [Legislative View for Women] was addressed to the French Constituent Assembly citing on its title page the following motion of the *Cahier de doléances* of the *Tiers Etat de la Ville de Paris* (1789): 'The Paris Assembly will undertake to find means to reactivate those regulations, which until now have proved ineffective, to crack down on the scandal of public prostitution.'[1] The section of the *Cahier* entitled *Municipalité*, from which this motion was drawn, contains detailed plans for civic improvements particularly in the fields of mental health, public hygiene and public morals (such as the elimination of gambling and the curbing of prostitution). Like the reformers drafting the *Cahier*, the author of *Vues législatives* was concerned with practical measures for the improvement of civic life. She called for the elimination of public prostitution, for the setting-up of a women's legislature with a jurisdiction over women in relation to family disputes, for the abolition of the *police des moeurs* (morals police), for the establishment of workshops and hostels for indigent women, and for the institution of the right to divorce.

This call for a women's legislative body to rule women, couched in explicitly Rousseauistic language, was the work of Marie Madeleine Jodin, a former actress turned *philosophe* and feminist who represents what Paul Vernière has termed an example of '*la contagion des lumières*' [the contagion of Enlightenment thought], operating on a woman whose origins in the artisan class placed her outside the usual constituency of the republic of letters inhabited by intellectuals and *salon-nières*.[2] Marie Madeleine was the daughter of Jean Jodin, a watchmaker from Genoa living near Paris, who had been a friend of Denis Diderot and had collaborated with him on technical subjects for the *Encyclopédie*. Diderot's friendship, which he extended to Jean Jodin's wife and daughter when they found themselves in difficult circumstances after the former's death, was to prove one of the enduring and liberating influences on Marie Madeleine's life. The other was her lifelong venera-tion for her father and her pride in his élite status as a citizen of the Republic of Geneva.[3] The Geneva concept of citizenship was to figure centrally in Marie Madeleine's petition to allow women to enter public life as full members of the newly emerging French polity. 'Et nous aussi', she reminds the members of the Constituent Assembly, 'nous sommes citoyennes' [And we too are citizens].

Vues législatives can be claimed as one of the first female-authored, signed, feminist works of the Revolutionary period, published, as it was, a year before Olympe de Gouges's *Les Droits de la femme* (1791) and two years before Mary Wollstonecraft's *Vindication of the Rights of Women* (1792). In submitting her treatise to the Assembly, Jodin was responding to the first, expansive, and for women, still favourable stage of the Revolution.[4] This discussion will focus on *Vues législatives* in the context of Jodin's own experience of arbitrary power and exclusion from citizen-ship and in relation to contemporary philosophical debates. Her plea for the right to citizenship for women emanated from an individual fully aware of the meaning of deprivation of rights: as the child of Protestants in France, as an unruly daughter imprisoned by her family for '*libertin-age*',[5] as an actress, denied civil and religious rights, and, finally as a woman confronting the legislators of the Constituent Assembly, who still could not count herself a full or 'active' citizen. The opening para-graph of *Vues législatives* focuses on an issue nowhere mentioned in *Cahier du Tiers* and absent from most discussions of constitutional reform. Indeed Jodin picks out the only specific, though negative, refer-ence to women (prostitutes) in the whole *cahier* and finds there the seeds of a feminist argument. Her treatise exposes an official silence over the inclusion of women in the new polity:

> When Frenchmen indicate their zeal to regenerate the State and to base its happiness and fame on the eternal bases of virtue and law, I have thought that my sex, which composes the attractive half of this great Empire, could also reclaim the honour and even the right to work towards public prosperity; and that in breaking that silence to which politics seems to have condemned us, we could usefully say: 'And we too are citizens'.
>
> (*Vues législatives*, iii)

If one compares Jodin's *Vues législatives* with Mary Wollstonecraft's *Vin-dication of the Rights of Women*, a notable difference is the absence of references to God or a supreme being in Jodin's text.[6] In all the appeals to natural law which underlie her concept of human rights, a ruling god is entirely absent. Jodin's atheism and anti-clericalism, particularly explicit in the final section on divorce, was arguably the product of her traumatic experiences when in 1750, as a child of nine, she was forcibly 'converted' to Catholicism. Separated from her Protestant parents and put under the guardianship of her Catholic aunt, she was sent to a convent, *la Maison des nouvelles catholiques,* for instruction. These convents which took Protestant girls for conversion, were known for their harsh regimes as well as their frequently disruptive pupils. 'Frequent conflicts and dramas sullied the work of this community, often cited in crime reports.'[7] It is evident that Jodin was by no means the only difficult child in her convent, but the strength of her rebellion can be gauged from the fact that in the course of the next six years she was ejected from this and five further convents for incorrigibly bad behaviour, and was on one occasion subject to an *Ordre du Roi* for her forcible detention.

Jodin's disastrous early educational experience illustrates some of the unintended consequences of the Revocation of the Edict of Nantes (1685) which had decreed that all French subjects must be registered at birth, in marriage and at death according to Catholic ritual. Protestant parents were under enormous pressure to allow their children to convert. Children were regularly taken from their parents to be placed in Catholic schools. Separation from the parental influence was seen as crucial. In 1750, the year of Marie Madeleine Jodin's conversion, a royal edict from Versailles: 'forbade mother superiors to allow children to speak or write or to have any relations with their mother or father or any other relations who had not done their duty towards the Catholic religion'.[8] On the other hand, incentives were also offered. Jodin's conversion gained her a life pension of 200 *livres* per annum, perhaps not a fortune, but an important sum to a watchmaker's family.

None of this seems to have made any difference to the girl herself. According to her family, throughout her youth she resisted convent discipline and 'refused conversion'.[9] This hostility to religious indoctrination as a child was to prove enduring and culminated in the story recounted by Diderot about Jodin's arrest for blasphemy in Bordeaux in 1769 when she was 28 years old. According to the exasperated Diderot, one of Jodin's staunchest defenders and friends, she had mocked a religious procession:

> Consider that she is the daughter of Protestants and draws a pension of two hundred *livres* as a new convert. Well, this 'new convert' who

every year receives two hundred francs for kneeling to the Good Lord when he passes by [Diderot is describing a religious procession] took it into her head to make fun of him when he was passing in the street. She was reported to the chief prosecutor, charged, arrested and thrown in prison from which she only emerged by bail payments or bribery.[10]

Diderot's chagrin was, one imagines, less to do with her mockery of the procession, than with Jodin's incredible recklessness. The memory of Chevalier de La Barre's execution for sacrilege three years previously was still fresh.[11] Jodin's visceral anti-clericalism, which had been shaped by her early experiences at her convent schools, was later reinforced by philosophic reading, culminating in her bitter attack on the Church and marriage laws in her *Vues législatives*. For example, citing Switzerland as a country free from the Catholic clergy's influence (though Jodin conveniently forgets to mention she is speaking of a theocratic state), she describes a country where: 'the idle and corrupt race of priests, abbots and monks do not proliferate' (*Vues législatives*, p. 66).

It was not only religious authority against which Jodin rebelled as a young girl. The authority of the family, second only to the authority of the king and based on the authority of God, were, as is well known, reinforcing modes of control and legitimisation in eighteenth-century France. As Jean-Louis Flandrin has noted: 'As late as the age of Louis XIV to say that an authority was "paternal" was to proclaim its legitimacy and the absolute duty of obedience on the part of those subject to it.'[12] Jodin, a disruptive child who nevertheless was deeply attached to both her parents throughout her adult life venerated the memory of her father and, under Diderot's urging, supported her mother. But during her teenage years she indubitably became *une enragée* in the domestic sphere. There is great pathos in the fact that in *Vues législatives* she reinscribes a wise maternal authority as the cornerstone of her reformed society. Her own mother, a gullible, spendthrift, though apparently good-hearted, woman was the antithesis of the ideal she was to construct in her treatise.

It would be quite misguided to construct Jodin as a victim; she resisted victim status at every stage of her life, which is partly what made her such a disruptive presence. The major influences from which she drew strength were her father and the republican ideal derived from his status as a citizen of Geneva. This was a meritocratic, élitist and by no means democratic concept. Jodin insisted on her right to an honourable status, as the daughter of a citizen of Geneva, especially understandable in the light of the humiliations of her *Salpêtrière* imprisonment from 1761 to 1763. Most women found themselves in *La Salpêtrière* for a gendered crime – prostitutes or 'libertines' were imprisoned, but not, unsurprisingly, their male clients. In addition, various intellectual influences, the 'contagion' of Enlightenment thought, are a key to understanding Jodin's development. The most immediate and powerful, after her father, must be counted the friendship of Diderot in whose 21 remarkable letters to her, between 1765 and 1769, we read an extended tutorial on the art of acting as well as intensive moral instruction.[13] Diderot, who judged Jodin to be a talented and intelligent individual, also demanded that she live up to the ethical standard of which he believed her mind and heart made her capable.

Diderot's concern for Jodin's welfare, which extended to the practicalities of becoming her man of business and investing considerable sums on her behalf, is attested to throughout their recorded correspondence. But it is in the area of reform of acting and in debates surrounding the status of actors and actresses that the letters are of the greatest significance to us here.[14] Seeking to render dramatic art more 'natural' or 'honest', Diderot argued against the static, declamatory style of classical French theatre. He attacked artificiality in acting, a paradox which he was later to explore more fully in his *Paradoxe sur le comédien* [Paradox on actors] (1777). His letters to Jodin, which offer a foretaste of the more developed *Paradoxe*, seamlessly combine aesthetic and ethical instruction. Diderot, in a rather proto-existential sense, clearly thought that to seem honest was to become honest. He continually urged *honnêteté* upon Jodin, this to a woman who must appeal to her public by artifice and to her lovers by charm. He warned her, however, not to play her roles of tragic queenly heroines off the stage, which she was prone to do. Indeed the language of these dramatic heroines infuses Jodin's prose, both in her *Mémoire sur délibéré* and in *Vues législatives* where we often hear the rhetorical cadences of her theatrical training.

In his letters to Jodin, Diderot was implicitly contesting Rousseau's philippic against the theatre and actors in his *Lettre à d'Alembert sur les spectacles* [Letter to d'Alembert on the Theatre] of 1753, part of the long-running *querelle du théâtre* between cultural conservatives, who saw the theatre as an evil influence, and progressives, like Voltaire and Diderot, who wanted to use the theatre as a vehicle for social reform. Both sides deplored the often scandalous behaviour of actors: conservatives saying that actors deserved their pariah status and progressives saying that their disorderly lives were a consequence of their exclusion from the sacraments of the Church and the protection of the State. Diderot, in a rather

Pygmalion-like spirit, seems to have seen Jodin as a test case to prove that there could exist a good actress who was also a good person. Authenticity in acting should, he suggested, spill over into her private life. For Rousseau, on the other hand, to pretend for one's living and for money, especially as a woman, was to be in essence a prostitute. Any 'public woman' or *'fille publique'* was a woman for sale. The status of the acting profession (outside the law), which the great tragedienne, Mlle Clairon, had unsuccessfully tried to rescue from infamy (its legal definition) in 1765, by petitioning the King, was not reformed until 1789 when actors were given citizens' rights. Yet when Jodin wrote her feminist treatise in 1789 and 1790, she must have realised that this victory for the profession did not extend to women, actresses or otherwise. Her experience of the contempt levelled at prostitutes and actresses lay behind her determination not merely to 'reform' prostitutes, *filles publiques*, who heretofore had defined women in public life, but to provide an honourable role for women as public figures.

In its immediate inspiration, *Vues législatives* can be interpreted in the context of the newly empowered Third Estate and its commitment to securing full rights for the middle ranks. The Parisian *Cahier du Tiers-Etat*, from which Jodin drew her theme about prostitution, was prefaced by its own *Déclaration des droits* which began: 'In all political societies, all men have equal rights'. But where, Jodin asks, were women in all of this? The deputies must be reminded of their inexplicable oversight. Addressing an all-male Constituent Assembly, products, as she flatteringly puts it, of *la vraie philosophie*, it is clear, Jodin purports to believe, that they would be too just and too rational, not to listen to her legislative views for women and to act upon them:

At a time when true Philosophy begins to enlighten all minds, when defeated Despotism leaves prejudices without any defence, prejudices which only existed thanks to Despotism, will the weaker sex which force alone has kept away from public deliberations reclaim in vain its imprescriptible [inalienable] rights? Should not this essential half of Society have any part in the Legislative Code promulgated in the name of all of Society? In response to these questions, I see Reason and Equity which motivate the august Assembly of Representatives of the Nation be astonished that they have not done so sooner, and hasten to welcome them. Let us then follow the general impulse which directs all ideas towards the goal of a re-conquered liberty which oppression had usurped from us [women] also.

(*Vues législatives*, p. 5)

In a text replete with philosophic references from Plato to Bayle, Rousseau, scourge of the theatre and apostle of women's exclusion from public life, is the philosopher most often invoked.[15] This is the Rousseau of *The Discourse on Inequality* and *The Social Contract* who promulgated theories of liberty and civic participation in passages such as the following:

> To renounce freedom is to renounce one's humanity, one's rights as a man and equally one's duties. There is no possible *quid pro quo* for one who renounces everything; indeed such renunciation is contrary to man's very nature; for if you take away all freedom of the will, you strip a man's actions of all moral significance.[16]

But Jodin's evident admiration for Rousseau posed difficulties in her overtly feminist text. Rousseau can be seen as the great seducer of eighteenth-century women intellectuals, who were drawn to his portraits of Julie in *La Nouvelle Héloïse*, where he legitimated both passion in women and the social importance of maternity. For Rousseau, women fell outside the parameters of self-determination which for him defined the ethical subject. As a consequence, he fashioned a gender-based ethic for them. In *Emile ou de l'éducation*, women were granted a separate ethical universe where qualities such as flattery and insincerity, judged vices in men, were seen as necessary feminine virtues. Mary Wollstonecraft, one of the few women writers of the period to confront the implications of this strategy, whilst praising Rousseau's concept of natural liberty, attacked his sexual double standard.[17]

Jodin's position is less clear cut. It seems clear that she identified powerfully with Rousseau, as the child of a Geneva citizen of the artisan class, as an autodidact and as an outcast and wanderer. She also identified with him, in writing her *Vues législatives*, in his role as legislator, a perhaps unique transposition of gender roles in this area.[18] In addition, she seems to take for granted aspects of Rousseau's sexual apartheid, speaking of '*le sexe faible*' (the weaker sex) and of female modesty or *pudeur* as the defining virtue of women as though she were paraphrasing passages from *Emile*. She would have been aware that to appeal to her audience, *Vues législatives* must embrace the language of the social contract and the cult of maternity, whatever she herself may have thought, but such phrases ring oddly in a document claiming women's capacity to rule themselves. Jodin resolves the issue of women's capacity for entering public life by identifying with their role as mothers – both to their families and to society, in the same way as paternal authority flowed from the king/state to the father/family and vice versa:

In France, where women have strengthened their influence by their talents and by the education which they have gained for themselves, they should hold in the administrative system, in that sphere of influence which I assign to them, authority solely over morals/manners, in the same proportion as a mother holds in the bosom of her family.

(*Vues législatives*, p. 52)

Jodin therefore proposes a women's legislature composed of well-educated and public-spirited women, to make laws dealing with women, and *une Chambre de conciliation*, a family court, less cumbersome than the standard judicial process, to settle domestic disputes. This body would be lodged in a vast *hôtel* where in a separate wing, indigent women could be given a basic education and taught a trade. Women legislators would become the public mothers of their wayward daughters, *les filles publiques*. Jodin's plan is detailed and utilitarian. In this it echoes the spirit and letter of the *cahiers de doléances* which focused on practical reforms to improve civic or village life.

Whilst following virtually to the letter the language of separate spheres ideology, namely the idea that women's procreative role defines them socially and ethically, Jodin subverts the doctrine in two ways. Firstly, she argues that women have been capable of far more than mere reproduction (listing examples of great women such as Elizabeth of England or Catherine of Russia). Secondly, she maintains that women's 'natural' maternal role can and must serve the wider social world, that the private world of the family is inseparable from the public sphere. This is the significance of Jodin's attack on 'public' prostitution, which demonstrably invades the supposedly sacred precincts of the bourgeois and working-class family with venereal disease, whilst destroying the hope of family life for the *filles publiques* who abandon their children to neglect. Jodin seeks to convince her audience that the private and public spheres are not separate; they form a seamless web.

Nevertheless, it is not entirely clear whether Jodin subscribes to an idea of separate 'natures' for women and men, or whether she believes sexual difference is a contingent rather than a necessary aspect of women's and men's humanity. Her discussions on the quintessentially female virtue of *pudeur* suggest that she sides with Rousseau, but on the other hand her comment on gender difference, taken largely from the seventeenth-century Cartesian feminist Poulain de la Barre,[19] points to a very different position:

> The love of one's country, of liberty and of fame stimulate our sex as
> much as they do yours, Sirs. We are not on this earth a different
> species from you. The mind has no sex, any more than virtue does.
> But the vices of the mind and the heart belong almost exclusively to
> yours.
>
> (*Vues législatives*, p. 19)

One may feel Jodin is trying to have it both ways: men and women are
equal in mind and soul, but men are responsible for more vice, the
reason being presumably that men control power and authority. Given
her insistence on a Rousseauistic image of women as the weaker, purer
sex, whilst denying their innate incapacity, it may be thought that Jodin
suffered from a certain philosophical ambivalence.[20] She internalised to
a very large extent Rousseau's legacy of separate spheres, particularly in
her rhetorical tropes, but nonetheless circumvented its most anti-
feminist implications.

Another source of ambivalence in *Vues législatives* arises from the
question of liberty versus order. We have seen that prostitutes are figured
as women who have lost the power of self-control. Similarly, the people,
or the lower orders, are characterised as lacking sexual and social control
brought about by the stimulus of pornography, licentious theatre and
public prostitution:

> In order to bring back a sense of decency to the common people who
> are susceptible to no morality when they have broken all restraints of
> subordination, and become from thence forward strangers to all hon-
> est feeling, to all social proprieties, it is necessary to remove from
> them those seductive objects which perpetuate this state of licen-
> tiousness and which beg for shameful excesses. The first object of
> reform, therefore, is to wipe out prostitutes [*filles publiques*] who
> destroy in the common people every instinct of modesty and the
> principles of physical and moral vigour.
>
> (*Vues législatives*, pp. 10–11)

In this passage Jodin links Revolutionary violence, which she herself
may well have witnessed in Paris in 1789, to sexual licence, suggesting
that passions unleashed in one direction may become uncontrollable in
another. The working class risks being fatally undermined in its usefulness and its moral character by 'these seductive objects who perpetuate
licentious behaviour and solicit shameful excesses'. Enlightenment
assumptions that liberty would lead to a new and better order could

only be borne out if all citizens internalised the fundamental laws. Public prostitution, contravening modesty, decency and social conventions, had in Jodin's account become the most glaringly visible symptom of social disorder.

Such concerns help to explain the morally prescriptive message of the first section of *Vues législatives* (cleanse our cities of these vermin prostitutes, of pornography and gambling). The second section on divorce is, however, more libertarian, arguing the right to sexual fulfilment and that marriage should not be a prison sentence to which both partners were condemned, but a mutual agreement which could be terminated at will. Jodin based her arguments on the two *Encyclopédie* articles on 'Divorce' and on 'Marriage', and included in her discussion a refutation of Marmontel's attack on an anonymous work advocating divorce, probably Hennet's *Du Divorce* (1789).[21] The tenor of these works is to historicise marriage and to detach it from the religious realm of the purely sacramental. Claims for the universality of the Christian position on indissolubility were also contradicted by contemporary European experience. Whilst prior to 1792 divorce was forbidden under French law, in most Protestant European countries it was permitted in some form, and even in Catholic Poland. In France, both the Church and the State enforced the doctrine of marital indissolubility, though in cases of extreme matrimonial cruelty on the part of the husband, judicial separations were possible, though they did not allow remarriage.

As in the arguments Jodin employs for restoring women to their original liberties, in her discussion on divorce nature is invoked as evidence against indissoluble marriage. 'At this moment when the rights of man, too long ignored, are the object of a new Constitution which restores them to them, there is none more timely than that claimed by Nature, namely the liberty to dispose of oneself' (*Vues législatives*, p. 67). Although her arguments in favour of divorce are not directly focused on women's rights *per se*, it becomes increasingly clear that their implications specifically apply to women. For example, 'the liberty to dispose of one's own person', was precisely that which the law did not accord to women, only to men. Divorce, by curbing the *'puissance maritale'* [marital power] of husbands over wives, had come to be seen as a feminist issue.

Marie Madeleine Jodin's *Vues législatives* was conceived by its author as a practical plan for the social and moral reform of prostitutes, whose lives she became only too well acquainted with during her prison sojourn. Beginning on a morally prescriptive note, she broadened her agenda to call for women's rights as citizens, following the logic of

Rousseau's views that one cannot demand morality from persons who have abrogated their liberty. She asked for the inclusion of women in the legislative process, though couching her appeal in conservative terms and offering an original version of separate spheres domestic ideology in the public sphere. Yet the implications for paternal authority by the admission of women to the responsible public sphere as legislators, even if 'only' over women, were radical. A woman's legislature would in theory legislate only for women, but in practice would be involved in many aspects of social and legal policy affecting both men and women. The proposal for a woman's legislature, like that for divorce reform, implied allowing women to control their own lives in a heretofore unprecedented fashion and would massively weaken patriarchal authority.

In her *Vues législatives*, Jodin attempted to appeal to the male members of the Constituent Assembly by a combination of flattery and rational argument. Her rhetorical strategies fall into the melodramatic pattern of *drame bourgeois* in which the Assembly is figured as a virtuous hero, who will rescue the heroine (women) from the villainous *police des moeurs* as well as from their own worst instincts. It is scarcely surprising, however, that her plan, no matter how rhetorically persuasive, fell on deaf ears. The reaction of Jean-Baptiste, Comte de Lynch (1749–1835), president of the Bordeaux Parliament, to whom she sent the first draft, can be read as typifying the probable reception of *Vues législatives* by the Constituent Assembly at large. He was both patronising and politely dismissive:

> I dare not promise you that the august Assembly will adopt your plan, but I have no doubt that they will appreciate it. It honours that sex which knows how to instruct and please and whose lessons have much more power over us than those of cold Philosophy.
>
> (*Vues législatives*, p. 44)

In particular Lynch was unhappy with Jodin's proposal for a family court with jurisdiction over marital and family disputes. He fully grasped its implications for patriarchal authority: 'I have a particular grudge against your Conciliation Chamber. Why do we need a Tribunal to patch things up with our wives? Would it not be better to prevent us from falling out with them?' (p. 44). Only allow the Assembly to formulate good laws, Lynch asserted, and sound morals would follow, especially if mothers charged themselves with the sound education of their daughters. Finally, in what was no doubt a reproof to Jodin who had in her text demonstrated her wide reading in ancient and contemporary philosophy, women should not dabble in 'cold Philosophy', a subject beyond their grasp and which could only diminish their charms and thereby their influence over men.

The fate of women's emancipation during the Revolutionary period, after the early flourishing of women's journals and the militancy of Revolutionary women, is well known. Nascent feminism was effectively crushed by the law of 4 Prairial, An II (1793) when women were ordered back to their homes and were forbidden to assemble in public in groups larger than five.[22] Nevertheless Jodin's arguments in favour of divorce were in tune with the reformist Assembly. The law of 20 September 1792, passed two years after her death, legalising divorce, was the most liberal in Europe, though it was modified under Napoleon and finally repealed in 1816.

Jodin's concept of citizenship was derived, as is indicated on her title page, *'Fille d'un citoyen de Genève'*, from the restricted political participation of eighteenth-century Geneva. Like Rousseau, she had gleaned from her father an idealised republican myth of Geneva government based on bourgeois virtue and a limited franchise. From the evidence of her surviving letters, it is evident that she always had a powerful and *élitist* sense of herself as someone with rights, not a common attribute, one imagines, of women of the artisan class in *ancien régime* France. 'We have the same rights as you', she informed a rejected lover as a young girl in Paris.[23] In Warsaw, in 1766, in a letter to the Court Chamberlain, Count Moszynski, following the dispute with her theatre manager, she invoked somewhat melodramatically: 'the sacred rights of society... the fundamental laws which make up the security of nations' as a means of appealing to his sense of justice.[24] Even writing to Stanislas Poniatowski, King of Poland, in 1777 (who, there is evidence to suggest, had been her lover during her Polish sojourn in 1765–66), she adopted a familiar and an egalitarian tone. Jodin entirely lacked, given her status as an actress and a woman, what many in the period would have considered to be a proper sense of subordination and humility.

Jodin's practical agenda, which she hoped would fit women for public life, though within the ambit of separate spheres ideology, foreshadowed the strategy of many nineteenth- and early twentieth-century feminists, who were to pursue their maternal role as teachers and educators of children as the route by which women might be granted a place in the public sphere. In her *Vues législatives*, Jodin applied Enlightenment principles of justice and human rights, to that one-half of the human race unaccountably overlooked by the new legislators of France. As

Condorcet would remark in his *Admission des femmes au droit de cité* [Admission of Women to Citizen's Rights] (1790): 'It was the strongest proof of the power of habit, even among enlightened men, to see the principle of equality of rights invoked in favour of three or four hundred men deprived of it by an absurd prejudice, yet forgotten in regard to twelve million women.'[25] Resting her case on theories of natural law, Jodin argued for inclusion of women in *le droit de cité*. She exposed the practical effects on ordinary women's lives of poverty, police harassment and marital oppression, but also insisted that women must attain a better moral standard to qualify for citizenship. Like Rousseau, she believed that the *raison d'être* of political life should be the moral improvement of society. 'The final objective...as stated in the *Contrat social*, is the attainment of moral freedom, "which alone truly makes a man master of himself".'[26] Jodin, like Olympe de Gouges, wished to make the word 'man' universal and generic, whereas for the Constituent Assembly, which she addressed in *Vues législatives*, it remained, in spite of the universalising rhetoric of 'The Rights of Man', gender specific. For all its rhetorical excesses and its curious structure, her feminist treatise is both revealing of Revolutionary debates, and predictive of struggles to come.

The elegiac vision of the future which ends the first section of *Vues législatives*, evokes Jodin, the actress, declaiming, as it were on the public stage, her vision of a France where the tree of liberty shelters all members of society, where the morals police no longer holds sway, and where women, no longer the slaves of others, have learned that capacity for self-governance which Rousseau saw as the necessary precursor to liberty. Though couched in the gloriously overblown rhetoric of the period, it is a moving testament of a woman who believed she was witness to a new dawn:

> Already, my soul enflamed by the sentiment of their justice soars into the future. Already, I see, rising on the scattered ruins of Despotism and Prejudice, the majestic tree of liberty whose branches spread out over all of society. Already I see this debased jurisdiction [the morals police] disappear which has so often protected scandalous disorders which fed its greed, replaced by an august College capable of lending all its lustre to public decency and to recall to order, thanks to its prudent regulations, those unfortunate, undisciplined women who are the shame of one sex and the ruin of the other.
>
> (*Vues législatives*, p. 34)

Notes

1 *Cahier du TIERS: Municipalité, Art. 34, Archives parlementaires de 1787–1860* (Paris, Paul Dupont, 1879), 1e série, vol. 5, p. 290; John Hardman, *French Revolution Source Book* (London, Arnold, 1999), pp. 75–123.

2 Paul Vernière, 'Marie Madeleine Jodin, amie de Diderot et témoin des Lumières', *Studies on Voltaire and the Eighteenth Century* (58, 1967), 1765; see also Dena Goodman, *The Republic of Letters: a Cultural History of the French Enlightenment* (Ithaca, Cornell University Press, 1994).

3 Linda Kirk, 'Genevan Republicanism' in David Wooton (ed.), *Republicanism, Liberty and Commercial Society 1649–1776* (Stanford, Stanford University Press, 1994), pp. 270–309; Clarissa Campbell Orr, 'A Republican Answers Back: Jean-Jacques Rousseau, Albertine Necker de Saussure and Forcing Little Girls to be Free', in Clarissa Campbell Orr (ed.), *Wollstonecraft's Daughters* (Manchester, Manchester University Press, 1996), pp. 44–60.

4 Marie Madeleine Jodin, *Vues législatives pour les femmes, addressées à l'Assemblée Nationale, par Mlle Jodin, fille d'un citoyen de Genève* (Angers, Mâme, 1790). Jodin published with the firm, Mâme, with whom she made contact when she performed in Angers in 1774. The lifting of censorship in August 1789 resulted in a flood of polemical books and pamphlets which included at least thirty feminist or quasi-feminist tracts. Most were by male authors or were probably satirising the idea of women in public life. See Madelyn Gutwirth, *The Twilight of the Goddesses: Women and Representation in the French Revolutionary Era* (Rutgers, Rutgers University Press, 1982); Jane Abray, 'Feminism in the French Revolution', *American Historical Review*, 80, 1 (February 1975), 43–62 and Paule-Marie Duhet, *Les Femmes et la révolution 1789–1794* (Paris, Julliard, 1971).

5 'Libertinage' had a wide range of meanings. Usually denoting debauchery and in women especially, sexual licence, it was also associated with free-thinking in a philosophical sense. Marie Madeleine's family accused her of both prostitution and of 'refusing conversion', that is, irreligious behaviour.

6 For the validation of natural law theories by notions of a deistic God see David Wisner, *The Cult of the Legislator in France 1750–1830* (Oxford, Voltaire Foundation, 1997), p. 36.

7 Martine Sonnet, *L'Education des filles aux temps des lumières* (Paris, Editions du Cerf, 1987), p. 182, who also cites the high mortality and escape rates from these institutions.

8 Samuel Mours and Daniel Robert, *Le Protestantisme en France du XVIIIème siècle à nos jours* (Paris, Librairie Protestante, 1972), p. 25. For a detailed discussion of the political and social background to the conversion of Protestants see Jeffrey W. Merrick, *The Desacralisation of the French Monarchy in the Eighteenth Century* (London, Louisiana State University Press, 1990), pp. 134–64.

9 Archives de la Bastille, 12, 124 (1761), f. 196.

10 Denis Diderot, lettre 570 'à Sophie Volland', 11 September 1769, in Georges Roth (ed.), *Correspondance*, IX (Paris, Editions de Minuit, 1963), p. 141.

11 The execution of the Chevalier de La Barre (1766) for sacrilege, though it can be argued that his death sentence was exceptional for the time, was one of the *causes célèbres* of eighteenth-century France. Merrick, *The Desacralisation of the French Monarchy*, pp. 39–40.

12   Jean Louis Flandrin, *Families of Former Times*, transl. Richard Southern (Cambridge, Cambridge University Press, 1979, first published 1976), p. 120.
13   Denis Diderot, in Georges Roth (ed.), *Correspondance* (Paris, Editions de Minuit, 1959–63), vols V to X.
14   For a discussion of Diderot's dramatic theories see P.N. Furbank, *Diderot, a Critical Biography* (London, Secker and Warburg, 1992), pp. 138–47.
15   One of Jodin's sources for her philosophic references was Pierre Le Moyne, *La galerie des femmes fortes* (1647).
16   Jean-Jacques Rousseau, *The Social Contract*, transl. Maurice Cranston (Harmondsworth, Penguin, 1968), p. 55.
17   Mary Wollstonecraft, *A Vindication of the Rights of Women* (1792). The vexed relationship of eighteenth-century women writers to Rousseau, a combination of enthusiasm and disapproval, has been traced in a number of works among them: Clarissa Campbell Orr, 'Cross-Channel Perspectives', in Clarissa Campbell Orr (ed.), *Wollstonecraft's Daughters*, pp. 1–42; P.D. Jimack, 'The Paradox of Sophie and Julie: Contemporary Response to Rousseau's Ideal Wife and Mother', in E. Jacobs, W.H. Barber, J.H. Bloch, F.W. Leakey (eds), *Women and Society in Eighteenth-Century France* (London, Athlone Press, 1979), pp. 153–70; Lynda Lange, 'Rousseau and Modern Feminism', ibid., pp. 95–111; Sara E.P. Malueg, 'Women and the *Encyclopédie*', in Samia I. Spencer (ed.), *French Women and the Age of Enlightenment* (Bloomington, Indiana University Press, 1984), pp. 250–70; Gita May, 'Rousseau's "Anti-feminism" Reconsidered', ibid., pp. 309–20; Gilbert Py, *Rousseau et les éducateurs* (Oxford, Voltaire Foundation, 1997), pp. 338–405; Joel Schwartz, *The Sexual Politics of Jean-Jacques Rousseau* (London, University of Chicago Press, 1984); Sylvana Tomaselli, 'The Enlightenment Debate on Women', *History Workshop Journal*, vol. 20 (1985), 101–24; Mary Trouille, 'A Bold New Vision of Woman: Staël and Wollstonecraft Respond to Rousseau', *Studies on Voltaire and the Eighteenth Century*, 292 (1991), 293–336.
18   For Rousseau and the role of the legislator, see David Wisner, 'The Anatomy of a Cult' in *The Cult of the Legislator in France*, pp. 39–61.
19   François Poulain de la Barre, *De l'égalité des deux sexes: discours physique et moral où l'on voit l'importance de se défaire des préjugez* (Paris, 1673), p. 109.
20   Jodin almost certainly lacked religious faith and was, like her mentor, Diderot, a philosophical materialist, not, as we know from contemporary and subsequent medical discourse, a particularly favourable position for women's emancipation. For a full debate on this issue see Geneviève Fraisse, *Reason's Muse*, transl. Jane Marie Todd (London, University of Chicago Press, 1994). Diderot was among the materialist philosophers who thought that women were ruled by their particular physiology. See Denis Diderot, 'Sur les femmes', in Roger Lewinter (ed.), *Oeuvres Complètes* (Paris, Le Club français du livre, 1997), pp. 29–60; Lisa Gasbarrone, 'Voices from Nature: Diderot's Dialogues with Women', *Studies on Voltaire and the Eighteenth Century*, 292 (1991), 259–91; Olwen H. Hufton, *Women and the Limits of Citizenship in the French Revolution* (Toronto, University of Toronto Press, 1992). On the feminist implications of Cartesianism, the author is indebted to: Siep Stuurmann, 'Seventeenth-Century Feminism and the Invention of Modern Equality', paper given to the 'Feminism and Enlightenment: 1650–1850' seminar, Institute of Historical Research, University of London, 2 December 1998.

21 For this and the following discussion relating to divorce law and the debate surrounding it see Roderick Phillips, *Putting Asunder* (Cambridge, Cambridge University Press, 1988), pp. 159–75. Jean-François Marmontel (1723–99) was an enormously prolific writer and journalist, best known for his *Moral Tales*. His review of this anonymous work on divorce appears on pp. 18–36 of the *Mercure de France* for February 1790. It refers to Hennet's *Du Divorce*, 1789, the first work in France to publish detailed proposals for divorce legislation. See Roderick Phillips, *Putting Asunder*, p. 173.

22 P.N. Furbank, '"And We are Citizens too" Diderot and Marie-Madeleine Jodin, Actress and Feminist', unpublished MS, p. 68.

23 Archives de la Bastille, 12, 124 (1761).

24 *Jodin Proçès*, letter 127, in Wierszbicka, 'Le Théâtre', Ch. XXII, AGAD, Warsaw, Manuscript.

25 'Condorcet's Plea for the Citizenship of Women', transl. John Morley, *Fortnightly Review*, 13 (1 June 1870), 719–24, reprinted in Susan Groag Bell and Karen M. Offen (eds), *Women, the Family, and Freedom, the Debate in Documents* (Stanford, Stanford University Press, 1983), vol. 1, p. 99.

26 David Wisner, *The Cult of the Legislator in France*, p. 60.

3
Representing the Sovereign People in the Terror

David Andress

By 'Terror', this chapter takes to mean the period approximately from the summer of 1793 to the summer of 1794, and the term is used in that sense as a marker, rather than a subject of analysis. The other three terms of the title, however, shall all be subject to analysis, singly and collectively, because 'representing the sovereign people' encapsulates in a phrase many of the most urgent concerns of the radical Revolution.

Representation, as a verbal assertion, has been made central to the political dynamic of the French Revolution by the analysis of François Furet. He stated that the primary political contestation of the period was over the claim to embody representation of the people as the sovereign, and that the Jacobins' and later Robespierrists' ascendancy relied precisely on the effectiveness of this verbal claim within a political language-game.[1] This analysis has, of course, been controversial, although it might be claimed to have had something of an ascendancy in the late 1980s.[2] In more recent years the work of a number of historians has suggested that for the Revolutionaries themselves, and for the culture of the late *ancien régime*, representation in a number of forms was a problematic concept, and one which provoked disquiet.

In the theatre, representation was a key theme of late eighteenth-century debate. For example, the way in which an actor could take on the identity of a character was for some philosophically troubling, especially when constructing visions of future civic communities. Restif de la Bretonne, author of endless utopian musings, planned to make actors either state slaves, or restrict acting to amateurs, tied to a single role in a limited repertoire, thus constraining either their civic existence or the mutability of their identity.[3] Similarly, what should be represented on stage, and in what fashion, was an active subject of philosophico-political debate, as Diderot and Sedaine made claims for the *drame bourgeois* and its presentation of 'real life' in an expressive mode that would engage an audience. That an audience might be 'engaged', and potentially transformed, by dramatic experience was itself a challenging notion, confronting an 'absolutist' conception of the unchanging ideal spectator to whom the drama was projected. This, of course, was in a real sense the king, just as theatres were sites of royal and corporate privilege, and to promote a new representational paradigm of interaction was an implicitly 'republican' approach with disruptive potential.[4] Theatres were already highly politicised places, both in their choice of repertoire and in the 'politics' of audience-constitution and behaviour.[5]

This is noteworthy in the context of discussion of the 'public sphere' more generally in the late eighteenth century. As modelled by Habermas, and elaborated in more recent works, the public sphere has tended to take on a rather contemplative, individual and indeed 'private' appearance, both in terms of how one can define the ways in which thinkers at the time perceived it, and in the echoes of this in more recent conceptions.[6] The theatre is a central site from which one might propose a more open, turbulent and collectively engaged public sphere in this period. (Another is the arena of the lawsuits pursued through sensational published *mémoires*, and the intense public demand these fuelled.)[7] One intriguing feature of the theatre in Paris during the eighteenth century was the extent to which earlier 'carnivalesque' forms of popular theatre were invaded by more moralistic values, as reforming playwrights seemed determined to impose didacticism on what had previously been somewhat Rabelaisian forms – Sedaine, one of the founders of the *drame bourgeois*, had begun his career writing for *opéra-comique*, which he and others turned from a pantomimic descendant of the travelling fair-theatre into something which lauded virtue in the context of scheming families and innocent love affairs.[8] The drive to make even such 'marginal' forms of theatrical entertainment 'serious' suggests that an implicit political element had entered this environment by mid-century at least, and would continue to grow into the 1780s.[9] This volatile and potentially disruptive public space lent itself immediately to metaphors for other kinds of participation, ones that were taken up eagerly, and worked almost to death, in the early years of the Revolution.[10]

A second theme, sovereignty, and the legitimacy of political action, was of key importance throughout the Revolution. Within the period addressed here, it may be noted that the fall of the Gironde was, at least in part, a contest over the expression and articulation of sovereignty, of centre versus periphery, political action in the capital versus the claims of a larger France, legal forms versus Revolutionary necessities. In the provinces, especially in Marseilles and Lyons, local groups and political and administrative structures fought for power based on such contested claims over sovereignty.[11] Within Parisian politics, a complex battle was fought out over the ground of popular assertions of rights over subsistence, in which the *enragés* championed the immediate popular response, while being increasingly politically marginalised by both the sectional movement and the Jacobins.[12] As the Terror drew to a close a year later, the circle of those within the 'sovereign people', worthy of inclusion in the new Republic, had narrowed to the point where only an imagined social realm of 'poor patriots' coexisted with a massive bureaucracy dedicated to watching itself for signs of faction. Here the representation of sovereignty, such an open question in early 1793, had contracted to the point where Furet's description of it seems immediately valid, as something captured within the phrases of a tiny leadership.

In the discussion of both sovereignty and representation, assertions concerning the identity of 'the people' were a crucial issue. 'The people' had been admitted into political action in 1789, largely because the insurrection of 12 to 14 July, and its provincial parallels made any other course implausible.[13] However, the word retained all its eighteenth-century ambiguities, and was not used in the constitutional formulations of 1789–91.[14] Here the 'Nation' was raised up as the sovereign body, the identity of which remained sufficiently abstract to, if necessary, remove substantial portions of 'the people' from political activity.[15] From 1792, and increasingly in 1793, 'popular sovereignty' was elevated as a slogan, and seen at work in events such as the fall of the Gironde. By now, however, 'the people' as a term had itself acquired a more restrictive, and hence politically useful, meaning. In the words of Robespierre on 6 April 1793, 'What is there in common between the people of Paris and a mob of women, led by valets of the aristocracy, by disguised valets: a gathering the fine *sans-culottes* took absolutely no part in ...?'[16] Food riots, such as the ones referred to here, are not a 'truly popular' activity, and therefore the concerns which prompted them could be ignored, until the more masculine and politically acceptable sectional movement also began to clamour for the maximum.

Separately, then, all of these terms were problematic, or contested. Collectively, however, they formed a conceptual package so powerful that it was accepted without question by almost every strand of Revolutionary thought, one in which these problems and contestations were persistently elided, ignored, or denied. It is this packaging, and the elisions it allowed, that are focused on here. It has been seen, in recent years, that it is possible to draw a wide variety of deeper conceptual structures out of the politics of the Revolution. A clear example is that of Lynn Hunt, who has proposed to us a picture of the Revolution as a Freudian 'family romance'. At a somewhat less single-minded level, Antoine de Baecque has catalogued the relationship of the Revolutionaries to the human body, as image, metaphor and occasional reality, expanding in so doing on the work of Dorinda Outram.[17] Another conceptual avenue of insight into the Revolution is proposed here – that of melodrama, or what more broadly it can be called, following Peter Brooks, the 'melodramatic imagination'.[18]

Melodrama as a theatrical genre was born precisely in the Revolutionary era, its first stirrings in the 1770s, and its acknowledged flowering in the years after 1800. Brooks has argued that in that latter period, the melodramatic imagination can and must be seen as wider than merely the theatrical production of specific plays and plots, that it underpinned deeper artistic and ethical concerns. Brooks suggests that 'melodrama may be born of the very anxiety created by the guilt experienced when the allegiance and ordering that pertained to a sacred system of things no longer pertains'.[19] This is, without doubt, a description applicable to the period after 1789, and especially after 1792. Melodrama as a literary and theatrical form attempts to compensate for this underlying anxiety by filling, and overfilling, its plots and situations with moral and ethical meanings – 'a search for a new plenitude, an ethical recentering'.[20] The earlier work of Lynn Hunt on the symbolic dimensions of Revolutionary culture has shown us the extent to which just this kind of 'overfilling' went on from 1789, accelerating into the period of Terror.[21] It shall be argued that the presence of melodramatic themes in the post-Revolutionary generation was a condensation, a de-politicisation, from a time when life itself, and most particularly the turbulent course of the Revolution, was seen in 'melodramatic' terms.[22]

There are several central components to a melodramatic plot. The first is virtue, often physically embodied as innocence, male or female. Then there is evil, of a radical, machinating kind, that will generally provide the impetus to the plot. This impetus takes the form of peril, moral and physical, inflicted on virtue. For the happy ending, a hero is necessary, sometimes individual, sometimes collective, but consummation is often achieved only with additional suffering, the peril of the virtuous sometimes extending to the point of illness, injury or mutilation.[23] It does not take a genius to superimpose these characteristics on the Revolutionary environment, and the Revolutionaries' collective self-representation, at a superficial level. In terms of an external representation, it is very easy to picture the events of the Revolution in melodramatic terms.[24] Certainly, the resort to plot as a political explanation, and the call to action on behalf of the people, were both at the forefront of Revolutionary rhetorical practices.[25] What shall be argued, however, is that the elements of moral identification just outlined were present in the internal representations of the Revolution – that Revolutionaries themselves possessed a set of conceptions that bound them into a 'melodramatic' plot, where 'the people' were the central, imperilled actor, and where individual Revolutionaries accomplished an identification which bound them to the perceived perils and fate of that actor.

This identification, and its employment within an implicitly melodramatic discourse, can be found at many levels of speech and writing. The writings of Jacques Roux, the *enragé* 'red priest' can exemplify this: in the summer of 1793 he took up the journalistic mantle of the assassinated Marat. At a time when the recently proscribed Girondins were beginning to foment what would become the Federalist revolt, and while the 'Jacobin Constitution' of 1793 was being proclaimed to the people, here is Roux writing of the threat to Paris:

> The enemies of the fatherland will be defeated; they are so persuaded that we shall triumph over their liberticide madness, if we draw ever closer the links of fraternity, that there are no means that they do not employ to divide us ... they engage the *départements* to march on Paris to annihilate that hospitable town, that virtuous and energetic city, which is the mirror of opinion, the depot of human knowledge, the sentinel and the mountain of the Republic, the cradle and the school of liberty and equality. Halt, halt, tiger thirsting for the blood of Parisians, Barbaroux, you shall not enjoy the fruits of your crimes. Know that to reduce Paris to slavery, you will have to pass over a million bodies; know that the terrible inhabitants who have lived for four years on iron and liberty shall not kneel as slaves before kings; learn at last that our warrior ardour redoubles at your baseness, responding to the threat to the public good ... the blood of Parisians will bring forth heroes fit to walk in their footsteps; our brothers in the *départements* will know how to avenge us.... [26]

There is immediately apparent in passages such as this a superficially 'melodramatic' tone, and this is far from the strongest example of this that one could cite from Roux's output. What we also have here, at a more structural level, is the trope of virtue imperilled, fighting free even at the cost of its own lifeblood. For authors such as Roux, this type of writing also carried a heavy weight of personal identification. He is here presenting himself effectively as the 'Shade of Marat', who was 'The People's Friend', and who died because of that. Roux himself suffered his own 'martyrdom' later in the summer of 1793, denounced by Marat's widow, and by Robespierre, for his intemperate needling of the Montagnard leadership. Roux reports on this as follows:

> But such is the fate of the friends of liberty, that when one no longer has need of their services, they are broken like a glass. It is natural that after having shown myself the implacable enemy of every kind of tyranny, having declared war on the moderates, the egoists, the thieves, the hoarders, all the scoundrels that starve us, and want to put the nation in irons, it is natural, I say, that I should be the target of the rage of the traitors of the old and new regimes.[27]

The self-melodramatisation that such comments reflect was far from unique to one political perspective. Moments of high drama could bring it out pithily in the speech of the Girondins, such as the well-known cry of Isnard from the chair of the Convention on 25 May 1793, that if Paris continued to threaten to rise up against the national representation, 'Paris will be destroyed... Soon they will be searching the banks of the Seine for a sign that Paris ever existed...'.[28] It was equally present, however, in longer and more considered observations, such as the speech of Vergniaud to the Convention, delivered on 13 March 1793, concerning the 'plot' underlying anti-Girondin riots on the 10th. He comments first on his own previous period of silence:

> Continually rained upon with calumny, I have refrained from speeches as long as I thought that my presence at the tribune could excite passions, and I could not hope to be useful there to my country. But today as we are all, I at least believe, united by the sentiment of a danger common to all: today as the entire National Convention is at the edge of an abyss into which the lightest push will propel it, and liberty, forever: today as the emissaries of Catiline do not merely show themselves at the gates of Rome, but have the insolent audacity to enter even into this chamber to deploy the signs of counter-revolution, I can no longer keep a silence which would become a veritable treason. Determined to avoid personal remarks unworthy of myself, and which would cast disorder into the Assembly, asking even that all its members refrain from applications which are far from my thoughts, I shall say what I know, what I believe true. I shall say it

without fear of the people, for the people love the truth. I shall say it without fear of assassins, for assassins are cowards, and I know how to defend my life against them.[29]

Thus, before he has spoken a word of his specific accusations, Vergniaud has dramatised his position, invoked plot and machination, and nodded towards the construction of a 'pure' blameless 'people', whose liberty is implicitly threatened as much as the lives of the Girondins. To maintain this blamelessness, he explains that the people are:

as if divided into two classes, of which one, delirious in the excess of exaltation to which it has been carried, works each day towards its own ruin; and the other, struck by stupor, drags out a troubled existence, in the anguish of unceasing terrors.

He goes on, having outlined briefly the perils of insurrection:

To the people there remain defenders who could still enlighten them: men who, since the first days of the Revolution, have been dedicated to its success, not through speculation, to conceal a criminal past, or to find under the banner of liberty means to soil themselves with new crimes: not to acquire houses and carriages, in declaiming hypocritically against the rich, but to have the glory of co-operating in the happiness of their fatherland, sacrificing to that single ambition their souls, conditions, fortunes, work, even family, in a word, all that they held most dear. Aristocracy has tried to destroy them by calumny. It has pursued them with perfidious denunciations, with impostures, with mad cries, either in infamous libels, or in even more infamous speeches from the tribune, in popular assemblies, in the public squares, each day, at all hours, at every instant.[30]

This type of rhetoric, self-glorifying, overtly denigratory of opponents, opposing the selfless to the selfish, the pure to the dishonest, the patriot to the traitor, is the single most typical trope of the entire Revolutionary era. This example comes at a time when, as later memoirs recalled, both Girondins and Jacobins had settled on the idea that the other faction was in league with either d'Orléans or Austria, or both. The Girondin Louvet observed that it was hard for some of his colleagues to admit this to themselves: 'Too-honest men, they could not believe in such crimes; though I did not cease to repeat to them that sooner or later they would be their victims ... '. Robespierre, as recorded by the Montagnard, later Thermidorian, Thibaudeau, was equally convinced of the Gironde's nefariousness: 'They made the motion to expel the Bourbons [after the declaration of the Republic] only because they well knew that it would not be adopted. They have only attributed to the Mountain the plan to raise Égalité [d'Orléans] to the throne in order to hide their design to place him there later.'[31]

In such an atmosphere, goodness had to be found somewhere, and we can observe Vergniaud, on an earlier occasion, in a speech tinged with bitter irony concerning the manipulation of concepts of sovereignty in the debate on the fate of the King, resorting to an idealisation of the people, and specifically their ability to conduct a referendum, in answer to his critics:

> They have spoken to us of discord, of intrigues, of civil wars; they have presented us with the most disastrous images. Discord! They think thus that the agitators exercise in the *départements* the same rule that a shameful weakness has allowed them to usurp in Paris?
> ... In the *départements* one obeys the general will. It is known that political and individual liberty is founded on that obedience ... The National Convention will proclaim the result of the general count, and I swear by the love of all Frenchmen for the fatherland, by their devotion to the cause of liberty, by their unshakeable fidelity to the law, that there is not one who will allow himself to murmur against the proclaimed result.[32]

Danton in this period could occasionally be found giving vent to melodramatic declamations along these same lines, although his speeches are generally noteworthy for their avoidance of such devices. On 12 August 1793 he forgot himself so far as to observe that: 'the just man gives no pardon to traitors', and to go on to announce that: 'it is the moment to make that great and last oath, that we vow ourselves all to death, or we shall annihilate the tyrants'.[33] Passing beyond the Federalist crisis, and into the Terror proper, he is found on 23 January 1794, perorating on a motion to ask the Committee of General Security to examine cases of arbitrary arrest: 'The Convention has only succeeded because it has been [of the] people; it shall remain [of the] people; it will seek and always follow public opinion; it is that opinion which must decree all the laws which you proclaim.'[34] To what extent by January of 1794 the Convention could any longer be said to be following any opinion but its own, or rather that which emerged from the play of factional leaderships, is a moot point, but clearly the people remain the central, ideal, point of reference.

Moving further, to the point when the 'factions' of the Revolution had been all but annihilated, we can find in the words of Robespierre a continuing echo of our melodramatic themes. Here, he speaks to the Convention on 18 floréal II (7 May 1794), 'On the Relation of Religion and Morality to Republican Principles'. Having first discussed the general progress of the human race, he turns his eyes to France:

> Yes, that delicious land that we inhabit, and which nature caresses with its favour, is made to be the domain of liberty and happiness; this sensitive and proud people is truly born for glory and virtue. O my country! If destiny had given me birth in a far distant land, I would have addressed to heaven continual prayers for your prosperity; I would have shed fond tears at the tale of your combats and your virtues; my attentive soul would have followed with an anxious ardour all the movements of your glorious Revolution; I would have coveted the fate of your citizens; I would have coveted that of your representatives: I am French, I am one of your representatives! ... O sublime people! Receive the sacrifice of all of my being: happy is he born amongst you! Even happier is he who can die for your happiness![35]

After this moving profession, he turns to his central themes:

> Vice and virtue make the destinies of the earth: they are the two opposed spirits which dispute there. The source of each is in the passions of man: according to the direction given to his passions, man rises to the heavens or sinks into murky abysses; now, the goal of all social institutions is to direct him towards justice, which is at once public and private happiness.[36]

Robespierre's personal sense of identification with the people would of course carry him all the way to the guillotine, unable to encompass those who opposed him within the narrowing scope of the republic of virtue. In the Thermidorian era, while so many political tendencies reversed, the melodramatic imagination remained central to political understandings.[37] The branding of Robespierre as a potential Caesar or Cromwell, undertaken as it was in an atmosphere of frantic self-justification, is testimony to the strength of the concept of machinating evil as a motive force in public life. The evils of the Terror had to be turned around and placed on the head of an individual, they could not be ascribed to circumstances, only a personal dénouement would suffice. If the Thermidorians later succeeded in placing 'Terrorists' as a category at the heart of their construction of blame, it was clearly by a process of individual assignment of guilt to, for example, Carrier, and by a process of elaboration of 'theatricalised' scenes of horror such as the mass drownings at Nantes. The late eighteenth century did not have many models available to it to account for public action.[38] When it looked to the theatre for its inspiration, portraying the political world as a stage, it was caught up into a complex of implied associations. Firstly, the stage of the 'representative public sphere', in Habermas's formulation, had already been for many years dominated by the notion of behind-the-scenes plot, cabal and influence, where action only occurs because of manoeuvre. Secondly, the language of the *drama bourgeois* and the proto-melodrama had created a model of individual activity on a plane of the conflict of vice and virtue. And thirdly, such a language, and such a world-view, had already begun to leak back into a 'politicised' sphere through the world of the law courts, and what Sarah Maza has characterised as 'domestic melodrama' in the presentation of affairs.[39] To think in such terms was already perceived as in some ways a challenge to power, if as yet an inarticulate one. Identification with the people, in a context of 'plot' that a later generation would refine and depoliticise as melodrama, was one of the underlying essences of a Revolutionary consciousness in the 1790s.

François Furet claimed that 'the "people" was not a datum or a concept that reflected existing society. Rather, it was the Revolution's claim to legitimacy, its very definition ... which it was nonetheless impossible to embody.'[40] From this point, Furet developed first his argument of the conflict between representation and direct democracy (or embodiment), and then his explanation for the descent into explanation via plot. Just as Antoine de Baecque has shown to what extent the imagination of the Revolutionaries could indeed 'embody' their collective identity, and that of their enemies, so it can be argued that the 'plot' component of the Revolution was not conjured out of its radical break with the past.[41] Rather, it reflected an attitude towards moral action found quite clearly in thought on the theatre of the pre-Revolutionary era, and arguably incorporated into 'pre-political' understandings that shaped the moral world of the Revolutionaries.[42] From being morally identified with the people, Revolutionary leaders would work their way towards identifying themselves as the people, its sovereignty as theirs, its enemies as theirs too. Revolutionary politics, so often labelled as paranoid, depicted the world as seen from within a melodrama. This was neither a conscious political articulation, nor the mental aberration of a few, but rather a collective drawing on pre-existing models, an assimilation of the mean-ing-saturated stage of Revolutionary politics to a meaning-saturated theatricality.

To pass beyond the Revolution, we can note that Robert Tombs, in his recent study of France in the nineteenth century, makes two observa-tions about French politics that are pertinent here – the first is that all political shades were effectively pursuing utopian goals, attempting at all times to remake society as they wanted it rather than trying to get along with a compromise system, and the second is that conspiracy theories had a central role to play in this system, offering a convenient explana-tion of the persistent failure to achieve any of these utopias.[43] If for 'utopia' we substitute 'dénouement', and for 'conspiracy', 'evil plot', we can perhaps see something of the persistence of the melodramatic mode within the politics of the nineteenth century.

Notes

1   François Furet, *Interpreting the French Revolution* (Cambridge, Cambridge University Press, 1981), esp. pp. 48ff.
2   See the forum on 'François Furet's Interpretation of the French Revolution' in *French Historical Studies*, 15 (1990), 766–802.
3   Scott S. Bryson, *The Chastised Stage; Bourgeois Drama and the Exercise of Power* (Saratoga, Anima Libri, 1991), pp. 84–6. Actors were, of course, excommunic-ate under the Catholic order, but this sanction derived from entirely other concerns.
4   See Downing A. Thomas, 'Architectural Visions of Lyric Theater and Spectator-ship in Late-Eighteenth-Century France', *Representations*, 52 (1995), 52–75; and Jeffrey S. Ravel, 'Seating the Public: Spheres and Loathing in the Paris Theaters, 1777–1788', *French Historical Studies*, 18 (1993), 173–210.
5   See for example the account of L.S. Mercier's travails as an author aspiring to write for the *Comédie française* in Gregory S. Brown, 'Scripting the Patriotic Playwright in Enlightenment-Era France: Louis-Sébastien Mercier's Self-Fashionings, between "Court" and "Public"', *Historical Reflections*, forthcom-ing 1999. The author is grateful to Dr Brown for allowing sight of a pre-publication version of this piece.
6   Discussion of this must begin with Jürgen Habermas, *The Structural Transforma-tion of the Public Sphere*, tr. Thomas Burger (Cambridge, Polity Press, 1989). A brief introduction to Habermas can be found in Benjamin Nathans, 'Haber-mas's "Public Sphere" in the Era of the French Revolution', *French Historical Studies*, 16 (1990), 620–44. Broader considerations of the formation of opinion are discussed by Keith Michael Baker, *Inventing the French Revolution* (Cam-

bridge, Cambridge University Press, 1990), chs 1, 5, 8; and Mona Ozouf, '"Public Opinion" at the End of the Old Regime', in T.C.W. Blanning (ed.), *The Rise and Fall of the French Revolution* (Chicago, Chicago University Press, 1996), pp. 90–110. See also 'Forum: the Public Sphere in the Eighteenth Century', *French Historical Studies*, 17 (1992), 882–950, with contributions by David Bell, Daniel Gordon and Sarah Maza. Daniel Gordon, *Citizens without Sovereignty; Equality and Sociability in French Thought, 1670–1789* (Princeton, Princeton University Press, 1994), strongly emphasises the 'apolitical' construction of discussion in the salon environment.

7 For this see Sarah C. Maza, *Private Lives and Public Affairs; the Causes Célèbres of Prerevolutionary France* (Berkeley, University of California Press, 1993).

8 See Robert Isherwood, *Farce and Fantasy; Popular Entertainment in Eighteenth-Century Paris* (Oxford, Oxford University Press, 1986), ch. 5, esp. pp. 113–21.

9 See here some of the thoughts of Sarah Maza, 'Luxury, Morality, and Social Change: Why There Was no Middle-Class Consciousness in Prerevolutionary France', *Journal of Modern History*, 69 (1997), 199–229, esp. pp. 224 ff.

10 See Angelica Goodden, 'The Dramatising of Political Theatricality and the Revolutionary Assemblies', *Forum for Modern Language Studies*, 20 (1984), 193–212; and Susan Maslan, 'Resisting Representation: Theater and Democracy in Revolutionary France', *Representations*, 52 (1995), 27–51.

11 See Paul R. Hanson, 'The Federalist Revolt: an Affirmation or Denial of Popular Sovereignty?', *French History*, 6 (1992), 335–55.

12 On this see the classic account by Albert Mathiez, *La Vie chère et le mouvement social sous la Terreur*, Paris, 1927, and the brief R.B. Rose, *The Enragés; Socialists of the French Revolution?*, Sydney, 1965.

13 Colin Lucas, 'Talking about Urban Popular Violence in 1789', in Alan Forrest and Peter Jones (eds), *Reshaping France: Town, Country and Region in the French Revolution* (Manchester, Manchester University Press, 1991), pp. 122–36.

14 'People' was an ambiguous concept in eighteenth-century thought: see Roger Chartier, *The Cultural Origins of the French Revolution* (Durham, Duke University Press, 1991), ch. 2, 'The Public Sphere and Public Opinion', esp. pp. 27–30; and the earlier full-length study by Harry C. Payne, *The Philosophes and the People* (New Haven, Yale University Press, 1976).

15 Maurice Cranston, 'The Sovereignty of the Nation', in Lucas, *Political Culture of the French Revolution*, pp. 97–104, esp. p. 103, demonstrates the interchangeability of 'nation' and 'people'. However, Pierre Nora, 'Nation', in François Furet and Mona Ozouf (eds), *A Critical Dictionary of the French Revolution* (Cambridge, Harvard University Press, 1989), pp. 742–53, can define that term at length without mentioning the concept of 'the people'. Pierre Rétat, 'The Evolution of the Citizen from the *Ancien Régime* to the Revolution', in R. Waldinger, P. Dawson and I. Woloch (eds), *The French Revolution and the Meaning of Citizenship* (Westport, Greenwood Press, 1993), pp. 4–15, documents the 'ambiguities and contradictions which surround' that term (p. 13), and its relations to *peuple, factieux, brigand*, and so on in the press discourse of 1789.

16 Cited in Carol Blum, *Rousseau and the Republic of Virtue: the Language of Politics in the French Revolution* (Ithaca, Cornell University Press, 1986), p. 198. For observations on the extent to which these riots were embedded within a pattern of distinctly 'Revolutionary' female activity, see Dominique God-

ineau, *The Women of Paris and their French Revolution* (Berkeley, University of California Press, 1998), pp. 116–18. (Orig. pub. as *Citoyennes Tricoteuses ; les femmes du peuple à Paris pendant la Révolution française* [Paris, Alinea, 1988]).

17 Lynn Hunt, *The Family Romance of the French Revolution* (London, Routledge, 1992); Antoine de Baecque, *The Body Politic; Corporeal Metaphor in Revolutionary France, 1770–1800* (Stanford, Stanford University Press, 1997), and Dorinda Outram, *The Body and the French Revolution; Sex, Class and Political Culture* (New Haven, Yale University Press, 1989).

18 Peter Brooks, *The Melodramatic Imagination; Balzac, Henry James, Melodrama and the Mode of Excess* (New Haven, Yale University Press, 1976).

19 Ibid., p. 200.

20 Ibid.

21 Lynn Hunt, *Politics, Culture and Class in the French Revolution* (Berkeley, University of California Press, 1984), esp. chapters 1 to 4.

22 Hunt, *Family Romance*, pp. 181–91, considers melodrama in its post-1800, and to an extent post-1795, theatrical manifestations, as a literary indicator of cultural attitudes. The author would wish to see the underlying tropes of melodrama operating much earlier, and more profoundly, than that however. Moreover, the link is more complex: as Brooks remarks, Freudian psychoanalysis is in many ways but 'a version of melodrama'. (*Melodramatic Imagination*, p. 201)

23 See Brooks, *Melodramatic Imagination*, ch. 1, esp. pp. 11–20. On the stage, many, indeed most, of these conflicts are based in and around the family unit, following on from the dramatisation of everyday life found in the *drame bourgeois*.

24 Emmet Kennedy, Marie-Laurence Netter, James P. McGregor and Mark V. Olsen, *Theatre, Opera and Audiences in Revolutionary Paris, Analysis and Repertory* (Westport, Greenwood Press, 1996), observes (p. 63): 'The Revolution itself can be said to have been a veritable melodrama with its scenes of eternal love between its king and its nation, its nation and its representatives, the ensuing carnage, and the Terror, when one never knew if the denunciation of one's neighbour would not make of oneself, tomorrow, the condemned person whom the charrette took off to the guillotine.' Nevertheless, plays which described themselves as 'mélodrame' amounted to only 0.7 per cent of those documented by this study. Nineteenth-century authors would of course find much melodramatic material in the Revolution, from Dickens' *Tale of Two Cities* to Baroness Orczy's *Scarlet Pimpernel*, and the social consequences of the Revolution are the underlying concern of Balzac's *comédie humaine*, to which Brooks ascribes melodramatic intensity: see *Melodramatic Imagination*, ch. 5.

25 See Furet, *Interpreting*, pp. 53–8.

26 Jacques Roux, *Le Publiciste de la République française*, no. 245, 21 July 1793, pp. 4–5; repr. In Walter Markov (ed.), *Scripta et Acta* (Berlin, Akademie-Verlag, 1969), pp. 176–7.

27 *Le Publiciste*, no. 259, 22 August 1793, p. 7, in ibid., p. 248.

28 Cited in John Hardman (ed.), *French Revolution Documents* (2 vols, Oxford, Oxford University Press, 1973), vol. 2, p. 67.

29 Cited in H. Morse Stephens (ed.), *The Principal Speeches of the Statesmen and Orators of the French Revolution, 1789–1795* (2 vols, Oxford, Oxford University Press, 1892), vol. 1, pp. 346–7.

30 Ibid., pp. 348–9.
31 Cited in Hardman, *Documents*, pp. 36, 53.
32 Vergniaud, speech on the *appel au peuple*, 31 December 1792, in Stephens, *Principal Speeches*, p. 334.
33 Ibid., p. 256, speech on the arrest of suspected persons.
34 Ibid. p. 275.
35 Ibid., pp. 394–5.
36 Ibid., p. 395.
37 See Bronislaw Baczko, *Ending the Terror: the French Revolution after Robespierre* (Cambridge, Cambridge University Press, 1994). Baczko does not shape his discussion in melodramatic terms, but its contents are clearly laid out, and amenable to this interpretation.
38 For a broader consideration of the themes in this paragraph, and others, see David Andress, 'Liberty and Unanimity: the paradoxes of subjectivity and citizenship in the French Revolution', forthcoming in a volume of papers from the conference 'Revolution and the Making of Modern Political Identity', Tel Aviv University, January 11–14 1999.
39 See Sarah C. Maza, 'Domestic Melodrama as Political Ideology: the Case of the Comte de Sanois', *American Historical Review*, 94 (1989), 1249–64.
40 Furet, *Interpreting*, p. 51.
41 On the general resort to plot as a political explanation in the eighteenth century, see Gordon S. Wood, 'Conspiracy and the Paranoid Style: causality and deceit in the eighteenth century', *William and Mary Quarterly*, 39, 1982, pp. 399–441. One should remember the Revolutionaries' classical training, and the extent to which the Roman historians in particular had insisted on the primacy of individual character and motive in historical and political events.
42 A parallel theme that there is not space to develop here would be the consequences for 'melodramatic' identifications and the erasure of ironic distances of the type of reading-practices discussed by Robert Darnton as common to the later eighteenth century: see *The Great Cat Massacre and Other Episodes in French Cultural History* (Harmondsworth, Penguin, 1984), ch. 6, pp. 209–49.
43 See Robert Tombs, *France 1814–1914* (Harlow, Longman, 1996), pp. 86–7, 94.

4
When the Revolution Had to Stop

Ian H. Birchall

In 1797 Filippo Buonarroti, on trial for his life, told the High Court at Vendôme that:

> The 1793 Constitution became my religion: I still remember with emotion, and this memory will certainly delight all men of good faith who are listening to me; I still remember, I say, the great assemblies of the people consecrated by it, the impulse given to the Nation towards the abandonment of prejudices, greed and pride, and towards sweet equality, open fraternity, friendship, sincerity, compassion, nature; I remember with emotion the abolition of servility, education in common, assistance guaranteed to the victims of poverty and misfortune, institutions which were to make the French into an astonishing people in happiness and friendship.[1]

It is a striking evocation of how 1793 was perceived by many Revolutionaries as a new dawn. But it was soon followed by the bleak sunset of Thermidor, an event which for many historians constituted the point at which the Revolution came to a halt. For Michelet the history of the Revolution ended with Thermidor; Napoleon (and Babeuf) appeared in the *Histoire du XIXe siècle*.

A more recent historian, Bronislaw Baczko, an associate of François Furet, gives a similarly negative picture of Thermidor:

> Thermidor was the point at which the Revolutionaries had only one desire left, were driven by only one remaining motivation: to finally put a stop to the Revolution. Revolutions age quite quickly... Thermidor is the unenchanted mirror which reflects to every new-born

Revolution the only image it would prefer not to see: that of the deterioration and decay which destroy dreams.[2]

Not so much a dawn as a weary and disabused bedtime: yet it was far from clear that the Revolution was in fact over. As Trotsky wrote of Kornilov's revolt in the summer of 1917: 'a Revolution needs from time to time the whip of the counter-Revolution'.[3] Thermidor forced those who wanted to continue the Revolution to reassess their strategy and goals. It was a confusing period for all concerned, but one which provoked new differentiations and new perspectives.

This chapter examines one of the political currents that crystallised amid the upheavals of Thermidor, that around Gracchus Babeuf and his co-thinkers such as Filippo Buonarroti, Charles Germain and Sylvain Maréchal, a current which, far from accepting that the Revolutionary process was over, set it new and ambitious goals. In terms of impact on immediate events the coalescence of the *babouviste* grouping, the short-lived conspiracy of 1796 and the dramatic trial of 1797 were marginal. Yet *babouvisme* represents one of the most significant 'new dawns' of the epoch, standing at the very inception of a 200-year tradition of Revolutionary socialism.

The importance and originality of Babeuf's political thinking have been underestimated by historians from all parts of the political spectrum. On the right, his ideas of radical equality have been dismissed with repulsion and disdain. François Furet described Babeuf as: 'a naïve and sentimental autodidact',[4] showing the peculiar hatred and fear which autodidacts evoke in professional academics, since they challenge their reason for existing.

Babeuf has not fared that much better with historians of the left. The whole Stalinist tradition, fearful of any challenge to the quasi-religious status of 'Marxism-Leninism', tended to downplay the originality of Babeuf's contribution to the socialist tradition. It was above all two dissident Marxists, Victor Dalin, who spent many years in Stalin's labour camps, and Maurice Dommanget, a Revolutionary syndicalist and sympathiser with the Left Opposition, who established the importance of Babeuf as a political thinker.[5]

This chapter does not purport to be a full study of Babeuf's thinking, but it is important to assert a few basic facts about Babeuf's originality before exploring his place in the debate about 'ending the Revolution'.

Firstly, Babeuf is often seen as no more than a belated Jacobin. It is true that he adopted the 1793 constitution as an agitational demand. But that constitution was never the programme of *babouvisme*, as Buonarroti wrote: 'It is regrettable that we find there the old, heart-breaking ideas on the right of property.'[6] Jacobinism always held tight to the defence of private property, while the *babouvistes* envisaged the total collectivisation of both consumption and production.

Secondly, Babeuf is often considered as a Utopian thinker. But if we take the term 'Utopian' in what the author understands to be its original Marxist sense of one who envisages an end without identifying the social forces that can achieve that end, then Babeuf was the very opposite of a Utopian. He dedicated himself, not simply to imagining an egalitarian future, but to constructing an organisation which could bring that future into reality.

Thirdly Babeuf was neither an ascetic nor an economic pessimist. He did not share Rousseau's hatred of luxury, though he raged against the ostentatious display of wealth by a privileged minority. The *babouvistes* did not reject technological progress but sought to mobilise its potential in the framework of a planned economy.[7] They showed particular enthusiasm for Claude Chappe's semaphore telegraph, which was allotted a crucial role in the democratic structures of a national community divided into regions and *départements*: 'Telegraphic lines accelerate communication between the administrations of the *départements* and the intermediate administrations, and between these and the supreme administration.'[8] We might be hearing of the alleged benefits of the Internet.

Babouvisme was not a fixed doctrine, crystallised within a single skull, but a set of ideas in full evolution which began to take shape during Thermidor under 'the whip of the counter-Revolution'. In his book *Comment sortir de la Terreur*, Bronislaw Baczko draws out the political complexity of the period initiated by Thermidor: 'At the end of Year II it is an obvious fact: *emerging from the Terror* is not an *act* but an agonising *process* with an uncertain outcome.'[9]

The claim that the Revolution was finished was not a new one in the Thermidorian period. Indeed, the Revolution had scarcely begun when some participants wished to proclaim it over. It was the most class-conscious of the Revolutionaries who were keenest to call a halt before the privileges they had won from those above them were claimed by those below.[10] As Marge Piercy puts it in her splendid novel of the Revolution, *City of Darkness, City of Light*: '... enlightened gentlemen ... imagined a Revolution that would be vigorous but polite, a matter of making speeches and passing laws and perhaps a referendum or two. They had never imagined that people who waited on them in stores and made boots for them, who carted off their waste and brought them water, would come to rule.'[11]

One of the most articulate advocates of the view that the Revolution was over was Isaac-René-Guy Le Chapelier, who had been *président* of the *Assemblée nationale* in 1789. In June 1791 Le Chapelier put forward a law to be adopted by the *Assemblée*, banning workers of the same trade from forming any collective organisation. In moving his proposal Le Chapelier created an image of violent pickets which has been recycled many times in the last two centuries by the enemies of trade unionism: 'They even use violence to enforce these regulations; they compel workers to leave their workshops, even if they are satisfied with the wages they are receiving.' Not a single speaker from within the Assembly opposed him.[12]

Le Chapelier's anxieties had been inspired by strikes of Parisian workers in April and May 1971 involving several tens of thousands of workers. Babeuf was not in Paris at this time, but a manuscript of his survives which reads: 'The workers of Paris are in revolt, they are issuing decrees, they are demanding a higher daily wage, and forcing those who are taking no part in their deliberations to stop work.'[13] While this contains no explicit approval of such action, it makes it clear that Babeuf took a keen interest in the evolving position of the wage-earning classes.

He was not alone in observing that there were class divisions within the Revolutionary forces. In April 1791 an article in *Les révolutions de Paris* declared that:

> We cannot escape from the fact that it was the proletarians who overthrew the Bastille and destroyed despotism, it was they who fought for their fatherland, while the comfortable bourgeoisie, steeped in the lethargy which comes naturally to them, stayed at home waiting to see which side would win the victory.[14]

A modern sense should not be projected back on the term 'prolétaire'. If the word *'prolétaire'* was in common currency in the 1790s, the collective term *'prolétariat'* did not enter the French language until 1832[15] – a reflection of the slow and tortuous process of class formation.

Nonetheless the article is of considerable interest, not least because one of the main contributors to *Les révolutions de Paris* was Sylvain Maréchal, later to be a leading figure in the 1796 conspiracy. Admittedly this article is not among those listed by Maurice Dommanget, Maréchal's biographer, as being definitely by Maréchal. But Dommanget tells us he has omitted articles about which there is 'the slightest doubt'.[16] In any case, the article originated from an editorial team including Maréchal, and expresses a current of ideas in which he actively participated.

Maréchal's ideas of class struggle went back to the pre-Revolutionary period, and in his 1791 pamphlet *Dame Nature à la barre de l'Assemblée Nationale* he repudiated those who claimed the Revolution was finished by insisting that it could not be over until economic equality had been established:

> The Revolution is not over; it will not be over as long as you remain in the circle of the same ideas, having changed only minor details . . . You declare the abolition of the nobility, but you preserve the relative conditions of the poor and of the rich, of masters and their servants . . . [17]

On 29 September 1791 Le Chapelier returned to the attack; now his target was the *sociétés populaires*, which he believed had served their purpose and should be limited in their activity. His report not merely set out lucidly his belief that the Revolution was now finished, but gave a very clear summary of what he and his political allies thought a Revolution consisted of:

> As long as the Revolution was still continuing, this state of affairs has almost always done more good than harm. When a nation is changing the form of its government, then every citizen rules; all deliberate and are obliged to deliberate on public affairs; and everything which urges on, strengthens and accelerates a revolution must be made use of. It is a momentary fermentation which must be supported and even intensified, so that the Revolution leaves its opponents in no doubt, and thus confronts fewer obstacles and reaches its goal more quickly.
>
> But when the Revolution has finished, when the Constitution of the regime has been fixed, when all public powers have been delegated, when all authorities have been appointed, then in the interests of the preservation of this Constitution, it is necessary for the most perfect order to be restored, for nothing to obstruct the operation of the constituted authorities, for deliberation and power to be located only where the Constitution has placed them, and for everyone adequately to respect both his own rights as a citizen and the delegated functions, so that he does not go beyond the former and never interferes with the latter.[18]

A Revolution, then, is simply a transition between two governments, in which the personnel holding power changes, but the basic form of rule remains the same. Spontaneity and mass involvement may be a necessary evil, but they are an inconvenience to be got rid of as soon as possible.

In winding up, Le Chapelier made his position even clearer:

> Everyone has sworn to accept the Constitution, everyone wants order and public peace, everyone wants the Revolution to be finished; from now on these are the unambiguous signs of patriotism. The time of destruction is over; there are no more abuses to be overthrown, no more prejudices to be fought against: from now on our task is to embellish this edifice of which liberty and equality are the cornerstones...[19]

Here Le Chapelier's rhetoric deconstructs itself neatly. If indeed *tout le monde* [everyone] wished the Revolution to be over, there would be no need to clamp down on the *sociétés populaires* [popular societies], no need to make the speech. It was only because some people patently did not wish the Revolution to be over that Le Chapelier had to be so eloquent in his insistence that it was. *Tout le monde* meant those who shared Le Chapelier's political perspectives and class interests; for them it might well be true that 'il ne reste plus d'abus à renverser' [there were no more abuses to overthrow]. Things doubtless looked somewhat different to the average water carrier or market porter.

Whereas nobody in the *Assemblée nationale* had defended the right of wage-earners to protect their livelihoods, this time round Le Chapelier evoked a prompt response from Robespierre himself, doubtless anxious as to his power base. He rejected the view that the Revolution was finished, although his speech was couched in terms of a typically vapid moralism, and gave little concrete indication of how he wished to take the Revolution forward:

> For my part, when I see on the one hand that the new-born Constitution still has enemies without and within; when I see that the language and the outward signs have changed, but that the actions have remained the same, and that hearts can have been changed only by a miracle; when at the same time I see intrigue and falsehood sounding the alarm, spreading confusion and discord; when I see the leaders of opposing factions fighting not so much for the cause of the Revolution as in order to make inroads into the power of dominating in the

name of monarch; when on the other hand I see the excessive zeal with which they banish the very name of liberty; when I see the extraordinary means they employ to kill the public spirit, by reviving prejudices, frivolity and idolatry; then I do not believe that the Revolution is finished.[20]

Le Chapelier won the vote but lost the war; the restrictions on the *sociétés populaires* were never in fact applied. A little over two years later the Revolution was in fact finished, as far as Le Chapelier was concerned. Having returned from a visit to England, he found himself suspected of conspiracy and went into hiding. In a move which must cast doubt on his political judgement, he wrote to his old adversary Robespierre, asking for help and giving his address. *L'Incorruptible* [the Incorruptible] was not a man to let old acquaintance stand in the way of Revolutionary virtue, and Le Chapelier was promptly sent to the guillotine.

In the period 1789–94 Babeuf regarded the Revolution as a process which could either be developed or cut short. His perspective was of an evolution towards a radically more equal society; he enthused over every step which seemed to move in that direction, and raged against whatever seemed to obstruct it, especially the preservation of privileges attached to wealth. As a journalist he exhorted greater efforts for equality and democracy, as an agitator he campaigned vigorously against such surviving unjust taxes as the *aides* [customs taxes] and the *champart* [tithes]. He had a highly optimistic view of the potential timescale of Revolutionary advance. In the spring of 1793 he wrote to his wife: 'This is exciting me to the point of madness. The *sans-culottes* want to be happy, and I don't think it is impossible that within a year, if we carry out our measures aright and act with all necessary prudence, we shall succeed in ensuring general happiness on earth.'[21]

Thermidor meant a dramatic change in perspectives for all participants in the Revolution. The Thermidorians wanted to mark a clean break with the policies of the Terror, while continuing to assert their Revolutionary legitimacy as the true heirs of the principles of 1789. To retain their hegemony they had to assert both continuity and change, an assertion which put the very fabric of language under enormous pressure. One of the more naïve Thermidorians, Edmé Petit, recognised this in a speech to the *Convention nationale* in September 1794. He accused Robespierre and his associates of perverting language: 'Let us remember that, beginning with the word 'revolution', they robbed all the words in the French language of their true meaning...'. And he concluded with a practical proposal to undo this damage: 'The Committee of Public

Instruction is given the task of producing a periodical publication designed to give the words which make up the French language their true meaning, and to restore to republican morality its true energy.'[22]

This linguistic anguish reflected a profound questioning of the basic concepts of the Revolutionary period. Babeuf and his colleagues were not exempt from this process. Babeuf's initial support for Thermidor – which has embarrassed many of his more hagiographic defenders – was very understandable in an unprecedented and confusing situation.

Babeuf's lucidity and courage were soon made clear in September 1794, when he attempted to make a dialectical assessment of the two Robespierres – 'Robespierre the apostle of freedom, and Robespierre the most infamous of tyrants' – something liable to endear him neither to the surviving Jacobins nor to the Thermidorians anxious to dismiss Robespierre merely with terms of abuse.[23]

From the very start Babeuf differentiated himself from the Thermidorian orthodoxy that the Revolution was finished. For him Thermidor marked, not the end of the Revolution, but its recommencement; he may have been naïve in his acceptance of Thermidorian rhetoric, but his Revolutionary commitment was unswerving:

> Five years ago we did indeed make a revolution; but we must have the honesty to recognise that since then we have allowed the counter-revolution to be carried through; and this latter event dates precisely from the time when we permitted the first attack on the freedom of opinion, whether in speech or in writing. 10 Thermidor marks the fresh point since when we have been in labour for a rebirth of freedom.[24]

Babeuf was not alone in challenging the idea that the Revolution was over. His paper, the *Tribun du peuple*, became a focus for those who wanted to see a continuation of the Revolution. Sylvain Maréchal contributed an anonymous article to Babeuf's journal in which he clearly set the final goal of the Revolution as the abolition of private property: 'But the Revolution will not be over as long as all men do not share the fruits of the earth just as they share the rays of the sun.'[25]

A little earlier, Babeuf had quoted with approval a paragraph from a contemporary journal, *Ami des lois*: 'They dare to claim shamelessly that they want to finish the Revolution. What am I saying? They dare to publish that it is over. Well, for my part, I shall say...that if the Revolution were over...the poor would be able to live.'[26] The *Ami des lois* was in fact a government-subsidised paper, but one of its leading contributors at this stage was Robert Lindet. Lindet was later accused at Vendôme along with the *babouvistes*, although he denied, with some plausibility, any connection with Babeuf.[27] *Ami des lois* was later to viciously attack the *babouvistes* as royalist agents.[28] Nonetheless the paragraph cited makes a vigorous point, showing the arguments that were current at the time.

In 1796 the *babouvistes* continued to reject the notion that the Revolution was over. In the widely fly-posted *Analyse de la doctrine de Babeuf* [Analysis of the Doctrine of Babeuf], the most authoritative statement of the conspiracy's aims, article XI stated: 'The Revolution is not finished, because the rich consume all the goods and monopolise power, while the poor work just like slaves, languishing in poverty and being as nothing in the state.'[29]

The papers seized at the time of Babeuf's arrest, which contained rough drafts and private jottings, reveal that Babeuf was still wrestling with the question of how Revolution was to be defined. He had copied Saint-Just's famous warning that 'Those who make revolutions halfway have only dug their own graves',[30] and its significance was clearly occupying his mind.

One draft in Babeuf's handwriting drew out one of the distinctive features of the *babouviste* concept of Revolution, namely that it was to be universal, not simply for some sections of the community: 'So you said to yourselves: "we too have the job of making a revolution; but this one must be the last one, since its outcome must be to satisfy the desires of every member of the Nation . . . to give everyone a destiny such that nobody will need to envy anyone else".'[31]

The monarchist constitution of 1791 had reserved democratic rights for active citizens, those who paid a certain sum in *contributions* [taxes] and were not domestic servants. (There were 4.3 million active citizens out of 7 million males of voting age.)[32] The constitution of 1793 had established universal male suffrage. The post-Thermidor constitution of 1795 again removed citizenship rights from servants and restricted them to those paying *contributions*. (Le Cour Grandmaison suggests that one reason for the exclusion of servants was that they were unproductive, that is, they did not make anything.[33] In this they were comparable to the unskilled workers who were generally excluded from citizenship by poverty.) In addition, it imposed an additional restriction, in that from Year XII young people being entered on the *registre civique* [civil register] must be able to read and write and to practise a *profession mécanique* [engineering profession].[34]

The *babouvistes* rejected any attempt to limit rights of citizenship on the basis of wealth, gender or literacy. They found their support primarily amongst groups excluded by those with a more limited conception of the Revolution. It would clearly be anachronistic to refer to the conspiracy as a working-class movement; the Parisian working class was still embryonic. But Babeuf and his comrades gave particular importance to wage earners.[35] For Buonarroti, the division between employers and wage earners was the fundamental cleavage in society:

> From the fact that there are many wage earners and few employers necessarily results the poverty of the former group. Ignorance is both a necessary condition for overloaded workers and a protection for those who have foisted their own burdens onto them. In our society poverty and ignorance give birth to slavery, which exists everywhere that men lack the power or the ability to make use of their will.[36]

Juste Moroy reported that in the twelfth *arrondissement* of Paris 'You hear sack-carriers and laundresses saying: 'We are sovereign.'[37] This assertion of citizenship on behalf of unskilled manual workers and women workers is typical of the *babouvistes'* target audience.

Literacy was linked to situation in the productive process. Whereas skilled artisans were generally literate, and left copious written records, the unskilled workers – market porters, dockers, water carriers and so on – were frequently illiterate. The *babouvistes* sought to initiate the illiterate into political life. At least two of those who stood trial alongside Babeuf at Vendôme were illiterate (Boudin and Clérex).[38] In 1796 Babeuf received a report that among soldiers stationed in Paris scarcely 10 per cent could read.[39] The response of the *babouvistes* was to develop forms of propaganda specifically addressed to the illiterate – songs, impromptu meetings in front of posters, and so forth.

One particular group excluded from reading may be mentioned here. In 1793 Valentin Haüy, a pioneer of education for the blind, drafted an address which read: 'We may lack a precious sense, the blind children cried, but we are nonetheless citizens.' Haüy's aim was that the blind should not be seen merely as victims, fit only to beg, but should acquire skills to overcome their handicap. While his links with *babouvisme* remain obscure, he was listed by the conspirators as a potential supporter.[40]

Babeuf had always distinguished himself from the Jacobins, and indeed from some of his own collaborators, in his defence of full political rights for women.[41] This is one of his most distinctive features, since, as

Le Cour Grandmaison points out: 'The exclusion of women is the most widely shared attitude among the revolutionaries.'[42] There were undoubtedly disagreements, even among the inner circle of *babouvistes*, about women's equality; but Babeuf's position clearly triumphed, since in the *Fragment d'un projet de décret économique* [outline of a plan for economic decree], published by Buonarroti as one of the conspiracy's policy statements, it is quite clear that women were to have full citizenship: 'Every French person of either sex who makes over all his or her property to the fatherland, and devotes his or her person and labour to it, is a member of the great national community.'[43]

In redefining the aims of the Revolution, the *babouvistes* were also obliged to redefine its means. To paraphrase William Morris, they saw the Revolution as being not simply 'for all' but 'by all'.[44] In his major speech at Vendôme, Babeuf set out his conception of the Revolution as he had come to see it:

> The Revolution – I went on as I addressed the people – must not be an action whose outcome is worthless. So many torrents of blood should not have flowed just to leave the people in even more straitened circumstances. When a people makes a revolution, it is because the operation of defective institutions has driven the best impulses in society to breaking point, so that the majority of its useful members can no longer go on in the same way. They feel ill at ease in this situation, they need change and they stir themselves in order to achieve it. Society is right to act thus, for it was only established in order to be, as a whole, as happy as possible: *The purpose of society is common happiness.*[45]

For the *babouvistes* the Revolution could not be considered as a simple transfer of power between one group and another. As early as 1790 a monarchist pamphleteer had accused Le Chapelier of wanting to make himself king,[46] and in the days after Thermidor there was a widespread rumour, false but plausible, that Robespierre had intended to proclaim himself monarch.[47] For the *babouvistes* Revolution meant, not a change of rulers, but a transformation of the conditions of life. As Babeuf put it in his popular paper *L'Éclaireur*, the aim was '...a Republic where the immense majority is in command and is sovereign; where every citizen enjoys the same rights; where we do not see unbridled luxury insulting the most terrible poverty; from which penury and corruption are banished; where every member of society can rely on subsistence, independently of the whims of fortune or of any individual; where virtue is honoured and crime punished; where in short true equality reigns, that is, *common happiness*.[48]

Such happiness could not be achieved on behalf of the majority by a minority of political activists; the *babouvistes* were alive to the danger of the development of a separate group of politicians, acting outside the direct involvement of the masses:

> If a class were formed in society which was exclusively acquainted with the art of running society, with laws and administration, it would rapidly discover in the superiority of its intelligence, and above all in the ignorance of its compatriots, the secret of how to create distinctions and privileges for itself; exaggerating the importance of its services, it would easily succeed in getting itself considered as the necessary protector of the fatherland; and disguising its impudent undertakings with the pretext of the public good, it would continue to speak of liberty and equality to its unperceptive fellow-citizens, already victims of a servitude which would be all the harsher for seeming to be legal and voluntary.[49]

Such a Revolution could not be carried through by palliatives or half measures; as Babeuf put it in one of his drafts: 'Partial popular laws, regenerative half-measures, these mere alleviations to which their desires seem to be limited, are always lacking in solidity.'[50] Nor could it be achieved through short-cuts; the provocateur Grisel proposed burning down castles outside Paris and assassinating the members of the Directory, but Babeuf opposed such acts.[51]

As Charles Germain argued at the Vendôme trial, the alleged 'conspiracy' was not a conspiracy at all, but an open campaign for a different concept of the Revolution:

> Is it conspiring to constantly inform the people of its rights; to give free rein to one's thoughts, to one's opinions? Is it conspiring to give one's fellow-citizens advice; advice which will be punished solely by contempt if they find it unsuitable, advice whose authors will be rewarded by public esteem if, after careful consideration, it is judged to be worthy and fitting?'[52]

Hence Revolution must be made by the oppressed, for only they could be the agents of their own emancipation. As Babeuf told the organisers in the various *arrondissements* of Paris:

Make the people understand that they will never do anything great, that they will never make revolutions for themselves, for their true happiness, except when there are no rulers involved in any way in their movement; they must not be so distrustful of their own resources, and they must convince themselves that they, the people, are sufficient to be able to carry out a great undertaking.[53]

The insurrection never took place, Babeuf was executed and the organisation smashed. A little later, when Bonaparte came to power, it could truly be said that the Revolution had been stopped. Yet although the *babouviste* conception of Revolution seemed to have disappeared the struggle had not been in vain. Babeuf's comrade Buonarroti never abandoned the task of organising and propagating the ideas of *bonheur commun* [common happiness] and *parfaite égalité* [perfect equality]. For many years Buonarroti's efforts seemed confined to the underworld of secret societies, but when in 1828 he published his history of Babeuf's conspiracy, the old mole reappeared.[54] In his last years Buonarroti was a constant associate of and adviser to the new generation of radicals who had emerged from the Revolution of 1830, and who would provide the leadership for the Revolution of 1848.

Among the documents published by Buonarroti was Maréchal's *Manifeste des égaux* [manifesto of the equals], which contained the stirring promise: 'The French Revolution is only the forerunner of another revolution which will be greater and more impressive, and which will be the last.'[55] This notion that the French Revolution had been incomplete in itself, and that it required completion by a further process, was taken up by socialists of the new generation. In 1839 Cabet wrote of Thiers' *Histoire de la révolution* 'it is the *bourgeois revolution* which the author is defending here; he is defending it against the innovations of *Democracy* as much as against the encroachments of the *Aristocracy*'.[56]

This notion of a 'bourgeois Revolution' to be followed and completed by a 'socialist Revolution' was taken up and developed by Marx and the Marxist tradition. As Daniel Guérin has shown, there is a direct line of continuity between Babeuf's concept of Revolution and Marx's: 'Long before Marx, he [Babeuf] had observed that the revolution is a single process, that it is permanent, that every revolution contains the seeds of a proletarian revolution, that the fundamental conflict is that between those who own property and those who do not.'[57]

And when François Furet set out to combat the noxious influence of Marxism in the historiography of the French Revolution, it is not surprising that he took his most famous soundbite: 'The French Revolution is over.'[58] from the tradition of Le Chapelier and the Thermidorians. Babeuf fought vigorously and unceasingly against the comfortable notion that the Revolution was over, and those today who wish to oppose Furet's interpretation of the Revolution will still find much in Babeuf that repays study.

Notes

1 *Débats du procès instruit par la haute-cour de justice contre Drouet, Babeuf et autres* (Paris, Imprimerie nationale, 1797, 4 vols), vol. 3, p. 217.
2 B. Baczko, *Comment sortir de la Terreur* (Paris, Gallimard, 1989), p. 353.
3 L. Trotsky, *The History of the Russian Revolution* (London, Pluto, 1997), p. 781.
4 F. Furet and M. Ozouf, *Dictionnaire critique de la Révolution française* (Paris, Flammarion, 1988), pp. 201–2.
5 I.H. Birchall, *The Spectre of Babeuf* (Basingstoke, Macmillan, 1997), pp. 107–21.
6 F. Buonarroti, *Conspiration pour l'égalité dite de Babeuf* (Paris, Editions sociales, 1957, 2 vols), vol. 1, p. 41.
7 Birchall, *Spectre of Babeuf*, pp. 142–6.
8 Buonarroti, *Conspiration pour l'égalité*, vol. 2, p. 210.
9 Baczko, *Comment sortir*, p. 58.
10 See R. Miliband, 'Barnave: a Case of Bourgeois Class Consciousness', in I. Mészáros (ed.), *Aspects of History and Class Consciousness* (London, Routledge and Kegan Paul, 1971), pp. 22–48.
11 M. Piercy, *City of Darkness, City of Light* (Harmondsworth, Penguin, 1997), p. 418.
12 P.-J.-B. Buchez and P.-C. Roux, *Histoire parlementaire de la Révolution* (Paris, Paulin, 1834–38, 40 vols), vol. 10, pp. 193–5.
13 V. Daline, Gracchus Babeuf (Moscow, Editions du progrès, 1987), p. 333.
14 *Les Révolutions de Paris*, No. 95, April 1791; cited S.M. Gruner, 'Le concept de classe dans la Révolution française: une mise à jour', *Histoire Sociale/Social History*, IX (November 1976), 417.
15 J. Grandjonc, *Communisme/Kommunismus/Communism* (Trier, Karl-Marx-Haus, 1989, 3 vols), vol. 1, p. 72.
16 M. Dommanget, *Sylvain Maréchal* (Paris, Spartacus, 1950), pp. 485–6.
17 Ibid., pp. 186–7.
18 Le Chapelier, *Rapport sur les sociétés populaires* (Paris, Imprimerie nationale, 1791), p. 4.
19 Ibid., p. 9.
20 *Gazette nationale ou Le moniteur universel*, No. 275 (2 October 1791), p. 9.
21 Letter of 17 April 1793, in R. Legrand, *Babeuf et ses compagnons de route* (Paris, Société des études robespierristes, 1981), p. 130.
22 *Gazette nationale ou Le moniteur universel* No. 360 (30 fructidor, an II [16 September 1794]), pp. 758–9.
23 *Journal de la liberté de la presse*, 17 fructidor, an II [3 September, 1794], p. 5.

24   Ibid., 19 fructidor, an II [5 September, 1794], p. 2.
25   *Le tribun du peuple*, No. 40, 5 ventôse, an IV [24 February, 1796], p. 255; for attribution see Dommanget, *Sylvain Maréchal*, p. 308.
26   *Ami des lois*, 9 frimaire, an IV [30 November, 1795], cited *Le tribun du peuple*, no. 36, 20 frimaire, an IV [11 December, 1795], p. 111.
27   *Second mémoire* pour Robert Lindet (Evreux, Imprimerie de Touquet, no date), p. 3.
28   J.D. Popkin, 'The Directory and the Republican Press: the Case of the *Ami des Lois*', *History of European Ideas*, 10 (1989), 429–42.
29   Buonarroti, *Conspiration pour l'égalité*, vol. 2, p. 106.
30   Haute cour de justice, *Copie des pièces saisies dans le local que Babeuf occupait lors de son arrestation* (Paris, Imprimerie nationale, an V [1796–97]), vol. 2, p. 72.
31   Ibid., vol. 1, p. 235.
32   O. Le Cour Grandmaison, *Les Citoyennetés en révolution* (Presses universitaires de France, Paris, 1992), p. 18.
33   Ibid., pp. 60–61.
34   Article 16. J. Godechot (ed.), *Les Constitutions de la France depuis 1789* (Paris, Garnier-Flammarion, 1970), pp. 104–5.
35   For a fuller discussion of Babeuf and the working class see Birchall, *Spectre of Babeuf*, pp. 147–51.
36   Buonarroti, *Conspiration pour l'égalité*, vol. 1, p. 27.
37   Haute cour de justice, *Copie des pièces*, vol. 1, p. 256.
38   *Débats du procès*, vol. 3, pp. 512, 524.
39   Haute cour de justice, *Copie des pièces*, vol. 1, p. 44.
40   Pierre Henri, *La vie et oeuvre de Valentin Haüy* (Paris, Presses universitaires de France, 1984), pp. 93, 115–16; Legrand, *Babeuf et ses compagnons*, p. 360.
41   See I.H. Birchall, 'Babeuf and the Oppression of Women', *British Journal for Eighteenth-Century Studies*, 20/1 (1997), 63–75.
42   Le Cour Grandmaison, *Les Citoyennetés*, p. 290.
43   Buonarroti, *Conspiration pour l'égalité*, vol. 2, p. 205.
44   'By us, not for us', letter to Daily Chronicle, 10 November 1893, in William Morris, *News from Nowhere and Selected Writings and Designs* (Harmondsworth, Penguin, 1962), p. 145.
45   V. Advielle, *Histoire de Gracchus Babeuf et du babouvisme* (Paris, Editions du comité des travaux historiques et scientifiques, 1990), vol. 2, pp. 29–30.
46   *Vie privée et politique du roi Isaac Chapelier* (Rennes, Chez l'auteur, 1790).
47   Baczko, *Comment sortir*, pp. 9, 17.
48   *L'Éclaireur* No. 4 [no date, approximately 7 germinal, an IV – 27 March 1796], p. 38.
49   Buonarroti, *Conspiration pour l'égalité*, vol. 1, p. 171.
50   Haute cour de justice, *Copie des pièces*, vol. 2, p. 21.
51   *Débats du procès*, vol. 2, pp. 90–91, 102–3.
52   Ibid, vol. 2, p. 151.
53   Haute cour de justice, *Copie des pièces*, vol. 2, p. 203.
54   The image is Marx's, in *The Eighteenth Brumaire of Louis Bonaparte*, in its turn borrowed from Shakespeare's Hamlet.
55   Buonarroti, *Conspiration pour l'égalité*, vol. 2, p. 95.

56 Cabet, *Histoire populaire de la Révolution française* (1839), vol. 1, p. vi; cited Grandjonc, *Communisme/Kommunismus/Communism*, vol. 1, p. 169.
57 D. Guérin, *La lutte de classes sous la première république* (Paris, Gallimard, 1968, 2 vols), vol. 2, p. 379.
58 F. Furet, *Penser la Révolution française* (Paris, Gallimard, 1978), p. 11.

5
The Uses of Democracy. Elections and Plebiscites in Napoleonic France

Malcolm Crook

Many scholars are acquainted with the plebiscites that took place in Napoleonic France between 1799 and 1815, but even among specialists a great deal of ignorance surrounds the elections that were held throughout the same period. Georges Lefebvre, for example, suggested that while provision was certainly made for electoral consultations, in practice they were rarely held.[1] Louis Bergeron, for his part, misrepresented the precise nature of the deliberately complex electoral system which was adopted under Napoleon.[2] These days there is no excuse for such errors, because a couple of decades ago Jean-Yves Coppolani produced a comprehensive introduction to the subject.[3] Unfortunately this fine work of scholarship spoils its own case by considering the Napoleonic electoral system as high comedy, a judgement contradicted by much of the material advanced to support it.

Besides underlining the fact that elections, like plebiscites, did indeed take place under Napoleon, this chapter will suggest that, for all their shortcomings when compared with today's polls, these consultations were more than just historical curiosities.[4] To be sure, their impact upon the exercise of power was minimal, for decisions were simply ratified by plebiscite, while elections proper merely named candidates for office, among whom government or administration made the final selection. This use of democracy provided a forerunner for those 'elections without choice' that have characterised authoritarian regimes of both Right and Left in more recent times. As the editors of a volume devoted to such contests suggest: 'the fact that elections do not have the same meaning when they are without choice is not evidence that they lack any meaning at all'.

The major purpose of twentieth-century elections of this sort is to serve as a source of legitimation for regimes which have reduced freedom of expression, an objective that was equally apparent in Bonapartist France. Nonetheless, under Napoleon it can be argued that the electoral practice facilitated by his various consultations served as a bridge between the more liberal regimes which preceded and succeeded his dictatorship. From the First Republic to the Bourbon Restoration there was no hiatus in electoral participation for the notables, and many ordinary French people too. The electoral apprenticeship begun in 1789 thus continued in Bonapartist France, and the resulting experiment offered something of a model for similar progress under the Second Empire later in the nineteenth century.[5]

The author's own interest in the topic stems from a forthcoming work to explore the development of a culture of elections in France from the Revolution to the Third Republic: *How France Learned to Vote*. What matters about this neglected episode in the wider process is the way in which because of the Napoleonic regime, as much as in spite of it, the electoral experience of the Revolution was transmitted to the nineteenth century. Too often the history of elections grinds to a halt in 1799 and only resumes in 1815, or even 1848. It will be suggested that there was an unexpected degree of electoral continuity across the apparent divide. To fully appreciate it, the Napoleonic practice of elections and plebiscites must be set in a broader context; Bonaparte twisted rather than termin-ated the Revolutionary heritage, and the Restoration in turn adopted a good deal of his legacy. Therefore, the nature of elections under Napo-leon, levels of participation in them and, finally, their contribution to the elaboration of an electoral culture in modern France will be discussed.

Those historians who have unwarily strayed on to the electoral terrain of Napoleonic France have frequently been confused by its complex nature. Yet within the wilfully Byzantine procedures that were employed, there appeared elements of experimentation which further extended the broad repertoire accumulated during the Revolution. Exactly how were elections conducted under Napoleon?

Three different systems emerged, each corresponding to a phase in the evolution of the Bonapartist regime: the first originated under the Con-sulate in the Constitution of 1799 (or the Year VIII, according to the Republican calendar) and introduced a system of electoral lists; the second was ushered in with the Life Consulate of 1802 (Year X), which restored electoral colleges; and the third was a fleeting accompaniment of the Additional Act concocted during the Hundred Days in 1815, after Napoleon had returned from Elba. Besides these elections proper, four plebiscites took place (they were actually referred to as 'votes on the Constitution'), in 1800, 1802, 1804 and 1815, to sanction the major constitutional changes of the era, from the establishment of the Consulate, to the Life Consulate, First Empire and, lastly, the 'liberal' Empire of 1815.[6]

Bonaparte immediately summoned the people to pronounce upon the constitution that was hurriedly issued at the very end of 1799, in the wake of his famous *coup d'état* in November (Brumaire, Year VIII). Following the Revolutionary precedents set in 1793 and 1795, the Constitution of the Year VIII was duly submitted to a plebiscite.[7] The novelty in January 1800, when voting took place throughout the Republic, lay in the fact that instead of meeting in assemblies, as tradition dictated, participants were asked to vote individually at a number of locations where registers were opened for them to sign. These included the *hôtel de ville*, notaries' premises, courtrooms and administrative headquarters in the larger towns or, in the many villages that in those days lacked a *mairie*, the mayor's house.

Whereas in 1793 and 1795 (as for all primary elections), voters had travelled to the *chef-lieu de canton*,[8] they were now able to vote in their own *commune* and they were allowed several days to do so, rather than awaiting a lengthy roll-call at the cantonal assembly on the appointed day.[9] Under Napoleon participants recorded their opinion, for or against the constitution, in a register. The business of voting thus became an individual rather than a collective gesture, though it also became more susceptible to official rather than communal pressure as a consequence.

These polling arrangements were maintained for the three plebiscites that followed later. However, a version of the individual ballot was also employed for elections proper, when lists of citizens eligible for office, the so-called *notables*, were compiled in 1801. This pyramid system, enshrined in the Constitution of the Year VIII and very much a product of Sieyès' thinking, was based on the decimal principle. It involved the primary or basic electorate nominating a tenth of its number to serve on the communal (or *arrondissement*) list. Those chosen at this level then selected a tenth of their number for the departmental list. Finally, these departmental notables selected a tenth of their number to form a national list. In future the local and central authorities were to choose all officials from the appropriate lists.[10] Precise arrangements for this process were presented to the Tribunate on 10 February 1801 and they became law on 4 March (13 ventôse IX). The electorate was divided into series of no less than 51 and no more than 150 citizens, who were to present themselves at the residence of the polling clerk to list a tenth of their number to go on the communal list. Roederer, a great ally of Bonaparte and a staunch supporter of this scheme, on which he claimed unrivalled expertise, suggested that these electoral regulations had rendered voting far easier than before:

> According to this system, no one is obliged to leave his commune, nor even his *quartier* in order to vote: nor is he constrained by the requirement to vote on a particular day or at a precise time, nor exposed to the vexations of a political rival or canvassing for his vote, nor condemned to any extraordinary expense. No time or money is lost, no opposition has to be endured.[11]

Voting at the second or third stages of the process, at *arrondissement* and departmental level, at the home of the oldest notary in the *chef-lieu*, obviously required displacement, but voting remained a solitary business.

Bonaparte himself was never especially enamoured of this complex scheme, which he found somewhat 'absurd', while Portalis was apparently in favour of its implementation only as a means of discrediting it.[12] Individual voting of a sort familiar to electors of the late twentieth century functioned effectively enough when it was simply a case of recording a yes or no verdict in a plebiscite. In the elections of 1801, by contrast, voters were expected to list a large number of names when they arrived at the polling station. Many prefects and sub-prefects, who were responsible for the organisation, complained bitterly about the difficulties of producing and counting the lists, given the limited and often illiterate personnel on whom they were obliged to rely. Computing the results subsequently gave rise to endless disputes, as much a consequence of confusion as of corruption, for pre-written lists were frowned upon and there were inevitably difficulties in distinguishing the handwritten names that voters inscribed on their ballot papers.[13]

It was a considerable achievement that these arrangements operated without any major disruption. The prefect of Mont Blanc reported with evident satisfaction that the:

> formation of *arrondissement* lists had been accomplished without any of those upheavals which accompanied preceding elections and which, during the Revolution, had contributed more than anything else to the discredit of the representative system and divisions among citizens...[14]

The First Consul was sufficiently impressed to compliment those who had taken part on their performance and rounded on the critics:

You all said that the system was inoperable and that only Roederer understood it. Well, the people have taken the trouble to understand it and execute it. Now you want to annul it all, and show lack of respect for the people who have shown such respect for your law.[15]

This voting procedure was repeated at communal level in the spring of the Year X (1802), when the ever-popular justices of the peace and their deputies were elected in the same fashion.[16] Turnout was relatively high, yet on this occasion Bonaparte expressed his displeasure at the outcome.[17] Indeed, he was quick to abandon the entire electoral list system as soon as he became Consul for Life later in 1802. The Constitution of 1799 was radically overhauled and a system of cantonal, *arrondissement* and departmental assemblies, or electoral colleges, similar to those employed during the Revolutionary decade, was established for the remainder of his regime. Individual polling was abandoned in favour of tried and tested collective procedures, though the voters' role remained restricted to the presentation of candidates from whom the authorities made the final choice.

According to the Constitution of 1802 (Year X), instead of composing lists of eligible citizens, the electorate was invited to assemble in the cantons in order to choose candidates to serve as justices of the peace and, in towns of more than 5000 inhabitants, municipal councillors. The same voters also selected members for the departmental and *arrondissement* electoral colleges, which were entrusted with the nomination of candidates for *arrondissement* and departmental councils, as well as for national parliamentary bodies. This was effectively a reversion to the two-tier system of the Revolutionary decade, when primary voters in the cantons had despatched second-degree electors to district and departmental assemblies. However, whereas this procedure had operated annually during the Revolution it was to do so less frequently under Napoleon, with each department following a rota roughly every five years. Moreover, members of the *arrondissement* and departmental colleges were elected for life, like the First Consul, and only replacements were chosen thereafter.[18]

These arrangements were modified in 1815. During the Hundred Days, besides reintroducing municipal elections in smaller communities (where the right to elect mayors and aldermen had been denied since 1800), Napoleon abandoned the presentation of candidates and reinstated the right of direct election from the *arrondissement* and departmental assemblies. This was a liberal gesture aimed at consolidating support for the returning hero and it was immediately put into effect in May 1815.[19] *Arrondissement* and departmental electoral colleges survived under the Restoration, though cantonal elections were abolished after 1815. However, a heavily restricted franchise was now applied at both levels and persisted until the Revolution of 1848 finally established both direct and democratic elections to the French legislature.[20] It is in 1848 that many historians begin their accounts of universal suffrage in France, yet only minimal restrictions were imposed on the adult male franchise after 1799, despite widespread expectations to the contrary.[21] Indeed, it is commonly asserted that Bonaparte restored universal male suffrage, which had been limited under the preceding regime of the Directory. The exiled journalist Mallet du Pan actually coined the term *'suffrage universel'* to describe the new electoral system, though women, paupers and domestic servants remained excluded.[22] Yet there were no qualifications for election to the lists of eligibility and only the stillborn Constitution of 1793 had proved more generous where the franchise was concerned. Fresh voter registers were drawn up during the Year IX (1800–01) to serve as a basis for electing Sieyès' short-lived pyramid of lists. The evidence suggests that roughly 20 per cent of the population was enfranchised.[23] Since it is generally accepted that adult males over 21 years old made up roughly a quarter of the total, up to a fifth of adult males were thus excluded. Even so, just over six million Frenchmen living within the boundaries of France in 1792 (before the expansion of the Republic) could vote under Napoleon. The figure is still higher when all territories are included, but because the annexed departments waxed and waned between 1799 and 1815, the rounded total of six million will be used to facilitate comparisons in the calculations that follow.

Most Frenchmen were thus eligible to vote during the Bonapartist period, and they were given the opportunity to do so on at least eight occasions. Although this was less frequently than during the Revolutionary decade, when there was a chance to vote each year (and during the early years of the Revolution several times each year), it still represents an average of more than once every two years. Moreover, the Napoleonic electorate was able to participate in a variety of votes from plebiscites to local polls, which are listed in Table 5.1.

How many citizens actually chose to participate? Turnout might seem easy to gauge in the case of plebiscites, since global figures were published by the regime. However, these should not be taken at face value. Systematic inflation of the results was practised in 1800, when real turnout was only 50 per cent of the official total, in order to produce a superior outcome to similar exercises during the Revolution. Such fraud continued to be perpetrated, albeit in a more episodic fashion, in both

Table 5.1   French Elections, 1799–1815

Consulate	
1800	Plebiscite on Constitution of the Year VIII
1801	Elections for the lists of *notables*
1802	Elections for justices of the peace
	Plebiscite on Life Consulate
Empire	
1804	Cantonal elections to *arrondissement* and departmental electoral colleges, which then convene to conduct their business
	Plebiscite on the Empire
1807	First series of cantonal, *arrondissement* and departmental elections
1808	Second series
1809	Third series
1810	Fourth series
1811	Fifth and final series
1812	Cycle of elections recommences
1813	Cantonal, *arrondissement* and departmental elections in second series of departments, plus election of justices of the peace and municipal councillors in towns of 5000 or more population, in *all* departments
Hundred Days	
1815	Plebiscite on Additional Act
	Elections in *arrondissement* and departmental colleges
	Municipal elections in communes with fewer than 5000 inhabitants

1802 and 1804.[24] Since verification of the figures is simply not practical for every single department, we must be satisfied with approximations. Excluding the questionable returns from the armed forces and the annexed departments, we can estimate 1.5 million participants in 1800, 3.5 million in 1802, 3 million in 1804 and 1.3 million in 1815:[25]

The overwhelming majority of these votes was affirmative, but it is instructive to measure opposition, or rather indifference to the regime by comparing levels of abstention. What emerges clearly is that turnout

Table 5.2   Turnout in Plebiscites in France, 1793–1815

Year	Total participants	Percentage turnout
1793	2 000 000	33
1795	1 300 000	22
1800	1 500 000	25
1802	3 500 000	58
1804	3 000 000	50
1815	1 300 000	22

was relatively poor in 1800, that it rose significantly in 1802, then fell back in 1804, before declining sharply in 1815. The official returns (which have not been used here) hide this trajectory because they over-play the turnout in 1800, and thus conceal the real increase that occurred two years later. Yet they also mask the loss of enthusiasm that greeted the establishment of the Empire, not only on account of fraud, but also because additional departments took part in the vote. On the other hand, even in the confused circumstances of the Hundred Days, some 1.3 million Frenchmen, representing more than 20 per cent of the electorate, still turned out to vote (excluding the army and navy in which many were enrolled). In the light of the Revolutionary decade this remained a relatively high level of participation.[26]

What of elections proper? Figures for turnout are harder to come by, since they require compilation by department and, in the absence of much deliberate sampling so far, the evidence remains somewhat sparse. Few general conclusions can be formulated at this stage for, as in the Revolution, levels of participation fluctuated wildly from one area to another. In 1801, for example, turnout at the communal level ran from 25 per cent in the Alpes-Maritimes to 75 per cent in the Nord.[27] The prefect of the Drôme bemoaned poor attendance in his department: 'The degree of participation was rather low; in some cases only nine votes were required to become a communal notable; the great majority of citizens, especially in the countryside, did not have sufficient under-standing of what was at stake... Yet the same prefect went on to say that for the departmental notability 'voters were much more numerous', and he reckoned that two-thirds of those eligible to vote had done so.[28] Likewise, in the Alpes-Maritimes and the Yonne over 70 per cent seem to have taken part in choosing a tenth of their number when it came to selecting names for the national list.[29]

More sustained interest at the secondary level of the electoral process was a familiar feature of the Revolutionary decade; it was only to be expected once polling was restricted to those with the time to devote to politics and the contest exercised an evident attraction for persons who were anxious to hold office. The same pattern of lower turnout on the part of first-degree electors was repeated in the elections which sub-sequently took place in the cantonal assemblies under the Napoleonic Empire. When the whole electorate was involved again, from 1807 onwards, participation often dropped to as low as 20 per cent.[30] Indeed, by 1813 it was falling to single figures in some cantons.[31] Still, it should be stressed that similarly low figures were sometimes recorded during the Revolutionary decade, in 1795 or 1799, for instance. Even a 10 per cent turnout of the broad electorate towards the end of the First Empire represented the participation of over half a million Frenchmen.

By contrast, attendance at *arrondissement* and departmental electoral colleges remained much more elevated, if not quite to the extent of comparable second-degree assemblies in the 1790s, when turnout of 80 and 90 per cent was not uncommon. In 1804 it was only the communal (or *arrondissement*) notables, elected in 1801 (and representing 10 per cent of the total electorate), who took part in choosing the first departmental and *arrondissement* colleges of the Life Consulate and turnout was usually 50 per cent or more.[32] Subsequent levels of participation at these electoral colleges might vary, but they rarely fell far below 60 per cent, at least until the special circumstances of the Hundred Days produced some exceptionally low returns of less than 20 per cent in the Midi.[33]

The electoral colleges of the Bonapartist system were retained under the Bourbon Restoration, and indeed down to 1848, though cantonal assemblies were abolished after 1815. The removal of the cantonal level initially reduced the total electorate to a mere 70 000 Frenchmen, but these colleges were now able to elect deputies directly, rather than simply propose candidates for the available offices.[34] It might be argued that under Bonaparte the fact that the final choice rested with the administration was a fundamental distortion of the whole electoral system, fully meriting the accusation of farce deployed by Coppolani. Election was no longer an entitlement, it had become an administrative duty; participants had effectively become *fonctionnaires*, mere cogs in the bureaucratic machine. There was no possibility of changing the government in office and those eventually chosen exercised little real power. To this extent there is no denying that the period did mark a hiatus in the electoral apprenticeship inaugurated in 1789. The Napoleonic regime was abusing rather than using democracy; these were elections which denied some fundamental rights of citizenship.

Yet the fact that the government retained the electoral process at all is significant, since it was clearly aware of the force of public opinion – otherwise, why inflate the results of plebiscites? – and hoped to draw significant conclusions from their outcomes. Of course, the value of elections in this regard was severely damaged by the constraints placed upon the exercise. Hence the lament of the sub-prefect at Toulon in 1813, reporting an abysmally low turnout: 'These days the electoral assemblies are very different from those of the Revolution. Then the people attached the greatest importance to voting and turned out *en masse*; as a result it was possible to discern the passions, opinions and even the most intimate thoughts of each class of citizen. Today, however, the people have come to realise that, on account of its expertise in assessing the contenders, the government alone should be entrusted with making the necessary choices.'[35]

Needless to say, this official was looking back through rose-tinted glasses, for participation had often been low during the 1790s. However, it remains possible to tease out some indication of public opinion by studying these Napoleonic consultations, not just in terms of relative levels of turnout, but also through the careful scrutiny of electoral behaviour. Members of the electoral colleges were required to explain absence or risk expulsion. The fact that some failed to offer apologies renders turnout a useful political indicator; participation in the Hundred Days reveals some especially stark regional contrasts, for example. If the outcome of a vote was contested and more than one round of balloting was required, then this too offers some insight into the presence of subterranean political division.[36]

The inscription of comments in registers employed for the plebiscites certainly renders their analysis more interesting than a purely statistical exercise. This practice represents a continuation of the tradition that linked debate and the formulation of *cahiers* to the process of voting. Indeed, in the consultations on the Constitutions of 1793 and 1795 participants were encouraged to submit resolutions relating to the document and many assemblies did so.[37] Individuals were unable to shake off the habit under Napoleon and some were prepared to make critical rather than congratulatory remarks. For instance, a landowner from Marayes, in the Aube, wrote *à propos* the Life Consulate:

> I would vote positively for the proposed question if the history of all peoples had not taught me never to give the supreme magistracy to one man for the unknown length of his life. Even in the most just hands, this can very often change the hearts and dispositions of the man who has assumed it. I say that such responsibility is nearly always dangerous to both the public and individual liberty and (my admiration for Bonaparte's talents) does not allow me to believe him as infallible as a god. Guided by these considerations I am not of the opinion that Napoleon Bonaparte ought to be designated Consul for Life.[38]

Even in 1815 the tradition remained alive and well. One former Revolutionary expended eight pages of text on his assessment of the vices and defects that he discerned in the Additional Act.[39] However, the essential purpose in considering these largely forgotten consultations of the Napoleonic period is to examine the procedure rather than its outcome: the preservation of the electoral system played a vital role in the process of political acculturation. Electoral practice was attenuated by contrast with the 1790s but it remained in being, conserving the heritage of the Revolution in this regard. Innovations appeared too: individual voting at a communal level was a particularly significant change from the traditional pattern of assemblies, which the Revolutionaries had retained from the *ancien régime*, and it was destined to become the norm later in the nineteenth century.

An element of political choice continued to be expressed and tensions were resolved within the electoral arena, without the violence that so often accompanied voting during the Revolutionary decade, and which had served to discredit the electoral system in the eyes of many Frenchmen. To that extent the claims of the Napoleonic administration were to be fulfilled. As the prefect of the Orne promised: 'You no longer have to fear the inconvenience that was inseparable from those tumultuous electoral assemblies of the past, where conflicting allegiances clashed violently and all too often presented such a shameful spectacle...'. The rules of the game were much more tightly drawn, but they accustomed those involved to play by them. This was true of the ritual of convocation, with the provision of a polling card, the practice of balloting, the successive rounds of voting in search of an absolute majority, and the universal adoption of the ballot box (though it continued to be symbolised by an urn) to regulate the counting of votes.[40]

Elections also offered some valuable political space, despite the official absence of candidates, canvassing and organised parties (which had been equally mistrusted during the Revolutionary decade). The address delivered by Roger Ducos, an accomplice of Sieyès in the *coup* of Brumaire, at the opening of the electoral college of the Landes in 1804, might have emanated from the 1790s: 'Each of us should search our conscience... to discover, wherever they may be found, those men whose modesty enhances their talents and virtues.' Presidents were nominated by the regime, but the assemblies restored after 1802 recovered the right to choose their own secretaries and scrutineers, and with it a certain sense of independence. These assembly officials often made a speech before balloting commenced and, though matters extraneous to the elections were formally excluded from the agenda, debate on a pressing local matter might well ensue. This could lead to the drafting of a petition and a deputation to carry it before the authorities, even to Napoleon himself. The contact between assemblies and the wider public was certainly less than during the Revolution, but reports on proceedings were carried in the newspapers, while the collective dimension and lengthy business of electoral assemblies sustained a much deeper sense of participation than the simple casting of an individual vote.

The notables naturally played a key role, as in preceding and succeeding regimes, both of which sought to encourage the wealthy to assume the burdens of office. After 1802 this was especially apparent in the stipulation that members of the Napoleonic departmental electoral colleges be drawn from among the 600 most heavily taxed individuals in the department. Curiously, *arrondissement* colleges were unrestricted in this regard, though it hardly affected their composition. Yet if Napoleon, like the Revolutionaries, sought to place essential power in the hands of large property owners, unlike the Restoration he invited the great majority of adult males to play a part in their selection. As Rosanvallon comments, this particular attempt to balance 'weight of numbers and rational principles' enabled the Napoleonic regime to constitute 'another stage in the democratic development of France'. The use of democracy in both elections and plebiscites during this period doubtless helps to explain the enduring popularity of Bonapartism in the years that followed.

Notes

1   G. Lefebvre, *Napoléon*, 3rd edn (Paris, Presses universitaires de France, 1947), p. 381.
2   L. Bergeron, *L'épisode napoléonien. Aspects intérieurs 1799–1815* (Paris, Editions du seuil, 1972), p. 85. P. Rosanvallon makes the same mistake in his excellent *Le sacre du citoyen. Histoire du suffrage universel en France* (Paris, Gallimard, 1992), p. 202.
3   J.-Y. Coppolani, *Les élections en France à l'époque napoléonienne* (Paris, Albatros, 1980).
4   Rosanvallon, *Le sacre du citoyen*, pp. 195–205, rightly accords a section to 'the Bonapartist model' in his survey of universal suffrage in France.
5   S. Hazareesingh, *From Subject to Citizen. The Second Empire and the Emergence of Modern French Democracy* (Princeton, Princeton University Press, 1998).
6   C. Langlois, 'Napoléon Bonaparte plébiscité?', in *L'élection du chef de l'état en France de Hugues Capet à nos jours* (Paris, Beauchesne, 1988), pp. 81–98, offers the only general study of these consultations.
7   J. Godechot, *Les institutions de la France sous la Révolution et l'Empire*, 2nd edn (Presses Universitaires de la France, Paris, 1968), pp. 556–7.
8   A canton is an administrative unit between commune and département in size.

9   M. Crook, *Elections in the French Revolution, 1789–1799: an Apprenticeship in Democracy* (Cambridge, Cambridge University Press, 1996), pp. 52–6 for an introduction to electoral procedure during the Revolutionary decade.

10 I. Collins, *Napoleon and his Parliaments, 1800–1815* (London, Edward Arnold, 1979), pp. 47–55, offers an excellent introduction to the somewhat perplexing system of lists.

11 P.-L. Roederer, *Mémoires d'économie publique, de morale et de politique* (Paris, Imprimerie du Journal de Paris, 1799–1801), vol. 2, p. 7.

12 Coppolani, *Les élections*, p. 30.

13 Archives nationales (AN) F1cIII Isère 1, Juge de paix de Voiron, 20 thermidor an IX (8 August 1801), or F1cIII Loir-et-Cher 1, Préfet au ministre, 9 fructidor an IX (27 August 1801), for example, and see Collins, *Napoleon and his Parliaments*, pp. 53–5.

14 AN F1cIII Mont Blanc 1, Circulaire préfectoral, 5 fructidor an IX (14 August 1801).

15 Cited in Collins, *Napoleon and his Parliaments*, p. 55.

16 Coppolani, *Les élections*, pp. 216–20.

17 Napoléon, *Correspondance de Napoléon* (32 vols, Paris, Imprimerie impériale, 1858–70), vol. 7, no. 6028, p. 547.

18 Collins, *Napoleon and his Parliaments*, pp. 90–106, for a summary of the new system.

19 Coppolani, *Les élections*, pp. 131–46.

20 A. Cole and P. Campbell, *French Electoral Systems and Elections since 1789*, 3rd edn (Aldershot, Gower, 1989), pp. 40–42.

21 R. Huard, *Le suffrage universel en France, 1848–1946* (Paris, Aubier, 1992), for example.

22 A. Aulard, *Histoire politique de la Révolution française*, 5th edn (Paris, 1901), p. 706.

23 Coppolani, *Les élections*, pp. 278–80. It is possible to calculate the numbers registered from the total of notables attributed to each department. These figures are located in the relevant cartons of AN F1cIII, departmental series.

24 C. Langlois, 'Le plébiscite de l'an VIII ou le coup d'état du 18 pluviôse an VIII', *Annales historiques de la Révolution française*, 44 (1972), 43–65, 231–46 and 390–415, brought this massive fraud to light. For a later example of malpractice, see A. Dubuc, 'Les consultations populaires de l'an X et de l'an XII en Seine-Inférieure', *Actes du 86e Congrès National des Sociétés Savantes* (Paris, 1962), pp. 190–91.

25 AN BII 853, Relevé des votes, an X et an XII.

26 F. Bluche, *Le plébiscite des Cent-Jours* (Geneva, Droz, 1974), pp. 36–8.

27 Coppolani, *Les élections*, pp. 213–15.

28 AN F1cIII Drôme 2, Préfet au ministre, 21 thermidor an IX (9 Aug. 1801).

29 Coppolani, *Les élections*, p. 215.

30 Ibid., pp. 225–34.

31 AN F1cIII Var 3, Liste des membres qui composent le collège électoral du département, 10 Nov. 1810, or *Archives départementales* (AD) Var, 2M7-3 2–5, Résumé des opérations électorales, July–Aug. 1813, for example.

32 Coppolani, *Les élections*, p. 224.

33 Collins, *Napoleon and his Parliaments*, p. 165.

34 AN C*II 383, Tableau comparatif des nombres d'électeurs et de votants depuis l'année 1815, 1846.

35 AD Var 2M2–1, Sous-préfet de Toulon par intérim au ministre, 17 September 1813.

36 J. Dunne, 'Chalk and Cheese or Bread and Butter: Political Culture and Ecology in the Seine-Inférieure during the Napoleonic Period', forthcoming in M. Cornick and C. Crossley (eds), *Problems in French History: Essays in Honour of Douglas Johnson* (London, Macmillan, 1999).

37 Crook, *Elections in the French Revolution*, pp. 112–15.

38 Cited in J. Horn, 'Bread and Circuses: Napoleonic Electoral Festivals in the Department of the Aube', in C. Crouch, K.O. Eidahl and D.D. Horward (eds), Consortium on Revolutionary Europe 1750–1850. Selected Papers, 1996 (Florida, State University Press, 1996), p. 57.

39 Reproduced in Bluche, *Le plébiscite des Cent-Jours*, pp. 140–46.

40 Coppolani, *Les élections*, pp. 198–210.

6
The Bishop of Pamiers: Political Thought and Experience from the Emigration to the Restoration

Munro Price

The career of the Bishop of Pamiers spanned the *ancien régime*, the Revolution, the Emigration and the Restoration. Charles-Constance-César-Loup-Joseph-Matthieu d'Agoult was born in Grenoble in 1747; he died in Paris on 21 July 1824. As a young man, with the bishopric of Pamiers, he was just approaching the higher reaches of the ecclesiastical world when the Revolution overturned the entire edifice. His new dawn only came 25 years later, with the Bourbon Restoration. In between, he played a major role in Louis XVI's secret counter-Revolutionary diplomacy up to the fall of the monarchy, and was one of the principal organisers of the flight to Varennes. After the restoration, his continuing links with Louis XVI's and Marie Antoinette's one surviving child, the Duchesse d'Angoulême, assured him an influential, if informal, status at the centre of the *Ultra* party. Throughout his life d'Agoult was also a prolific pamphleteer, specialising in constitutional issues, finance and political economy. He has been completely ignored by historians.

Yet d'Agoult's experience is not just one more individual example of aristocratic vicissitudes during the Revolution to set alongside those of a Talleyrand or a Mme de Staël. His life and ideas may have a wider significance than that. D'Agoult was the most prominent political confidant of Louis XVI and Marie Antoinette during the Revolution to survive to play a role under the restored monarchy. His career provides one of the few means we have of assessing what direct legacy, if any, Louis XVI's policy during the Revolution left to the Restoration. More concretely, we can gauge how d'Agoult's own political thought developed from one reign to another through three pamphlets that he wrote, one in his youth, the other two in his old age. The first, *Principes et réflexions sur la constitution française* [Principles of, and Reflections on the French Constitution], written in 1789, examines the nature and composition of the Estates-General. The second, *Lettres à un jacobin* [Letters to a Jacobin], which appeared in 1815, is a detailed comparison of the Charter of 1814 with the 'antique constitution' of the old monarchy. Both works illuminate an important yet neglected strand of royalist political and constitutional thought, closely associated with Louis XVI and Marie Antoinette themselves, from its genesis at the outbreak of the Revolution, to its finish as a slightly uneasy element in *Ultra* doctrine under Louis XVIII.

The third pamphlet is more mysterious. The author stumbled on it by chance some years ago in Paris, in the collection bequeathed by the Abbé Grégoire to the Bibliothèque de Port-Royal. It was ironic finding d'Agoult's work there, among the papers of this radical priest and deputy to the Convention who had approved the execution of Louis XVI, in a manuscript library devoted to a Jansenism that had always been anathema to French royalism. The pamphlet itself is entitled *De l'intérêt des puissances de l'Europe, et celui de la France, au rétablissement de son antique forme de gouvernement* [On the Interests of the European Powers, and those of France, in the Restoration of its Former System of Government]. It is anonymous, but under the printed title the Abbé Grégoire has written in his own hand: '*par Mgr. d'Agoult ancien évêque de Pamiers*' [by Mgr d'Agoult, former Bishop of Pamiers].

The first point of interest about this work is its extreme rarity. It cannot be found in any of the major French or British libraries; most likely, the copy in the *Bibliothèque de Port-Royal* is the only one that still exists. Its second, and most exciting aspect, is that it is probably based on conversations that d'Agoult had with Edmund Burke in 1793, at the beginning of his English exile. *De l'intérêt des puissances de l'Europe* thus offers a tantalising intellectual link between those French royalists closest to Louis XVI and Marie Antoinette, and the organic conservatism of the greatest British political thinker of his day.

Throughout his life, d'Agoult answered perfectly to the description of worldly prelate. In this sense, he always remained a product of *ancien régime* rather than Restoration culture. It is difficult to see that he had any religious vocation at all; his writings all dealt with entirely secular themes. For him, the Church seems to have been essentially a means to a political career. Appointed to the Diocese of Pamiers on 13 May 1787, at the outbreak of the Revolution, he was clearly on the way to becoming one of those administrative bishops so characteristic of the period, in the mould of Brienne of Toulouse, Dillon of Narbonne and Boisgelin of Aix. Like them, he assiduously kept up his political contacts at Versailles. By the mid-1780s, he had found a patron, who was to bulk large throughout his later life, the minister of the *maison du roi*, Baron de Breteuil.[1] This long-lasting relationship was cemented by a further example of the Bishop's worldly tastes; for most of his life he had a permanent mistress, and this, conveniently, was none other than Mme de Matignon, the Baron's daughter.[2]

By 1789, d'Agoult's personality was formed. In many ways, he was impressive, highly intelligent, handsome, capable and erudite. His particular forte was political economy, to which he seems to have devoted considerable private study in his youth.[3] His debut at Pamiers also revealed him as a talented administrator. Yet these qualities were compromised by an immense arrogance, typical of his time and his class, which commentators were to underline throughout his life. His open affair with Mme de Matignon, too, raised eyebrows even in the tolerant atmosphere of Versailles. As the marquis de Bombelles, who looked askance at both d'Agoult's personal and political tastes, put it cuttingly in his journal: 'The pretty girls have turned this young head less dazzled by modern philosophy than swept away by the taste for pleasure.'[4]

After this life of pleasure, the Revolution was a rude awakening. The fall of the Bastille forced the flight of the Baron de Breteuil, whose fleeting appointment to head a conservative ministry after Necker's dismissal had been the signal for the revolt of Paris.[5] By this time, too, d'Agoult's arrogance had begun to have unwelcome effects; his own clergy, tired of his haughty manner, failed to elect him as their representative to the Estates-General, despite his public and brass-necked checking of which of them had voted for and against him. A few months later, horrified by the October days, d'Agoult joined his patron in exile in Switzerland, the second episcopal *émigré* of the Revolution. From Solothurn, installed with his patron and his mistress, the Bishop published his adhesion to *Exposition des principes des évêques de l'assemblée* [Explanation of the Principles of Bishops in the Assembly] drawn up by Boisgelin of Aix, formally opposing the civil constitution of the clergy. Five months later, he issued a final ordinance and pastoral letter to the faithful of his diocese, denouncing the election of the *curé* of Serres, Bernard Font, to succeed him as constitutional Bishop of the Ariège.[6]

By this time, d'Agoult had found a more secular outlet for his talents. He and Breteuil were horrified by the progress of the Revolution, and by the personal danger in which it now placed Louis XVI and Marie Antoinette. In their exile they concocted a detailed project for the escape of the royal family from the capital; in October 1790 d'Agoult slipped back incognito to Paris to present it to the King and Queen.[7] The result of this mission was a secret accreditation from Louis XVI for Breteuil, authorising the Baron to negotiate in the King's name with the European powers to further his personal policy, 'which is the restoration of my legitimate authority and the happiness of my peoples'.[8] In practical terms, this was a mandate to organise the rescue of the King and his family from Paris. On his way back to Switzerland, the Bishop stopped off in Metz, where he confided the plan to General de Bouillé, whose loyal troops in Lorraine were Louis XVI's destination and the chief proposed means of the restoration of his authority. Nonetheless, d'Agoult did apparently reassure Bouillé that the success of the project would not mean a return to despotism.[9]

Even after the plan's disastrous failure at Varennes, d'Agoult continued to act as an emissary between Louis XVI and Breteuil, who remained the King's secret minister charged with organising European support for the counter-Revolution. In December 1791, at great risk to his life, he went back to the Tuileries for a last meeting with the royal family. His ineffable self-esteem was quite undaunted either by the danger of his situation or the exalted, if threatened, rank of his hosts. The Queen was treated to a harsh lecture on the folly of her current intrigues with the more moderate Revolutionaries led by Barnave. As she confided to her admirer and probable lover Count Fersen in a letter smuggled out soon afterwards:

I cannot tell you how happy I was to see the Bishop; I found it difficult to leave him . . . He will have much to tell you of me, and especially about my new acquaintances and connections. I found him very severe with me; I thought I had already done a lot and that he would admire me: not a bit of it.[10]

From Brussels, where Breteuil and Mme de Matignon had moved after the flight to Varennes, d'Agoult continued to work tirelessly on behalf of the King and Queen until their deaths. Throughout these trials he remained alert, optimistic and insufferably self-important. The best portrait of him at this time comes from the pen of his colleague in counter-Revolutionary diplomacy, Bombelles. It is not flattering; Bombelles was a remarkable diarist but also a malicious gossip, and may well have resented his displacement by the younger man as Breteuil's principal protégé. Yet d'Agoult's qualities as well as his defects are acknowledged in this careful and unsparing description:

I am sad to see that a man capable of performing real services, a man endowed both with talent and that firmness necessary in high positions, will probably cut a poor figure in them, because he will render himself ridiculous through excessive presumption. He had no hesitation in telling me that he will take on the finance ministry because he has become convinced, after a thorough examination of all those known for their expertise in this field, that none of them combined as he did all the qualities needed for success in this delicate area. The day after this modest admission, the Bishop of Pamiers further assured me that six months of research in the manuscripts of the royal library had made him more knowledgeable about French history than all our most erudite writers. This worthy bishop, still ambitious, but in a good cause, did not have, or at least did not admit to having, such a prodigious self-confidence when we were together at Solothurn and I took pleasure in observing the success of his administrative apprenticeship.[11]

Had the Austro-Prussian invasion of France in the summer of 1792 been successful and Louis XVI and Marie Antoinette liberated, d'Agoult would, as Bombelles predicted, have become finance minister in a ministry headed by Breteuil. This was made clear by Fersen in one of his last letters to Marie Antoinette, one of the more spectacularly premature examples of political planning during the Revolution, written exactly a fortnight before the fall of the monarchy:

> Here is the Baron's plan for the ministry: he wants to control it himself, to avoid dissension...he is giving the foreign ministry to Bombelles, Paris to La Porte and the finance ministry to the Bishop of Pamiers to avoid any rigid doctrines and install a firm man of order, with a six-man council.

Even read today, the Queen's reply, written in invisible ink, betrays a faint note of exasperation:

> The King's life as well as the Queen's have clearly been threatened for some time...Amid so many dangers, it is difficult to devote time to choosing ministers.[12]

D'Agoult's years of emigration after 1792 were spent in England and Germany, and ended in 1802 when he returned to France under Napoleon's amnesty for the *émigrés*. His English experience in particular marked him profoundly; he remained fascinated by the English constitution and fiscal system, publishing in 1817 a lengthy comparison of taxation in France and England. It even affected his taste in architecture. The chateau of Courtalain, where he often stayed under the empire and the restoration, is today approached via a Strawberry Hill Gothic gatehouse, and surrounded by an English landscape garden, both of which he designed.

Throughout the Bishop's wanderings, one thread of continuity was provided by his unorthodox menage with Mme de Matignon and Breteuil. When Mme de Matignon left their household in early 1802 to pay court to the rising sun of Bonaparte, d'Agoult rather touchingly kept his ageing patron company at weekends, sharing his lunchtime cutlet with him. When Breteuil followed his daughter back to France later that year, d'Agoult went back with him. The link survived until Breteuil's death in 1807; one of the few keepsakes the old politician bequeathed in his will was a diamond-mounted watch to the Bishop of Pamiers.[13]

Despite the ties of friendship, politics remained d'Agoult's chief passion. Under the Consulate and the Empire, having finally resigned his bishopric, he lived in discreet retirement, though one senses that he retained some influence among the reviving *salons* of the Faubourg St Germain. The first restoration, however, and the triumph of the monarchy in which the Bishop had never ceased to believe, paved the way for his return to political life. In this new world, d'Agoult had one particularly strong card to play: the continuing affection of Louis XVI's and Marie Antoinette's daughter the Duchesse d'Angoulême, who never forgot his efforts on behalf of her parents during their last years. This link was reinforced by the closeness to the Duchesse of other members of d'Agoult's family; his brother the Vicomte d'Agoult was her first equerry, and his sister-in-law the Vicomtesse was her first lady-in-waiting and greatest friend.[14] From this anchorage in the royal household the Bishop was able to wield considerable influence behind the scenes. By this time he had evolved into a moderate *Ultra*, if that isn't a contradiction in terms. His best-documented political initiative, in 1818, was an attempt to reconcile the Duc de Richelieu's shaky centrist ministry with the *Ultras* led by Villèle, to whom d'Agoult was close. The price of this bargain was to be a revision of the electoral and press laws to make them more favourable to the *ultras*. This intrigue failed, but it marked a stage towards the ultimate goal reached at the end of 1821, of a ministry headed by Villèle.[15]

D'Agoult's adult life was emblematic, and sometimes very dramatically so, of the experience of French *émigrés* and counter-Revolutionaries from republic to monarchy. Yet his ideas also evolved in response to the unprecedented challenges of the period, and this is where his true significance lies. The best way of assessing this is to compare the two most important pamphlets he wrote on the French constitution, *Principes et réflexions sur la constitution française,* published at the outbreak of the Revolution, and *Lettres à un jacobin,* which appeared at the outset of the second restoration.

The *Principes et réflexions* came out at the beginning of 1789, just as the debate over the relative powers of the privileged orders and the Third Estate in the forthcoming Estates-General was gathering pace. As a statement of political faith from someone as close to the royal government as d'Agoult, it is surprising, since it is a stinging denunciation of ministerial despotism, very much in the spirit of the *révolte nobiliaire* of the previous two years. Its centrepiece was a plea for taxation henceforth to be raised by consent, rather than through the absolute will of the monarch. As d'Agoult himself put it:

> Our kings, unwise enough to aspire to a despotic authority, must learn that a people of slaves can never patiently support a heavy tax burden, and that the liberty of the nation to vote taxes has the great advantage of removing from the monarch the odium of these impositions, which even seem less heavy to the taxpayer when they are a product of his free will... A long succession of finance ministers has had more difficulty raising forced taxation than our kings ever experienced in obtaining voluntary contributions.[16]

This assertion led back to d'Agoult's central theme, which never varied and had become his swansong by the time of the Restoration, that France had always had a constitution, and that its cornerstone was liberty. To quote his own summary:

> The King in France enjoys the plenitude of royal authority, but his power extends neither over the liberty nor the property of any of his subjects. The nation is made up of three orders of citizens, distinct in rank, equal in rights. These are the two principles of the French constitution, from which are derived, as from a rich source, all the diverse relations between the monarch and his subjects, all their reciprocal rights and obligations.[17]

In the context of 1789, this led d'Agoult to two essential conclusions. First, it was contrary both to natural rights and to national precedent to levy taxation without consent; in this sense absolutism was an aberration in the history of the French monarchy. D'Agoult was thus by definition arguing for a constitutional monarchy with a parliamentary veto over the budget, and one suspects that here his fascination with the English model was already working its spell.

These sentiments chimed in well with those of the emerging Third Estate; d'Agoult's second conclusion, however, emphatically did not. This was that the separation of orders in the estates general must at all costs be preserved. Here d'Agoult was above all defending hierarchy and rank in a corporate society; to preserve it the first two orders should sacrifice everything else, and first of all their fiscal privileges. To those in the Third estate who argued that without the abolition of distinction of order in the estates the nobility and clergy would never give up their tax exemptions, his response was ingenious: since the origin of all taxation in France was voluntary, and the privileged orders had used this to gain their own exemptions, the Third Estate should simply refuse to pay the *taille* until the nobility and clergy agreed to pay their share.[18] It was an original, if slightly impractical, solution to the first great crisis of the Revolution.

All of this marks d'Agoult out as a champion *par excellence* of a conception of aristocratic liberty against the menace of both royal despotism and democracy alike. Indeed, one could see him as a representative of what used to be called the 'aristocratic reaction', except that the phrase does not do justice to the diversity of noble political thought at the end of the *ancien régime*.

Twenty-five years later, in *Lettres à un jacobin*, d'Agoult returned to the same themes, in a completely different political context. The continuity of his preoccupations was underlined by the subtitle of the work: *Réflexions politiques sur la constitution d'Angleterre et la charte royale, considérée dans ses rapports avec l'ancienne constitution de la monarchie française* [Political Reflections on the English Constitution and the Royal Charter, Considered in Respect of the Former Constitution of the French Monarchy]. Yet at the time of writing, during the Hundred Days, d'Agoult's ideals faced almost as many challenges as they had in the 1790s. A 15-year tyranny had been replaced in 1814 by a constitutional monarchy which fulfilled at least some of his prescriptions, yet after only a year it had been swept away by Napoleon's return. What had gone wrong? D'Agoult pondered this agonizing question deeply, and in the resulting 170-page treatise he stuck stoutly to his constitutional guns; the Charter had succeeded where it had remained faithful to the principles of the antique constitution, and had failed where it had not.

The *Lettres à un jacobin* is thus a meditation on the strengths and weaknesses of the restoration political settlement, in the light of the constitutional principles d'Agoult claimed to discern in the pre-1789 monarchy and which had been so brutally interrupted by the Revolution. The Charter's main strength, in d'Agoult's eyes, was that it finally restored the key principle which had determined Louis XVI to make his journey to Varennes, and which the constitution of 1791 had denied him: the right of the King, and not an assembly, to initiate legislation.[19] On the powers of the chamber of deputies, the Bishop was equally emphatic; these should be limited simply to the right to vote on the taxes and laws presented to it by the government.[20]

What of the issue that a quarter of a century before had first precipitated d'Agoult into the counter-Revolution, the composition of the national representative body? The Bishop never lost his nostalgia for the old Estates-General with its three separate and distinct orders, and there is some evidence that he attempted to influence opinion in favour of its reintroduction at the first restoration.[21] A year later, *Lettres à un jacobin* compared favourably the three chambers of the old French estates with: 'the constitution of our neighbours, in which the House of Lords finds itself accidentally involved in legislation'.[22] Yet d'Agoult was also a realist, able to abandon what it was no longer possible to reimpose, and reluctantly accepted the best solution available for the time, a bicameral legislature in which a chamber of peers acted as a brake on the elected assembly. Having held up the pre-1789 constitution as his ideal, he added with resignation:

> But it is foolish to pretend otherwise, the original elements of this constitution are no longer with us. Since all property in France is now of the same nature ... we find ourselves obliged to have only one national chamber; but at least let us not allow the levellers to root out from among us the institution of nobility.[23]

Elsewhere in *Lettres à un jacobin* d'Agoult sketched out a conservative interpretation of the provisions of the Charter. He felt the taxpaying qualification for electors should be set at 500 francs, not 300 francs, and he devoted only a few ambiguous sentences to the burning issue of the *biens nationaux*.[24] Yet he retained enough pragmatism to recognise that the old regime was gone forever, and that compromises had to be made if the essential, a monarchical system, were to survive. D'Agoult made the point almost poetically, in a passage one feels was deliberately aimed at royalists more intransigent than himself. Having warned against the dangers of too radical constitutional change, he added:

A no less dangerous folly after a Revolution of twenty-five years would be to attempt to retrace our steps along a path made impassable by obstacles, to arrive back at the place where we began and whose ruins would offer no shelter from storms.[25]

The third pamphlet, *De l'intérêt des puissances de l'Europe,* sits uneasily with the other two. To begin with, it is the only one not published at the time of writing. First composed in 1793, it was dusted down and brought out by d'Agoult at the beginning of the first restoration, almost certainly in an attempt to influence the public debate about the form of the future French government.[26] Despite his fascination with the English constitution, d'Agoult's main purpose was to argue passionately that its introduction into France would gravely menace both the stability of France and the security of her neighbours. His own unambiguous prescription was contained in the pamphlet's second proposition: 'that the interest of the rival powers to France dictates the restoration of her antique government without change or modification'.[27] The chief interest of the work, however, lies in the possible link it provides between the political thought of the Bishop of Pamiers and that of Edmund Burke. The evidence for this connection comes in d'Agoult's entry in Michaud's *Biographie universelle* of 1843, an indispensable source for the period, and particularly for the lives of its lesser-ranking public figures. His entry lists six of his published pamphlets that are available in the *Bibliothèque Nationale* and other major libraries, and one that is not. This last is described as follows: 'Michaud, *Biographie universelle, Conversation with E. Burke, on the interests of the European powers.* The author, during his period in England, had had some contact with this celebrated publicist.'[28] As far as is known, there is no copy extant of a pamphlet with this precise title. There are, however, strong grounds for believing that the anonymous work attributed to d'Agoult by the Abbé Grégoire in the *Bibliothèque de Port Royal* is at least a version, and the only surviving one, of it. For a start, the similarity in the titles is striking, between *Conversation avec E. Burke sur l'intérêt des puissances de l'Europe,* and *De l'intérêt des puissances de l'Europe, et celui de la France, au rétablissement de son antique forme de gouvernement.* In addition, even though Burke is nowhere directly mentioned in *De l'intérêt des puissances de l'Europe,* many of the ideas it contains could certainly have been the product of conversations with the great political philosopher: denunciation of the principle of the sovereignty of the people, arguments for the restoration of the *ancien régime* in France more or less *in extenso,* and a lengthy historical disquisition on the growth of political stability in England that betrays a strong Whig bias.

If Burke and d'Agoult did indeed meet, there is unfortunately no historical record of the fact. Although Burke was active on committees for the relief of the *émigré* French clergy in England during the Revolution, this work does not appear to have brought him into contact with d'Agoult.[29] Neither is d'Agoult mentioned in Burke's voluminous correspondence preserved in the Sheffield City Library. However, in a long letter of circa 6 August 1793 to the Comte de Mercy Argenteau, former Austrian ambassador to Versailles and a close collaborator of Breteuil's in the French royal family's secret diplomacy, Burke expresses ideas that may conceivably have been suggested by d'Agoult. He strongly urged to Mercy the proscription of the newspaper *Assignats*, which was one of d'Agoult's obsessions at the time: 'The utter destruction of *Assignats* and the restoration of order in Europe are one and the same thing.' Burke also trumpeted the praises of that embattled élite which d'Agoult had earlier joined, the *émigré* French clergy:

> We have had opportunities of knowing and considering them, in all points of View; and, if their reestablishment were not a valid claim of Justice, yet their personal merits, and the rules of sound policy, would strongly recommend it. We did not believe, before we had an opportunity of seeing it realised before our Eyes, that, in such a multitude of men, so much real Virtue had existed in the world.[30]

Most significant of all, one of the central arguments in d'Agoult's pamphlet echoes strikingly a key paragraph in Burke's letter to Mercy. The central assertion of *De l'intérêt des puissances de l'Europe* was that a restoration of the traditional French monarchy, which would take years to regain its former health, presented far less of a menace to the other powers than the national energies that a revived constitutional monarchy or a continuation of republicanism in France could mobilise. As the Bishop put it himself:

> The restoration of our antique government, without change or modification, is the sole means open to the powers to retain the advantage over France that her Revolution has given them. The calamities of all sorts that this Revolution has visited upon her, are nothing in comparison to what her government has suffered; as a monarchy France today is nothing but an immense empty space: this ancient body, exhausted by its abuses, and still more by the remedies of charlatans,

pierced by the rebels with a thousand mortal wounds, is henceforth condemned to languish ... a century of prudence will not restore to the French monarchy what she has lost in five years of troubles.[31]

Compare this to Burke's far pithier summary, part of his attempt to convince Mercy that Austria's interests would in no way be threatened if she recognised the dead Louis XVI's brother the Comte de Provence as regent of France:

> The French Monarchy, if it ever can be restored, languishing, feeble, and tottering, with an infant King, and a convalescent Royalty, will for a long time be rather an object of Protection than Jealousy, in any of its Magistracies, to [the emperor] or to any foreign power.[32]

The similarity of these two passages is remarkable, even down to each man's use of the same verb, 'languish', or 'languir', to describe the future state of a restored monarchy. It is very tempting to think that d'Agoult was recalling a conversation with Burke when he wrote *De l'intérêt des puissances de l'Europe*.

If d'Agoult was calling in 1793, and by implication also in 1814, for a restoration of the antique constitution 'sans changement ni modification', he took care to be specific about what this meant. The King was the source of all authority and had sovereign power, he stressed, but taxes could only be levied by a vote of the representatives of the people. At one point in the pamphlet d'Agoult seems to assign to the *parlements* a role in this representation,[33] but otherwise his sentiments on these key constitutional issues echo those of his earlier and later works. In this endorsement of a traditional monarchy that nonetheless fell some way short of absolutism, d'Agoult was at least consistent. And, as ever, he was emphatic in distancing himself from any accusation of despotism:

> From the fact that we refuse to admit the absurd principle of the sovereignty of the people, it would be very mistaken to conclude that we are partisans of despotism: by the antique constitution of the State, the French nation has its liberties and freedoms, the authority of the monarch its limits.[34]

If d'Agoult's political thought at the Restoration shows a basic continuity, his political activity after 1814 is more mysterious. Michaud's *Biographie universelle* claims that at the second restoration in 1815 there was a move to make him finance minister.[35] Presumably his candidacy had the support of the Duc and Duchesse d'Angoulême. It is probably no coincidence that the Bishop chose this moment to publish a project for a new national bank, which he claimed he had first submitted to Louis XVI in 1791.[36] It is also significant that this pamphlet appeared under the imprint of Adrien Egron, printer to the Duc d'Angoulême. In the light of this suggestive evidence that d'Agoult retained both political ambitions and powerful backers, one should take with a pinch of salt the modest disclaimer in his preface:

> The restoration of Louis XVIII to the throne of his fathers, in fulfilling the dearest and most ardent of my wishes, has certainly not affected my resolution never to come out of retirement and return to public life; my age has in any case reinforced this vow that I took after the loss of Louis XVI.[37]

Our last picture of the Bishop of Pamiers, and the best evidence we have that he most definitely did not 'vivre étranger aux affaires publiques' after 1815, comes in the memoirs of Count Molé, minister of the marine in 1817–18, and eventually one of Louis-Philippe's prime ministers. Molé recounts a secret meeting in December 1818, in the dying days of the Duc de Richelieu's ministry, with d'Agoult and Villèle, at the Bishop's little house in the former orangery of an *hôtel* in the rue de l'Université.[38] The aim of the intrigue was to gain *Ultra* support for the ministry in the wake of worrying liberal electoral gains. Villèle did the negotiating, and his terms are not without interest: the substitution of full septennial elections for the current system of renewal of deputies by fifths, a new press law, the removal of the *Ultras'* bugbear Decazes from the ministry, and the replacement of Marshal Gouvion St-Cyr at the war ministry by General Lauriston. The discussions got nowhere, and Richelieu and Molé resigned later that month. Yet as far as d'Agoult is concerned, the chief interest of this recollection lies in the splendidly vituperative portrait Molé draws of him. Molé, who had never met him before, presents him as vain, shallow, mediocre and obsequious. One suspects, however, that Molé was influenced by a literary conceit. He was concerned to draw a contrast between the old and the new royalism, between the elegant but obsolete bishop of the old regime, and the unprepossessing, plebeian, but infinitely more farsighted Villèle. The result, at the least, is a marvellous vignette:

> This interview, as has been shown, had little result, but my passion for observation found much to satisfy it. The elegant Bishop, an old relic

of the corruption of an age which could never return, and the plebeian royalist, himself the child of a Revolution whose principles he attacked, formed a most instructive and piquant contrast. The first, handsome, polished, powdered, solemn, obsequious, but hollow, ignorant, narrow, blinded by prejudices and hardened by personality. The other, of an ignoble ugliness, increased by his clumsiness and untidiness, yet composed in manner, free in spirit and language, at bottom shrewd and contained beneath an artless appearance, contemptuous of the Bishop and all his kind, who were humiliating themselves before his genius and expecting him to ensure the triumph of their most cherished interests.[39]

Molé's prose and conclusions are damning, as they were intended to be. They are also unfair, since d'Agoult's writings clearly show that he did not simply want to turn the clock back to 1788. D'Agoult's appearance and his manners, so redolent of pre-Revolutionary Versailles, clearly repelled Molé, whose own life was devoted to remaining one step ahead of the present, not looking back fondly at the past. Yet they also blinded him to what lay beneath the Bishop's unfashionably powdered exterior. Always emotionally attached to France's 'antique constitution', the Bishop recognised that it had to evolve if it were to survive. Above all, he had no nostalgia for absolute monarchy, and consistently championed the right of national assemblies to vote or refuse taxation throughout his career. For d'Agoult, Louis XVIII's granting of the Charter was of a piece with his elder brother Louis XVI's decision to call the Estates-General, and both were in the spirit of the true French constitution, which was grounded on the liberty of the subject. One may question just how accurate an interpretation this was of the real motives of either Louis XVI or Louis XVIII, and indeed just how far France's pre-Revolutionary political arrangements could ever have been described as a constitution. Yet this is to miss d'Agoult's real aim, which he pursued all his life, which was to use the past to create roots for what in France, at least, was the most fragile of plants, constitutional monarchy. Elegant, arrogant and libertine, the Bishop of Pamiers was also a serious and significant political thinker. He remains an unjustly neglected representative of an unjustly neglected period.

Notes

1 No biography of Breteuil has yet been written. In its absence, there is one institutional study of his period at the *maison du roi*, R.-M. Rampelberg, *Le ministre de la maison du roi; baron de Breteuil, 1783–1788* (Paris, Economica, 1975).

2 Marquis de Bombelles, in J. Grassion and F. Durif (eds), *Journal* (4 vols, Geneva, Droz, 1978–98), vol. 1, p. 136.

3 See below.

4 Bombelles, *Journal*, vol. 2, p. 170.

5 See P. Caron, 'La tentative de contre-révolution de juin–juillet 1789', *Revue d'histoire moderne et contemporaine*, 8 (1906–07), 5–34 and 649–78, and M. Price, 'The Ministry of the Hundred Hours: a Reappraisal', *French History*, vol. 4, (1990), 317–39.

6 N. Aston, *The End of an Elite: the French Bishops and the Coming of the Revolution, 1786–1790* (Oxford, Clarendon Press, 1992), pp. 148, 207; L.G. Michaud, *Biographie universelle* (Paris and Leipzig, 1842–65), vol. 1, p. 239.

7 Comte Louis de Bouillé, *Souvenirs* (3 vols, Paris, Picard, 1906–11), vol. 1, p. 180.

8 The original of this accreditation, the famous *plein-pouvoir*, is today in the château de Breteuil, Yvelines, France; it is published in P. and P. Girault de Coursac, *Enquête sur le procès du roi Louis XVI* (Paris, La Table Ronde, 1982), p. 208.

9 Bouillé, *Souvenirs*, vol. 1, p. 181.

10 Baron R.M. Klinckowström (ed.), *Le comte de Fersen et la cour de France* (2 vols, Paris, Firmin-Didot, 1877–78), vol. 1, p. 268.

11 Bombelles, *Journal*, vol. 3, pp. 381–2.

12 Klinckowström (ed.), *Le comte de Fersen*, vol. 2, pp. 340–41.

13 Archives Gontaut-Biron, château de Courtalain, Eure-et-Loir, France, *Compte d'exécution testamentaire de feu M. de Breteuil*.

14 J. Vier, *La comtesse d'Agoult et son temps* (Paris, Armand Colin, 1955), pp. 82–3.

15 See below.

16 C.-C. d'Agoult, *Principes et réflexions sur la constitution française (1789)*, pp. 26–7.

17 Ibid., p. 8.

18 Ibid., pp. 21–2.

19 Published in J. Hardman, *The French Revolution: the Fall of the Ancien Régime to the Thermidorian Reaction, 1785–1795* (London, Arnold, 1981), pp. 127–8.

20 C.-C. d'Agoult, *Lettres à un jacobin; ou réflexions politiques sur la constitution d'Angleterre et la Charte Royale, considérée dans ses rapports avec l'ancienne Constitution de la Monarchie Française* (Paris, Egron, 1815), pp. 79–80.

21 This was probably one of the reasons why he published *De l'intérêt des puissances de l'Europe*, considered below, in 1814.

22 D'Agoult, *Lettres à un jacobin*, p. 154.

23 Ibid., pp. 154–5.

24 Ibid., pp. 165–6.

25 Ibid., p. 117.

26 C.-C. d'Agoult, *'De l'intérêt des puissances de l'Europe, et celui de la France, au rétablissement de son antique forme de gouvernement'* (Paris, 1814), [Editor's note:

'The text we publish today was never intended for the public. Composed in 1793, its purpose was purely political. We can confirm, and supply proof, that it has remained completely unaltered since that date.']

27 Ibid., p. 6.

28 Michaud, *Biographie universelle*, vol. 1, p. 239, '*Conversation avec E. Burke, sur l'intérêt des puissances de l'Europe*, Paris, Egron, 1814, petit nombre d'exemplaires. L'auteur avait eu, pendant son séjour en Angleterre, quelques relations avec ce célèbre publiciste.'

29 P.J. Marshall and J.A. Woods (eds), *The Correspondence of Edmund Burke, January 1792–August 1794* (Cambridge, Cambridge University Press, 1968), pp. 207–8.

30 Ibid., pp. 389, 390.

31 D'Agoult, *De l'intérêt des puissances*, pp. 30–31.

32 Marshall and Woods (eds), *Correspondence of Edmund Burke*, p. 393.

33 D'Agoult, *De l'intérêt des puissances*, p. 40.

34 Ibid., p. 39.

35 Michaud, *Biographie universelle*, vol. 1, p. 239.

36 C.-C. d'Agoult, *Projet d'une banque nationale* (Paris, Egron, 1815).

37 Ibid., p. ii.

38 Marquis de Noailles (ed.), *Le comte Molé, 1781–1855, sa vie – ses mémoires* (8 vols, Paris, Edouard Champion, 1925), vol. 4, pp. 188–91.

39 Ibid., p. 191.

7
Painters and Public Patronage in the First French Republic: the Ministry of the Interior and the Art of the French Revolution[1]

David Wisner

At the salon of 1798, the French painter Louis Lafitte exhibited a large sketch of *Pericles awarding Prizes to Artists before the Odeon in Athens*. Hopeful of obtaining a public commission through the agency of the Ministry of the Interior, Lafitte sought vainly to inspire the Revolutionary authorities to award his work a prize. The subject of the sketch no doubt had something to do with the artist's relationship with important figures in the French theatre, such as Marie-Joseph Chénier, whose portraits he also painted. More importantly, Lafitte later claimed that his work was the fruit of an unwritten agreement with a Minister of the Interior, Pierre Bénézech, to produce a painting for the State. In his correspondence with the Ministry, Lafitte mentions that his enormous composition (3×4 metres) was initially meant to serve as a design for a curtain at the *Théâtre Français*, but had remained uncompleted owing to the painter's poor health and a lack of support for the project. Lafitte ultimately felt compelled to write to a subsequent Minister of the Interior, Nicolas François de Neufchâteau, to plead his case:

> Pericles is already distributing prizes and I await the first penny of mine in order to paint the crowns... You will recall Pericles in the French Odeon, Phydias and Zeuxis in our museums, in aiding in the efforts of young artists.[2]

Lafitte's pleadings fell on deaf ears: he began but never finished his project, and indeed, seems never to have received any of the 6000 francs he had allegedly been promised. As for the sketch, it eventually made its way, ironically enough, into the private collection of the prolific Danish collector Bruun-Neergaard, while the canvas itself remained unfinished – and went unsold – at Lafitte's death.[3]

Artists like Lafitte frequently had to deal with the Ministry of the Interior during the Revolution as they struggled to find alternatives to the system of court patronage demolished along with the *ancien régime*. Indeed, by the mid-1790s the Ministry of the Interior had become nothing less than a prototypical Ministry of Cultural Affairs, especially active in the realm of artistic patronage. As early as 1791, with the inaugural salon of the Revolutionary era, the Ministry had been charged with overseeing the first such affair to be open to academicians and non-academicians alike; previously the salon had been a closed affair. Similarly, the famous Revolutionary *concours* and *prix d'encouragement* were managed by the same Ministry. The Ministry played a central role as well in the mobilisation of national patrimony, through the creation of museums, national clearing houses for sequestered patrimony (*dépôts*), and a variety of other 'republican institutions'. Finally, the organisation of Revolutionary festivals, which Mona Ozouf has claimed constituted the essential cultural link throughout the Revolutionary decade, was again largely the province of the Ministry of the Interior.[4]

The single most important type of republican patronage administered by the Ministry of the Interior was the *prix* or *travail d'encouragement*. This was awarded in most cases by a jury of prominent artists charged by the government, through the intermediary of the Ministry of the Interior, to inspect works shown at the salon. In theory, works which benefited from receipt of an award or a prize were products of a democratic and egalitarian competition in which individual artists functioned first and foremost as citizens of the Republic. Some of the more familiar projects undertaken in this system include Jean-Jacques-François Le Barbier's *Courage of Young Desilles* and François Gérard's *Insurrection of 10 August*. Yet throughout the Revolutionary decade any number of artists would become involved in the Ministry's patronage schemes.

A great deal has been written recently about the salons and *concours* of the Revolutionary decade, and part of the documentary record was published in 1989 in the third volume of the exhibition catalogue *La Révolution française et l'Europe*.[5] Much less has been said, on the other hand, about the crucial relationship between the Ministry of the Interior and its artists, especially during the Directory (1795–99). This chapter considers a few of the more interesting cases, which reveal above all both the range of republican patronage, and the difficulties artists, particularly painters, had in dealing with the new system. Also examined more specifically are what efforts were made to replace *ancien régime* institutions and to overcome the mentality ingrained in artists accustomed to the mechanisms of court patronage: more fundamentally, how to best characterise the system of republican patronage in the 1790s. A brief survey of the activities of artists like Lafitte and a representative sampling of others should show that if they were on the whole less instrumental in the formation of cultural policy than the Ministry personnel they worked with, some did nonetheless attempt to clear a tentative space for innovative, if not republican, gestures. At the same time, an analysis of republican patronage from this precise vantage point will also provide a view of the process by which a court system gradually came back into place, even before the advent of Napoleon and the subsequent return of the Bourbons.

In many ways the figure of Pericles, which Lafitte evoked so dramatically, was emblematic for the Revolution. For example, three painted versions of *The Friendship of Pericles and Anaxagoras* appeared in the early years of the Revolution, the first two by Jean-Charles-Nicaise Perrin and Nicolas-Guy Brenet at the salon of 1791, the third, a *travail d'encouragement* by Augustin-Louis Belle *fils* in 1793 and again in 1796; the theme would also be the subject for the sculpture *concours* in 1799. The anecdote forming the basis for this particular scene could in fact be applied to nearly the entire Revolutionary decade. According to Plutarch, Pericles came one day to consult with Anaxagoras, his friend and former mentor. The philosopher, on a hunger strike after having previously been abandoned by Pericles, pointed to a burned-out lamp and remarked that if light were wanted oil would be needed to fill the lamp.[6] By extension, from the point of view of individual artists the degree to which an organ like the Ministry of the Interior could provide the necessary sustenance to its artists would serve as a gauge for the larger success of the Revolution itself.

In this respect Lafitte's case is particularly instructive. Considered in retrospect his career would be one of modest yet solid success. He was an able portraitist and history painter, the last of the younger cohort of neoclassicists to be accorded the *Grand-Prix de Peinture* by the Royal Academy of Painting and Sculpture and thus be allowed to study in Rome at royal expense. Study in Rome he did, even through the troubles brought about by the Revolution. After the rise of Napoleon in particular he received numerous commissions for a variety of art forms, including interior *décors*, tapestry cartoons, and designs for porcelain painting and medallions. He managed to maintain his standing during the Restoration, when he was appointed to a position as royal artist (*Dessinateur du Cabinet du Roi*) and elected into the Legion of Honour.

The Revolutionary years, in relative contrast, were lean ones for Lafitte, but not for want of trying. Indeed, he had shown himself to be willing and eager, perhaps too much so, to accommodate his art to the needs of Revolutionary propaganda. Throughout the 1790s he executed a series of portraits and scenes inspired from contemporary events related to the Revolution – like his depiction of Pericles – apparently in search of some great government commission; a few of these were also engraved for popular audiences. Yet it was only with the restoration of forms of court patronage in the post-Revolutionary period, channelled through an updated version of the Ministry of the Interior, that Lafitte was able to engage more fruitfully in his artistic activities.[7]

The careers of Perrin and Belle also reflect the efforts needed by artists to cope with the often desperate straits occasioned by the collapse of the *ancien régime* networks of patronage. Like Lafitte, Perrin had been trained as a history painter in the Royal Academy. Come the Revolution, he sought to find work as best he could. Thus in 1789 he collaborated with a number of other young painters in publishing a collection of portraits of deputies at the National Assembly. At the salon of 1791, as we have seen, he exhibited his *Pericles and Anaxagoras*. In May 1792 he was one of a group of artists to receive a royal commission to paint a scene from French history to be exhibited in 1793. Meanwhile the Terror intervened and this commission came to naught. More bad news followed: in 1794 a jury for the Gobelins judged Perrin's *Death of Seneca*, painted in 1788–89 for the King, to be unsatisfactory for reproduction, despite the painting's 'republican spirit'. Sometime during 1795 nonetheless Perrin was named assistant director of the school of decorative arts, which he came to head in 1806.[8]

In 1799 Perrin exhibited a painting entitled *The First Inhabitants of the Earth*, inspired from a reading of Lucretius. Notable for the parallel it provides with Jacques-Louis David's better-known *Intervention of the Sabine Women*, Perrin's painting was not actually awarded a prize by the jury. Rather, it was supported by ministerial discretion upon inspection of a preparatory drawing. It was subsequently sent to the museum of the French school at Versailles. Two years later Perrin won another prize, this time from the jury, for a painting of *Socrates saving Alcibiades from the Arms of Indulgence*. This he was eligible to receive after exhibiting another painting, *Cyrus condemned by Astiages* in 1802, although not before he was obliged to solicit final payment for his earlier effort from the Minister of the Interior.[9] Apparently succeeding ministries were hard pressed to accommodate initiatives taken by their predecessors.

Belle, too, was a product of the Academy. He worked principally at the Gobelins factory, however, and at one point petitioned the Minister of the Interior to keep his painting of *Pericles and Anaxagoras* there in order to make a tapestry cartoon from it; the same painting was later sent by the Ministry of the Interior to decorate the chambers of the Council of 500, whence it was eventually returned to the Louvre by way of Coutances. The painting itself was still not fully paid for in 1796. Belle was awarded another prize in 1799, which he finally received in 1801 for a painting entitled *Mars crowned by Venus.*[10]

Even the most celebrated works of the Revolutionary decade were the products of similar confusion. One of these, Le Barbier's *Courage of Young Desilles*, was commissioned in 1791, largely as the result of the artist's own lobbying efforts with government officials, but was not exhibited publicly until 1795.[11] This painting was one of two *prix d'encouragement* won by Le Barbier, doubtless among the most industrious and resourceful painters of his generation. Le Barbier was an academician and the author of a moderate plan to reform the Academy in 1790.[12] Much of his personal success as an artist was due, however, to the fact that he was willing – and able – in fact to bypass the necessity of falling back on the principal organs of State patronage, such as the royal commissions channelled through the Academy or the *Direction des Bâtiments* in the *ancien régime* or the quasi-charitable *travaux d'encouragement* administered by the Ministry of the Interior during the Revolution. This he did partly by striking out on his own, through the media of the press and the decorative arts (including *papier peint*), and partly by appealing to other, less visible sources of government patronage. In 1793, for example, Le Barbier was commissioned by Gilbert Romme to produce a frontispiece for a Revolutionary almanac published by the Committee of Public Instruction.[13] Even so, the second half of the Revolutionary decade was still difficult for Le Barbier. He did win another *prix d'encouragement* in 1798, although there is no record of his following up on it.[14] In this instance Le Barbier seems actually to have abandoned his engagement with the ubiquitous Ministry of the Interior.

While some painters turned voluntarily to the decorative arts to supplement the meagre earnings they could muster from their principal artistic activities, others were actually patronised for ephemera. A notable case of the 'flexibility' of Republican patronage concerns Gérard, who was awarded first prize in the great *concours* of the Year II for his sketch of *The Insurrection of 10 August*; he was also granted a monetary prize for another composition at the same *concours.*[15] Gérard's project never reached fruition, partly for want of proper support and payment, but he was eligible for recompense from the Ministry of the Interior for another, unrelated affair. In 1796 Gérard and another fellow pupil of David's, Gioacchim-Giuseppe Serangeli, requested payment from the

Committee of Public Instruction for materials furnished for the festival in honour of Bara and Viala in the summer of 1794. Both artists had been invited by David to paint banners for the festival, which had remained in the Feuillants Church during and after their master's imprisonment. The Committee approved the request, but no action was taken. In 1796 the same artists again presented a request, this time to the Ministry of the Interior, either for payment or retribution of their material. Neither was paid, although the banners were eventually returned.[16]

David himself managed, on the other hand, to make something of a career working with, for, or around the Ministry of the Interior.[17] David was in fact extraordinary for the degree to which he was able to balance – for want of a better word – the needs of the Revolutionary government with his own ambitions, both before and after Thermidor. David was awarded only one *prix*, in 1791, which he immediately rejected so that it might be divided among other artists. Yet David's major history painting of the decade, the *Sabines* (1799), was in part the fruit of a protracted series of negotiations with the Minister of the Interior, particularly François de Neufchâteau, the object of which was to procure space in a public building for a private exhibition – one with an entrance fee no less.[18] Meanwhile David also petitioned the Ministry on more than one occasion on behalf of his students, whom he had exempted from military service or allowed to copy art works stored in national collections; by the same token he also offered his support selectively to other artists seeking lodgings or other services from the government. He even had the audacity during the Directory to seek payment from the Ministry of the Interior for two students who had engraved *Marat* and *Le Pelletier*, both of which David had donated to the government during the height of the Terror but which he now kept jealously hidden in the recesses of his studio.[19] It would seem that the minister complied in this instance. In more constructive moments David was also a perennial member of the juries which reported to the Ministry. In this context, too, David, like many other artists, worked as a commissary for the Ministry, specifically during the Directory, either on projects that he was commissioned to do as an individual, such as the official costumes he designed, or on tasks undertaken in conjunction with other artists. This latter activity manifested itself most often in the form of visits in teams to studios of artists requesting payment for a *travail d'encouragement*, upon which the commissary would be called upon to attest to the State that the work in question had been completed and was of artistic merit. In similar fashion artists like David were also invited to evaluate a variety of other government commissions and projects, including in such institutional contexts as the Museum and the National Institute.[20]

While some artists had thus to depend in one away or another on the goodwill of an often impoverished Ministry of the Interior to continue their work, others were involved in the more fruitful activity of collecting and conserving national patrimony. Here, too, the Ministry of the Interior was an omnipresent force, particularly in the creation and administration of the multiple *dépôts* which served as national clearing houses, but also in the development of patrimonial policy itself.[21] In the case of the *dépôts*, artists, scientists, and men of letters all became civil servants in an embryonic and often confusing governmental structure, in which the Ministry of the Interior was a central linchpin. One of these civil servants was the painter Jean Naigeon, who had a variety of dealings with the Revolutionary bureaucracy, first and foremost as the keeper of the Dépôt de Nesle in the heart of Paris.[22] Naigeon was a pupil of David's in the 1780s. He was one of the beneficiaries of the prize given to David in 1791 but subsequently divided among three other artists. Naigeon never received this particular prize, according to correspondence with the Ministry of the Interior in 1800. On at least two other occasions he did receive patronage from other sources in the government, however. In 1793 he was commissioned by the Committee of Public Safety to produce an anti-British caricature, while during the Directory and again in the Consulate he contributed letterhead designs to the executive branch.[23] Yet Naigeon's main effort in the Revolution was as an official collector and keeper. Most of the details of his job were the direct province of cultural agencies such as the Committee of Public Instruction and its Temporary Commission of the Arts, although on any number of occasions Naigeon had also to report directly to the Ministry of the Interior. Naigeon was eventually rewarded for his diligent service with the curatorship of the newly formed Luxembourg Museum in 1802, but not before sending several demeaning petitions to the Ministry of the Interior seeking employment and/or lodgings.[24]

In this respect it is possible to see the activities of the Ministry of the Interior in the domain of patrimony as constituting yet another form of patronage. Contemporary French artists whose work had been excluded from the Louvre, could nonetheless be thankful for at least two initiatives taken by the Ministry of the Interior during the Directory. In 1797 Bénézech implemented the creation of a museum in Versailles dedicated to the French school. Two years later François de Neufchâteau authorised the decoration of the chambers of the Council of 500 at the Palais Bourbon with more works by living French painters and sculptors (including Belle's *Pericles and Anaxagoras*). Many of the works involved in both projects had actually passed through *dépôts* like the Dépôt de Nesle before arriving at these destinations. If the artists did not receive pecuniary compensation, at least they could increase their personal glory and that of French art. In certain cases, artists were in fact reticent to comply.[25]

Given this dimension of ministerial patronage, it is perhaps not inappropriate to consider briefly the question of private patronage as well. As Colin Bailey has indicated, the Revolution wiped out the efforts of a generation of private collectors to sponsor contemporary French art.[26] Some individual artists did manage, with considerable toil, to find success outside the State-run apparatus set in place to compensate for the collapse of both the academies and the market. Painters of landscapes, genre, and portraits like Louis-Léopold Boilly, Jean-Louis De Marne, Jacob Sablet, and Gérard struck a chord in the tastes and sensibilities of the Directory bourgeoisie, while history painters such as David, Le Barbier, and Jean-Baptiste Regnault endeavoured to approach the public by means of a variety of personal initiatives; David even made a considerable fortune in the process.

Certain ministers of the Interior also addressed the issue of the market directly or indirectly. Early in the Revolution the liberally inclined Jean-Marie Roland insisted that the Ministry of the Interior not displace the public sphere and the market. Although he wished to see the State multiply the cultural institutions under its authority, he also emphasised the need to support privatisation and decentralisation.[27] Yet another minister, Lucien Bonaparte, profited – apparently – from his position to build his own personal collection while in office; in so doing, he employed any number of willing artists to evaluate the fruits of the art market.[28] Some of the art may well have been auctioned off by the government, as authorised by the Ministry of the Interior, from the unwanted stores kept in *dépôts* like the Dépôt de Nesle.[29]

Nonetheless, the general tendency was one of centralisation, in which individual artists' initiative was curtailed by the imperatives of republican policy, particularly as the decade drew to a close. Indeed, by the end of the Directory the Ministry of the Interior found itself in a paradoxical situation. It had gradually become the focal point of artists' contact with the republican government. Unable to pay its artists for public works, it still found it advisable to increase the centralisation of the art world, in part by eliminating the open salon; as Udolpho van de Sandt has shown, it was precisely the Ministry of the Interior, under François de Neufchâteau, which would begin this process in 1799.[30] The experiment with democratic, if not egalitarian, forms was rapidly coming to a close, even before Napoleon assumed office. The artists, the fiascos of republican patronage behind them, had little choice but to follow suit. Even the arch-republican David would become a court artist for Napoleon, if only half-heartedly.[31]

'Artists, honour a Nation which honours you', exhorted François de Neufchâteau, Minister of the Interior, in 1798.[32] This statement, by one of the most ambitious and energetic ministers of the Interior of the First Republic, captures well all of the ambivalence of republican patronage. For while François was exemplary in the degree to which he could encourage those under his direction – Ministry personnel and artists alike – to take initiatives in their work, he was also singularly responsible for the centralisation of republican cultural policy.[33] Régis Michel has intimated in fact that this policy was never anything more than an exercise of State control: 'The Salon, as an ideological apparatus of the State, reflects *exactly* the power emanating therefrom.'[34] What did eventually transpire as a result of ministerial involvement in cultural affairs was a substantial loss of autonomy among the makers of cultural artefacts, at least until the art market could restore itself in the first decade of the nineteenth century; arguably, this development is symptomatic in a broader sense of what Howard Brown has recently described as a shift from the liberal democracy of the First Directory to the 'liberal authoritarianism' of the Second Directory and the Consulate.[35] Nonetheless, Michel's statement is extreme if taken at face value, for it fails to account for the potential 'republicanism' of State patronage in the middle years of the Revolution, when something resembling a 'republic of culture brokers' emerged to take a leading role in the creation and diffusion of Revolutionary culture.[36]

The contours of republican policy may come more clearly into focus if, for example, we look ahead to the post-Revolutionary period for a moment. Late in 1799 Napoleon Bonaparte, just named First Consul, requested of his brother Lucien, then Minister of the Interior, the names of the best artists in France, those whose talent made them worthy of government support.[37] Already during the Italian campaigns Napoleon had begun to attract artists and men of letters to his side. His strategy was simple: he would keep his artists busy and paid, and they would serve as cogs in one great propaganda machine. As for the Ministry of the Interior, it would be staffed by equally busy and obedient civil servants.

In matters of patronage, Napoleon's intention made itself known rather quickly. Early in 1801 Charles Meynier was commissioned to paint an allegorical scene representing *Titus dedicating the Temple of*

Peace, in which he had assembled the Masterpieces of Art on a ceiling in the Louvre. This subject, apparently Lucien's idea, was obviously intended as a paean to Napoleon's patronage of the Louvre, and as a tribute to his peace initiatives; as such it provides an interesting foil to the earlier scenes of Pericles discussed above. Napoleon would brook no whining, however. Several months later the commission was changed by a new Minister of the Interior, Jean-Antoine Chaptal; the scene would now represent *The Earth receiving from the Emperors Adrian and Justinian the Laws of the Romans dictated by Nature, Justice, and Wisdom*, which Meynier duly finished early in 1803, and for which, by all accounts, he was promptly paid. Chaptal seems to have derived his inspiration for the change from Louis de Fontanes, then *rapporteur* in the artistic division of the Ministry of the Interior and a notoriously precocious Napoleonic apologist, if not from the master himself. Indeed, this particular scene reveals one of Napoleon's role models, Justinian, whom he consciously imitated in his codification of civil law. Clearly Napoleon was looking forward to bigger and better things, and art would be one of many vehicles used to help him attain his goals.[38]

A similar environment of sovereign control and propagandising would be the goal of the Bourbon Restoration, albeit with less perfect results. The Restoration reverted, in the spirit of the *ancien régime*, to a Ministry of the Royal Household. But the efficiency of the Napoleonic regime was forsaken for a spoils system, particularly during the reign of Charles X, in which loyal *Ultras* were rewarded with positions of responsibility with considerable overlap and room for conflict. One conspicuous example is the double royal commission to decorate the Musée Charles X and the Council of State in the Louvre in 1825. The idea for the commission was due to a veritable Minister of Fine Arts (fancifully dubbed the King's Pleasures), Sosthènes de La Rochefoucauld, whose position had been carved out of his father's Ministry of the Royal Household. La Rochefoucauld had to struggle for two long years with the Director of the Royal Museums, the Governor of the Louvre, the President of the Council of State, the Minister of Justice, the Director of Royal Furniture, and the Director of Royal Buildings, all of whom bickered constantly with each other almost to the ruin of his grandiose conceptions. And of course the funding for the project was as hard to come by as ever. Ever the pragmatic *Ultra*, La Rochefoucauld admits in his memoirs that his primary concern was to keep his artists and writers busy and well fed. Not surprisingly, *his* artists (including the young Delacroix) all reviled him (as did many fellow *Ultras*), not least of all for the coercive tactics he was willing to resort to.[39] Yet they took the work, for the market would not support a history painter, and the prestige of obtaining a public commission was ever so great. A similar story could be told of nearly all the regimes of nineteenth-century France.[40]

Against this brief *aperçu* of post-Revolutionary cultural management certain cogent features stand out with regard to the specific tenor of cultural life in the First Republic. The system of patronage installed in the 1790s was republican in name and, in certain dimensions, in spirit, despite the numerous obstacles faced by the Revolutionary authorities. Many artists struggled with the new order of things, yet some attempted sincerely to make it part of their artistic language. To be sure, the republican system seemed to function better from the ministerial side than from that of the artists, and the eventual failure of the Revolution to bear fruit in this respect owed much to the material deficiencies and unstable personnel of the republican regime. Nonetheless, while republican patronage more often than not failed to satisfy the needs of the artists themselves, who had little or no public market to which to turn (even if some exceptions did prevail), certain artists did in fact engage, however momentarily and ambivalently, in a refreshing variety of activities, frequently in conjunction with the Ministry of the Interior.

In contrast, the post-Revolutionary regimes quickly attempted to snuff out all traces of the Revolutionary experiments in Republican democracy. The Napoleonic Empire and the Bourbon Restoration both retained the *étatisme* inherent in the policies of the Revolutionary Ministry of the Interior while inverting the process of legislative sovereignty which had been such an integral part of the Revolutionary moment. Thus in 1817, after the Ministry of the Interior had undertaken an initial survey of transformations to be made on edifices previously occupied by republican (and imperial) organs of government, Alexandre-Evariste Fragonard *fils* was commissioned to replace an allegorical figure of the law (*lex*) in a bas relief decorating the façade of the Chamber of Deputies with a figure of the King (*rex*).[41] Significantly, the Ministry took its orders directly from the King and his closest entourage, and promptly paid its painter. This neo-absolutist proclivity to subsume the law under the person of the King was indeed a familiar motif in the Restoration. What alternatives did an artist have? Fragonard complied, as did Lafitte, Perrin, Le Barbier, Gérard, and so many others, while a few, like Fragonard *père*, Naigeon, or Belle, gave up painting, in some cases altogether; David, ever one to buck trends, emigrated to Brussels and lived out the rest of his life bitter and in relative seclusion.

How might one account for this subsequent state of affairs, for what might be taken as the failure of republican patronage in the Revolution?

This is hardly the place to launch into a detailed analysis, but one might propose three significant factors in the process in guise of conclusion. First, if the verdict of Alexis de Tocqueville is accepted, then the primary consequence, if not *raison d'être*, of the Revolution was the enhancement of State power and administrative centralisation begun already in the reign of the Sun King, Louis XIV, if not earlier. In the world of art, this translated in large part into the restoration after 1796 of the Academy and its normative classicism.[42] Then again, as a new public sphere rose out of the debris of the *ancien régime*, some alert politicians and bureaucrats actually built up their own networks of artist-clients. This gradual restoration of court forms, beginning, arguably, in the circles of Paul Barras and then of Lucien Bonaparte during the Directory, greatly facilitated the return of the sovereign court under Napoleon and then the restored Bourbons.[43] Finally, and perhaps most fundamentally, the patterns of behaviour ingrained in artists accustomed to working through circles of patronage as courtiers – or beggars, as the poet André Chénier disparagingly called them[44] – took considerable time to disappear, if at all, despite the anti-academic rhetoric so prevalent throughout the 1780s and 1790s. As T.J. Clark has noted, the same patterns of behaviour are clearly visible well into the nineteenth century: artists had to stoop to soliciting commissions and seeking protectors, without which it was next to impossible to survive.[45] It would require several decades, and a handful of generations, into the nineteenth century before the experiments of the mid-1790s could show any results.

By then, however, a concurrent 'Revolution in red tape', to paraphrase Clive Church,[46] had already run its own course. Already when Charles X acceded to the throne in 1824 the elements for State intervention in the various regimes of the nineteenth century were firmly in place: an overweening State apparatus replete nonetheless with a potential for internal conflict and contradiction; a status quo in cultural production epitomised by the Academy and the salon; a private sector increasingly alienated by official taste and policy. To all this the public careers of Delacroix, Courbet, Manet, and a host of other nineteenth-century artists clearly attest. Seen from this perspective, then, the Revolution of 1789–99 was, almost despite itself, the critical moment in a long-term evolution in the French cultural-bureaucracy, for better or worse, truly a new dawn.

Notes

1   An earlier version of this paper was presented in April 1997 at the Association of Art Historians conference held at the Courtauld Institute. The author is grateful to Robert Oresko, Mary Hollingsworth, Edouard Pommier, Philippe Bordes, Antoine Schnapper, and Yveline Cantarel-Besson for their support.

2   Archives nationales (hereafter AN), F17 1056, doss. 14.

3   *Catalogue des tableaux, dessins, estampes, livres, médailles, coquilles et curiosités du cabinet de feu M. Louis Lafitte* (Paris, 1828).

4   M. Ozouf, *La Fête révolutionnaire* (Paris, Gallimard, 1976).

5   *La Révolution française et l'Europe 1789–1799* (Paris, Grand Palais, 1989), vol. 3, pp. 830–902; also the papers in P. Bordes and R. Michel (eds), *Aux armes et aux arts! Les arts de la Révolution* (Paris, A. Biro, 1988); and J.-F. Heim *et al.*, *Les salons de peinture de la Révolution française* (Paris, C.A.C. S.A.R.L. Edition, 1989).

6   Plutarch, *Life of Pericles*, ch. 16.

7   See E. Bénézit, *Dictionnaire critique et documentaire des peintres, sculpteurs, dessinateurs et graveurs de tous les temps et de tous les pays*, new ed. (Paris, Grund, 1948–55), vol. 6, p. 372; Bibliothèque nationale, Cabinet des Estampes (hereafter BN Est.), Dc 53, 'Oeuvres de Lafitte'; AN F17 1056, doss. 5, 14; *Catalogue des tableaux*; also P. Bordes, 'L'art et le politique', in *Aux armes et aux arts!*, pp. 118–19; *La Révolution française et l'Europe*, vol. 3, p. 839; and P. Marmottan, 'Lucien, Ministre de l'Intérieur, et les arts', *Revue des études napoléoniennes* (1925), 29–30.

8   Bénézit, *Dictionnaire critique*, vol. 8, p. 235; *Un peintre sous la Révolution. Charles-Nicaise Perrin (1754–1831)* (Montargis, Musée Girodet, 1989), pp. 51–3 (ill.). For the ventures alluded to in this paragraph see *Collection complète des portraits de MM les Députés à l'Assemblée nationale de 1789* (Paris, n.d.; Perrin's portraits include Ducret, Lamy, Langlier, Molien, Pradt, Saurine, and Séalt); AN, O1 1925b, no. 17; AN, O1 1931; *La Révolution française et l'Europe*, vol. 3, p. 903; P. Vitry, 'L'amphithéâtre des chirurgiens et l'Ecole des arts décoratifs', *Gazette des Beaux-Arts* (1920), 207.

9   AN, F17 1056, doss. 15; *La Révolution française et l'Europe*, vol. 3, p. 849; Catalogue de Tableaux, Dessins, Esquisses, Croquis de feu M. Perrin (Paris, 1831); *Un peintre sous la Révolution*, pp. 59, 60, 62 (ill.).

10   AN F17 1056, doss. 16; Y. Cantarel-Besson, *La Naissance du Musée du Louvre. La politique muséologique sous la Révolution d'après les archives des musées nationaux* (Paris, Réunion des Musées nationaux, 1981), vol. 2, p. 147; *La Révolution française et l'Europe*, vol. 3, pp. 834, 853 (ill.).

11   See especially F. Pupil, 'Le dévouement du chevallier Désilles et l'affaire de Nancy : essai de catalogue iconographique', *Le Pays lorrain*, 2 (1976), 73–110 (ill.); also Bénézit, *Dictionnaire critique*, vol. 6, pp. 501–2; *La Révolution en Haute-Normandie, 1789–1802* (Rouen, Editions du P'tit Normand, 1989), 275–80; D. Wisner, 'Une esquisse peinte de J.-J.-F. Le Barbier l'aîné: *Lycurgue présentant aux Spartiates leur nouveau Roi (1791)*', *Gazette des Beaux-Arts* (1990), 129–36.

12   AN AA 34, no. 1040.

13   *Cincinnatus returning to his Plough*, frontispiece for the *Almanach du cultivateur* by Gilbert Romme (Paris, Year III); also BN Est., 'Halbou'.

14 *La Révolution française et l'Europe*, vol. 3, p. 846.

15 AN F17 1056, doss. 14; AN F21 569, pl. 6, nos. 48–56; *La Révolution française et l'Europe*, vol. 3, pp. 837, 840, 858–9, no. 1079 (ill.); also M. Moulin, 'François Gérard, peintre du 10 août 1792', *Gazette des Beaux-Arts* (1983), 197–202; and D. Wisner, 'Deux images de la République: le *Serment du Jeu de Paume* de David et l'*Insurrection du 10 août* de Gérard', in F. Demichel (ed.), *Saint-Denis, ou, Le Jugement dernier des Rois* (Colombes-La Garenne, Editions de l'Espace européen, 1993), pp. 397–405.

16 AN F17 1242, doss. 'Gérard et Serangeli'; *La Mort de Marat* (Avignon, Musée Calvet, 1989), pp. 61, 65–6, 163–4.

17 *La Révolution française et l'Europe*, vol. 3, pp. 830 ff.; *Jacques-Louis David 1748–1825* (Paris, Louvre, 1989), pp. 323–38, 589 ff.

18 The essential archival sources are: AN F13 1195; AN F13 1196; AN F17 1056, doss. 7; Archives de Seine, DQ 10, 37, doss. 4097; Institut d'Art et d'Archéologie, Fondation Doucet (hereafter Doucet), carton 10, peintres, no. 3611, 'David'; also Cantarel-Besson, *La Naissance*, vol. 2, pp. 21 ff.

19 AN F17 1056, doss. 14.

20 AN F17 1056, doss. 14, 'Hennequin', 'Réattu', doss. 17 'Dumarest'; AN F17 1057, doss. 6, 7; AN F17 1232, doss. 3; AN F21 569, pl. 5, no. 5, pl. 6, nos. 71, 104; AN AD VIII; Archives de l'Académie française, cartons 5B 1, 5B 2, 5B 3.

21 See especially E. Pommier, *L'art de la liberté. Doctrines et débats de la Révolution française* (Paris, Gallimard, 1991), p. 108.

22 See D. Wisner, 'Jean Naigeon at the Dépôt de Nesle: a Collector and Culture-Broker in the First French Republic', *Journal of the History of Collections*, 8 (1996), 155–65; also *La Révolution française et l'Europe*, vol. 3, p. 834.

23 AN AFII, 66; *Description de l'oeuvre de Barthelémy Joseph Fulcran Roger graveur en taille douce*, BN Est., Yb3 386.

24 Doucet, carton 22, peintres, 'Naigeon'; BN, mss Fonds Lesouëf, 167, doss. 27, ff. 158–9; Archives de Seine, DQ 10, 385, doss. 6471; Archives des Musées nationaux, AA3, 229; and Bibliothèque municipale de Beaune, ms 278.

25 AN F21 569, pl. 4, no. 71, 73; AN F21 584, doss. 1, nos. 3–7; and cf. *Jacques-Louis David*, p. 225.

26 C. Bailey, '"Quel dommage qu'une telle dispersion": Collectors of French Painting and the French Revolution', in *1789: French Art during the Revolution* (New York, Colnaghi, 1989), pp. 11–26; and now S.L. Siegfried, *The Art of Louis-Leopold Boilly: Modern Life in Napoleonic France* (New Haven, Yale University Press, 1995).

27 *Compte rendu à la Convention nationale par Jean-Marie Roland, Ministre de l'Intérieur* (Paris, 1793), pp. 223–4.

28 See F. Piétri, *Lucien Bonaparte* (Paris, Plon, 1939), pp. 112–13; also R. Michel, 'Meynier ou la métaphore parlementaire. Essai sur *La Sentence de Ligurius*', *Revue du Louvre*, 3 (1987), 88–200.

29 See Wisner, 'Jean Naigeon', pp. 158–9.

30 U. van de Sandt, 'Institutions et concours', in *Aux armes et aux arts!*, p. 158.

31 See W. Roberts, *Jacques-Louis David, Revolutionary Artist: Art, Politics, and the French Revolution* (Chapel Hill, University of North Carolina Press, 1989), ch.

4. For another revealing case see F. Beaucamp, *Le Peintre lillois Jean-Baptiste Wicar (1762–1834). Son oeuvre et son temps* (Lille, E. Raoust, 1939); also *Le Chevalier Wicar, peintre, graveur, dessinateur et collectionneur lillois* (Lille, Musée des Beaux-Arts, 1984).

32 Cited in van de Sandt, 'Institutions et concours', p. 160.

33 See C.H. Church, *Revolution and Red Tape: the French Ministerial Bureaucracy, 1770–1850* (Oxford, Clarendon Press, 1981), pp. 164–5.

34 R. Michel, 'L'art des salons', in *Aux armes et aux arts!*, p. 94.

35 H.G. Brown, 'From Organic Society to Security State: the War on Brigandage in France, 1797–1802', *Journal of Modern History*, 69 (1997), 661–95.

36 See Wisner, 'Jean Naigeon', pp. 161–2; also L. Hunt, *Politics, Class, and Culture in the French Revolution* (Berkeley, University of California Press, 1984), especially ch. 6; and E. Kennedy, *A Cultural History of the French Revolution* (New Haven, Yale University Press, 1989), pp. 185–92.

37 Van de Sandt, 'Institutions et concours', p. 160. For an overview of Napoleonic patronage, see R. Rosenblum, 'Painting under Napoleon', in *French Painting 1774–1830: the Age of Revolution* (Detroit, Institute of Fine Arts, 1975), pp. 161–73; also *La Révolution française et l'Europe*, vol. 3, pp. 911–21.

38 See N. Munich, 'Les plafonds peints du Musée du Louvre. Inventaire de documents d'archives', *Archives de l'art français*, 26 (1984), 108–9, 112–13; and D. Wisner, 'The Napoleonic Lawgiver: Myth and Reality 1796–1815', *Proceedings of the Annual Meeting of the Western Society for French History*, 21 (1984), 107–21.

39 See for example, AN O3 1417; also *Mémoires de M. de La Rochefoucauld, duc de Doudeauville* (Paris, M. Levy, 1861–4), vol. 7, p. 156, vol. 8, pp. 487 ff., vol. 9, p. 366. For a discussion of the commissions see K. Simons, 'Die Dekoration des Musée Charles X im Louvre: Offizielle Kunst, Stilwandel und Salonkritik zwischen Restoration und Julimonarchie', *Idea: Werke, Theorien, Dokumente*, Jahrbuch des Hamburger Kunsthalle, 9 (1990), 161–210; D. Wisner, 'Law, Legislative Politics, and Royal Patronage in the Bourbon Restoration: the Commission to Decorate the *Conseil d'Etat* Chambers, 1825–1827', *French History*, 12 (1998), 149–71; and J.P. Ribner, *Broken Tablets: the Cult of Law in French Art from David to Delacroix* (Berkeley, University of California Press, 1993), pp. 50–62.

40 See especially T.J. Clark, *The Absolute Bourgeois: Artists and Politics in France 1848–1851* (London, Thames and Hudson, 1973); P. Mainardi, *Art and Politics of the Second Empire: the Universal Expositions of 1855 and 1867* (New Haven, Yale University Press, 1987); also M. Marrinan, *Painting Politics for Louis-Philippe: Art and Ideology in Orleanist France, 1830–1848* (New Haven, Yale University Press, 1988).

41 AN F21 584, nos. 49–77, 88.

42 A. de Tocqueville, in J.-P. Meyer (ed.), *L'Ancien régime et la Révolution*, new ed. (Paris, Gallimard, 1967); also A. Boime, *The Academy and French Painting in the Nineteenth Century* (London, Phaidon, 1971); and P. Grunchec (ed.), *Les concours des Prix de Rome de 1797 à 1863* (Paris, Ecole nationale supérieure des beaux-arts, 1983).

43 See P. Mansel, *The Court of France 1789–1830* (Cambridge, Cambridge University Press, 1988).

44 *La République des Lettres*, in P. Dimoff (ed.), *Oeuvres complètes d'André Chénier* (Paris, 1908–12), vol. 2, p. 215.

45 Clark, *The Absolute Bourgeois*, especially ch. 2.

46 *Church, Revolution and Red Tape.*

Part II

8

The History of a Renaissance: the French *University*[1] from the Revolution to the Restoration (1792–1824)[2]

Jean-Claude Caron

The history of the universities does not attract a great deal of interest in France. With a few exceptions, those most closely concerned, the universities themselves, display very little enthusiasm for writing or prioritising research into their own history.[3] As far as studies giving a general overview of the situation are concerned, these amount to no more than a few notable, but rare, examples, of which the most recent are two works, the first edited by Jacques Verger,[4] and the second, more ambitious from the standpoint of subject-matter although more constrained by its format, edited by the same historian in association with Christophe Charle.[5] Nothing comparable, in fact, to the interest directed in the Germanic world towards the universities as institutions, but also as locations for the interaction of socio-professional groups, or as places where the élite of the nation's youth can come together. It would seem that the highly centralised constitution of the French state even before the French Revolution may have acted against the creation of a sense of patriotism at the university level, a feeling which is incomparably stronger in Germany – rather like the feeling that was to emerge in France with the birth of the *grandes écoles* during the revolutionary era.

Both universities and students have produced a small number of works, some prosopographical, others statistical which, however important they may be from the point of view of innovation, have failed to give rise to any genuine lines of research in this field.[6] Finally, while French historians have written extensively on the education system, one cannot fail to observe a marked imbalance between works on the primary school sector, which is still the subject of very keen interest,[7] and works on other sectors. Is this simply the reflection of a problem of size: quantity (primary school pupils) is favoured over privilege (secondary school pupils, sixth formers, students)?; or is it the expression of a deeply rooted culture, that of the primary school as the common vehicle for the civic and republican ideal?

The period from 1792–1824 established the legislative framework which gave birth to the French *University*. From that time onwards, a multiplicity of questions has arisen. While some of these can be easily resolved (the reasons for the abolition by the Republic of the 22 universities of the *ancien régime*, for example), others need to be seen from a perspective which would take us outside the time-frame of this book, even though, in essence, the terms of the debate which were set under the Republic, the Consulate, the Empire and the Restoration remained unchanged thereafter right up to the end of the nineteenth century. For, in the end, 'each era has had to resolve the recurring dilemma of preserving past knowledge while assimilating innovation, of evaluating skills and of changing the criteria of assessment'.[8] Such is the case for the years 1792–1824, which saw a succession of different political models, all of them, however, confronted with these two alternatives. Finally, there needs to be some agreement as to what is meant by *University*, a word whose polysemous nature sometimes prevents the engagement of apparently homogeneous discourses, which appear to be the same, but which do not, in fact, refer to the same thing. We are touching here on one of the major distinctions between the periods before and after 1789, something not always taken into account.

Up to 1789, and even, at least in theory, as late as 1793, there were universities in existence which constituted so many autonomous teaching bodies. If they were not independent of the political establishment (on the contrary, they contributed at times to its legitimisation: the role played by the Sorbonne in the conflict between Gallicans and Ultramontanists, or in the war against Jansenism, is a case in point), it is true, nevertheless, that they clung fiercely to their privileges, the more so because their role during the Enlightenment was undoubtedly being eroded, and reduced, as it was at times, to proclaiming the proscription or destruction of 'immoral' books, or to setting themselves up as *de facto* defenders of absolutism in the name of the age-old alliance between throne and altar. Conversely, the *University*, as it emerged under the First Empire, was made up of a centralised authority which administered the whole of the education system. So, whether in terms of concept or scope, it is clear that the change was both quantitative and qualitative. In a way, the word *University* was misappropriated by the imperial authorities to make it correspond to a policy of unity and obedience which was the exact antithesis of the notions of diversity and (relative) liberty which had prevailed before. It can therefore be claimed legitimately that, from their abolition in 1793 up to the major legislation of 1896, France was without universities or, to be more exact, that the *University* set up by Napoleon I was an institution whose role consisted solely in the administration of all state education in France, special and higher education being embodied within groups of Faculties, the number varying from town to town (Paris, Strasbourg and, to a lesser extent, Toulouse, each with five Faculties, being for many years the best endowed). There were also certain specialist establishments (*écoles spéciales*), which provided instruction in a particular field of knowledge, and which were outside the tutelage of the University, such as the military academies (the *Polytechnique*, St Cyr and so on) attached to the War Office or the *Arts et Métiers*, linked to Trade and Agriculture.

The state of the universities in *ancien régime* France varied a great deal. While the weight of Paris remained crushing (except for Medicine, in which Montpellier, founded in 1289, was outstanding), a marked distortion can often be observed between the scientific and intellectual ambitions of these establishments, in which exceptional teachers sometimes operated, and the unflinching practice of the most common venality in the awarding of university degrees. Such a case is that of the Faculty of Law at Rheims, which held 'the national record for graduates by prerogative of age',[9] or the Faculty of Medicine at Besançon, 'lavish and automatic dispenser of university degrees, but also at the same time a centre for serious study pursued over a long period with a view to effective training in the practice of medicine'.[10] Quite a common situation, in fact, which clearly reveals the 'cohabitation' of two practices which, at first sight, seem antithetical, whereas they both fall within an economic and social reading of *ancien régime* France: on the one hand, the difficult problem of survival for small and medium-sized establishments, reduced to commercial practices, such as the sale of grades: on the other hand, the pressure from young people anxious to gain access to a lucrative position in society at the most reasonable cost.

For a period of about twelve years, France had neither universities nor *University*, but was not entirely bereft of higher education.[11] When, in 1791, the Le Chapelier law was passed, providing for the abolition of the guilds, it was clear that the survival of the *ancien régime* universities was at stake. The latter were in fact attached to these ancient bodies, the symbols of pre-revolutionary archaism. On 15 September 1793, the Convention ratified the abolition of the colleges and faculties, which *de facto* entailed the disappearance of the universities. However, it was not until the decree passed by the Convention on 20 March 1794 that the University of Paris (the Sorbonne, in other words) and the provincial universities were officially dissolved. The education system of the *ancien régime* had benefited, so to speak, from the vagaries of domestic and foreign policy so as to survive until the *Montagnard* Convention, at least officially. Neither Talleyrand's report on the state education system in 1791, nor Condorcet's in 1792, resulted in any concrete measures. The education system was totally disorganised as a result of attacks on the body which had been the principal player in the field before the Revolution; namely the Church. From 1793 onwards, the latter was replaced by the state as provider of funds, of premises (released by the nationalisation of the assets of the clergy) and of staff.[12] This was the beginning of a long-standing rivalry between the two institutions.

In 1794, and despite the burden of war, civil and external, the Convention set up the *Ecoles spéciales*, the first elements of a higher education system which was particularly necessary since the Revolution lacked the managerial talent needed to promote the realisation of its projects. For this reason, a decree of 4 September 1794 created three *Ecoles de santé*, in Paris, Montpellier and Strasbourg.[13] These were to become Faculties of Medicine,[14] their number remaining unchanged up to the time of the Third Republic. They had places, at the time, for about 550 students, the majority destined for the Army or the Navy. But 1794 was also the year in which the *Conservatoire nationale des arts et métiers*, the *Ecole normale supérieure* and the *Ecole polytechnique*[15] were created; the following year saw the foundation of what would become the *Ecole des langues orientales*, the *Conservatoire nationale de musique* and the *Institut national* (now the *Institut de France*), which replaced the former academies, as well as the *Ecoles centrales*, conceived as an antechamber to higher education, which replaced the colleges. In relation to these years 1794–95, therefore, one can speak of a real renaissance of higher education, envisaged primarily as a breeding-ground for élites. In the words of Janis Rangins, 'The Republic needed educated men.'[16] What the Convention had started, the Directory was to continue, taking advantage of a somewhat calmer climate. As early as Year III, Daunou drew up a *Rapport sur l'organisation des écoles spéciales*, in which he revealed himself to be in favour of 'not destroying any existing establishment',[17]and ensuring that 'the *écoles spéciales* are deployed in such a way that all parts of the Republic have more or less equal access to the enjoyment of the benefits of education'.[18] They were embarking on a scheme of conservation and extension, but without really giving themselves the means to put it into effect. Nobody, at the time, saw the need for an institution to oversee the whole education system, even though the role of the State, at least in secondary education, was being reinforced.

If the concern for rapid action was the rule as far as medical education was concerned, the same cannot be said of legal training. France had to wait until the Acts of 1 May 1802 (creation) and 13 March 1804 (organisation) – and for a few months, therefore, under the regime of the Consulate – for the foundation of 12 Law Schools, of which nine were within the 1789 frontiers. The First Consul needed qualified legal personnel to administer an enlarged France, soon to be an empire of 130 departments. Objectively, it was a matter of providing a uniformity of training, fixed by regulations from which no one could depart. This was particularly true of medicine, prompted by the expansion of knowledge, but also by the need for personnel for the armies. 'No-one will be able to enter the profession of physician, surgeon or Medical Officer of Health without having sat or passed an examination,' affirmed the decree of 10 March 1803 on the practice of medicine. The stakes were high: on the one hand in terms of recognition of equivalent competence over the whole of the territory (the desire for uniformity) and, on the other hand, in terms of access to learning and therefore to a position in society based, theoretically at least, on ability and not social origin. In general terms, however, none of the higher education establishments founded during the decade 1794–1804 formed either universities or the *University*. Each school possessed its own particular statute. Here there is a paradox, a contradiction even, between the often repeated affirmation of the quest for unity, uniformity even, and the absence of any sovereign regulatory authority. Within the logic of imperial educational policy, indeed of the policy of the regime as a whole, the foundation of the *University* did not come before change, but completed a transformation which originated in a clearly stated political act of will.

The creation of the *University* conceals an ambition which goes far beyond the aim of this chapter which will be limited to observing its effects on higher education. Originally, however, the Imperial *University* was concerned with all levels of education. It was created in two stages: the decree of 10 May 1806 and the decree of 17 March 1808. The first three articles declare at the outset: 'Public education [to be understood here as something that does not fall within the sphere of the family], is entrusted exclusively to the *University*. No school, no educational establishment whatsoever may be formed outside the Imperial *University*, or without the authorisation of its head. No one may open a school or teach publicly, without being a member of the imperial *University*.' It was really a question, as summarised in Pierre Larousse's *Grand dictionnaire encyclopédique du XIXe siècle*, of the foundation of 'a major public body of which all members were appointed by the government'.[19] For this purpose the country was divided into 'academies', headed by a Rector, supported by an administration composed mainly of General Inspectors, and by an academic council whose particular jurisdiction was over all matters relating to discipline. This monopoly appears in line with imperial political practice, in whatever area.

In practice, however, this monopoly was quickly destroyed in the field of primary education (the *petites écoles*), the state having at its disposal neither the material means, nor the political and moral will, to take on this heavy responsibility. It relinquished the task to the local authorities, beginning with the town councils, and to the teaching orders, which came back into favour (the brothers of the *écoles chrétiennes* as early as 1803, for example). In contrast, the monopoly was applied strictly in the case of secondary education, as signified by the creation of the *lycées* in 1802 (replacing the *écoles centrales*, whose curriculum and teaching methods were deemed too innovative) and by the maintenance of colleges in the smaller towns, and also in the case of higher education. Fourcroy was the overseer of this global reorganisation of the education system. The power of the Grand Master of the *University* (the first incumbent of this kind of proto-Ministry of Education was Louis de Fontanes) was considerable: nobody could practise without his authorisation, and he was supported by a University Council which had total power over the entire territory, and the whole of the teaching staff.

The bases, or principles, inspiring the education imparted were clearly defined, and in accordance with a carefully established hierarchy: firstly, the precepts of the Catholic faith; next loyalty to the Emperor, to the imperial monarchy and to the Napoleonic dynasty; finally, compliance with the statutes of the teaching profession. In order to test this last requirement, and to give it a binding and universal form, the decree of 17 September 1808 established the oath that every individual had to swear in order to be accepted as a member of the *University*:

> I swear before God to fulfil all the duties placed on me, to use the authority entrusted to me only to train citizens attached to their religion, their prince, their country and their parents, to further by all the means in my power the advance of knowledge, good habits of study and high moral standards; to perpetuate these traditions to the glory of the reigning dynasty, the happiness of the children and their fathers' peace of mind.

The significance of this text, characterised by a shrewd balance between references to the public and to the private spheres, lies also in the continuity which it strove to establish between the pre- and post-1789 periods, and also between generations. In this sense, it is a revealing indicator of an ideology which clearly expects the teaching profession to play a role in bringing unity, and even uniformity, to society by means of the education of its children.[20] It is precisely on this point that the Revolution was soon denounced by its opponents, who roundly condemned those who 'concentrated all their efforts on corrupting and infecting the young and innocent minds' of children, who were 'like soft wax, easily handled, and as malleable as one wishes'.[21]

The network of faculties expanded considerably under the Empire. The number of faculties reached 91 around 1810, of which 38 were in the conquered territories,[22] and 53 within the France of 1789. Among the latter, one can point firstly to 22 Faculties of Arts and ten Faculties of Science, whose principal task consisted of organising the annual *baccalauréat* examinations in arts and sciences respectively; and secondly, to nine Faculties of Law and three Faculties of Medicine, which specialised in supplying administrative and medical personnel for the civil and military services. There were also seven Faculties of Catholic Theology and three of Protestant Theology: the former were at that time, and for a long time afterwards, in serious decline, facing competition from the major seminaries (a concession granted to the Church in the climate of religious conciliation embodied in the signing of the Concordat of 1801), which were specifically exempt from the tutelage of the *University*. The redistribution of Faculties across the country gave rise to hopes which were often dashed. While Besançon, for example, regained a Faculty of Arts from 1810, it possessed a Faculty of Science only between 1810 and 1815 (re-established in 1845), and it obtained only a minor School of Medicine in place of the Faculty which had been its pride and joy.[23] In addition, certain faculties had difficulty in attracting students. While the Faculties aiming at professional qualifications filled up rapidly, those with academic aims had a greater number of casual attenders at lectures (the curious, the enthusiasts, those with time to spare) than of students in the strict sense of the word. At Toulouse, for example, 'no student enrolled in the Faculty of Science during the first decade of existence'.[24] The town could not, and would not, get its Faculty of Medicine back until 1878. The paucity of funds allocated by the local authority and the competition from Montpellier provide a partial explanation for this long absence. On a wider scale, it is interesting to note that no faculty was created in France between 1815 and 1834.

It is legitimate to claim that in the case of the imperial *University*, it was not a question of 'science as teacher, as in Germany, but the State as teacher, as in Sparta', and that its members were for this reason, 'Jesuits of the state'.[25] Born of political will, the *University* was always at the heart of a wide-ranging debate which, far from being silenced by the return of peace, was intensified by it. The central question was as follows: as was the case with other institutions of Napoleonic origin, should the Restoration preserve the *University* or not? If the question arose, it was because the new *régime*, confronted by the evidence of its own fragility, as witness the episode of its double restoration, was torn between the twin realities of preserving an instrument of control over the education system which would bear the mark of imperial institutional genius, and of having to support the players acting within it, whose political commitment it feared. The same applied to the commitment of the administrators (Rectors) much as that of the teachers and, of course the students, who were all suspected of being agents of liberalism, Bonapartism, even republicanism – in short, of what can be summed up in the word 'patriotism'.

In addition, there was no lack of voices, that of Chateaubriand for example, to denounce 'the twin evils of despotism and democracy'[26] within the *University*. From Lamennais to Benjamin Constant, there were those who inveighed against the monopoly of the *University*, which appeared to be an intolerable survival of imperial despotism. For this reason, an edict dated 17 February 1815, provided for the replacement of the imperial *University*, and of the 27 existing academies,[27] with 17 regional universities, somewhat on the German model. The office of Grand Master was also abolished, and replaced by an 11-member Council. Decentralisation, but also the return to favour of the Church, clearly shaped the desired objectives. The Hundred Days, however, did not allow the system envisaged to be set up on a permanent basis. With the Second Restoration, the situation changed. Louis XVIII understood what an ideal instrument of control the Imperial *University* represented. The latter, renamed 'royal', was maintained 'provisionally' by an edict dated 15 August 1815, then confirmed definitively in 1822. At the same time, a Committee of Public Instruction was set up, becoming in 1820, the *Conseil royal de l'instruction publique*. Furthermore, in 1822, the office of Grand Master was re-established, and conferred on Mgr. Frayssinous, titular bishop of Hermopolis, who cleansed the *University* of dissident administrators, teachers and students: nine rectors, five inspectors from the academies, nine lecturers in law and medicine were removed from office;[28] seventeen Faculties of Arts and three Faculties of Science were abolished, officially because of excessive cost. Lastly, about seventy-five students, deemed guilty of participation in the protest movements of the

Jeunesse des Ecoles at the beginning of the 1820s, were excluded temporarily or permanently from various Faculties. The zeal of Mgr. Frayssinous earned him elevation to the rank of Minister of Public Instruction and Ecclesiastical Affairs (the combination is significant), a new post created in 1824, of which he was the first incumbent.

To sum up, the *University*, although it had become 'royal' under the Restoration, still bore the deep imprint of its imperial origin; it appears to be a particularly typical example of a state institution on the French model. The aborted plan of 1815 to split the *University* into several universities was not taken up again until 1896, with the avowed intention of limiting the power of Paris in this field, in the name of much-needed decentralisation. The results of this reform were all the more disappointing, even in the eyes of its promoters. It is difficult, in whatever country, to fight against a deeply rooted politico-administrative culture such as the one that exists in France, and which is a constituent element of her history – one might almost say of her essence. The Guizot decree of 28 June 1833 gave official recognition to the end of the *University*'s monopoly of primary education (in practice, this had already been the case since the First Empire) and the Falloux decree of 15 March 1850 put an end to its monopoly of secondary education. As for higher education, a similar law passed in July 1875 at the time of the 'moral' Republic failed to survive the triumph of the Republic of republicans which began immediately after the general election of 1876. In 1880, Jules Ferry restored the *University*'s monopoly in the award of degrees, and banned private establishments from calling themselves universities. It was not until the decree of 10 July 1896 that it was again possible to speak of universities (plural), although the autonomy of these institutions was in no way comparable to that of their predecessors.

The political issues which underlie all government action relating to higher education also coincide with socio-economic considerations. Successive governments, from the Empire to the Restoration (and, of course, beyond), took great care not to train too many qualified professionals in relation to the state of the labour market, if one may venture such an anachronism.[29] The theme of 'poverty dressed in black' became a recurrent motif from the earliest years of the Restoration, and a particularly virulent one since the *Jeunesse des Ecoles* was seen as one of the social groups in the forefront of the battle for liberalisation. By the decree of 5 July 1820, Faculty administrators were endowed with an effective arsenal of repression which placed the *Jeunesse des Ecoles*, and also their lecturers, under close surveillance. But how was control to be exercised over the continuous stream of young people arriving on the benches of the Faculties? Overall, the number of students in Paris increased from about 2300 in 1814 to 4500 in 1821, and 5000 in 1830, the maximum being reached in 1835 with nearly 7500 students.[30] Faced with this expansion in numbers, a deputy declared as early as 1825 that there was 'an overabundance of physicians and surgeons, either qualified or currently in training', while, three years later, the *Nouveaux tableaux de Paris* asserted that 'there will never be enough courts for those who want to be magistrates, enough practices for those who want to become solicitors, enough cases for those who want to distinguish themselves at the Bar'.[31] The question is not to decide whether these words belong to the realm of reality or fantasy. They were the expression of a fear of the social consequences of class changes within a liberal society that had put the notion of social advancement at the heart of its ideology.

Founded in 1806, abolished in 1896, the Napoleonic *University* testifies in an exemplary fashion to the profound changes in French society since the Revolution of 1789. Having entered, at one and the same time, into the era of triumphant individualism, and the heyday of social categorisation of individuals, France was trying to fuse together two apparently conflicting elements. It was a case of proclaiming the reign of liberty (including that of changing social status) and of equality (on a strictly legal level), while assigning to each individual a place and a role which would guarantee the continuity of the established order. The organisation of the *University*, overseeing all tiers of the education system, met these twin criteria exactly. Firstly, it organised these tiers into a hierarchy to which the different social classes corresponded. Guizot set out the facts bluntly: 'Primary education is designed for all subjects of the State (...), as much in the interests of the state as in that of the individual'. Secondary education was reserved for 'men who are destined for leisure and ease, or who take up higher professions such as commerce, the arts, etc'. Finally, specialist or higher education must allow for the development of 'superior minds', and therefore provide the priests, military personnel, administrators, magistrates and the doctors which French society needed.[32] Secondly, the *University* allowed these changes in the social order to be channelled, controlled and limited. In this connection, it offers a most convincing illustration of the idea that the Age of Revolution must give way to that of Evolution; in other words, that the time of violence as a way of organising social relationships must yield to a time of peaceful organisation of the body politic. This ideal, as is well-known, was far from being achieved, since the nineteenth century, particularly in France, is still seen as 'the age of revolution', to repeat

Eric Hobsbawm's classic phrase.[33] Finally, it is a not inconsiderable paradox that this periodically revolutionary country has shown itself to be so
keenly attached, for so long a period, to the maintenance of that venerable institution, the French *University* – so much so that that it still
survives here and there of course, inside the current framework of the
French education system. Homage paid to Napoleon's genius?

Notes

1 The term is italicised to indicate its specialised usage as a centralised authority
  with control over the sector of higher education as a whole, and to differenti-
  ate it from its other meaning as a specific institution.
2 Jean Clark and David Williams translated this chapter from French.
3 See, for example, A. Tuillier, *Histoire de l'Université de Paris et de la Sorbonne*
  (Paris, Nouvelle Librairie de France, 1994), 2 vols; *Histoire de l'Université de Paris*.
  Exhibition catalogue of the Chapelle de la Sorbonne (Paris, Chancellerie de
  l'Université de Paris, 1973); J.M. Burney, *Toulouse et son université. Facultés et
  étudiants dans la France provinciale du 19e siècle* (Toulouse, Presses universitaires
  du Mirail and Editions du CNRS, 1988). For bibliography, see L. Parker, *Institutions of Higher Education. An International Bibliography* (New York, Greenwood
  Press, 1990). On the *ancien régime*, see S. Guenée, *Bibliographie de l'histoire des
  universités françaises des origines à la Révolution* (Paris, Picard, 1978–81), 2 vols.
4 J. Verger, *Histoire des universités en France* (Toulouse, Privat, 1986). This super-
  sedes S. d'Irsay, *Histoire des universités françaises et étrangères des origines à nos
  jours* (1933–35). See also G. Weisz, *The Emergence of Modern Universities in France
  (1863–1914)* (Princeton, Princeton University Press, 1983); J. Minot, *Histoire
  des universités françaises* (Paris, PUF, 1991); A. Renaut, *Les révolutions de l'université. Essai sur la modernisation de la culture* (Paris, Calmann-Lévy, 1995).
5 C. Charle and J. Verger, *Histoire des universités* (Paris, PUF, 1994); see also L.
  Stone, *The University in Society* (Princeton, Princeton University Press, 1974–75)
  2 vols; K.H. Jarausch, ed., *The Transformation of Higher Learning (1860–1930)*
  (Stuttgart, Kletta Cotta, 1983). In progress: *A History of the University in Europe*
  (Cambridge, Cambridge University Press), 4 vols.
6 See also D. Julia, J. Revel and R. Chartier, *Les universités européennes du XVIe au
  XVIIIe siècles. Histoire sociale des populations étudiantes* (Paris, Editions de
  l'EHESS, 1986–89), 2 vols. See also J.-C. Caron, *Générations romantiques. Les
  étudiants de Paris et le quartier latin (1815–1851)* (Paris, Colin, 1991); C. Charle,
  author of several prosopographical works on professors in the Faculty of Arts
  and the Faculty of Science in the University of Paris, as well as in the *Collège de
  France*, including *La République des universitaires* (Paris, Seuil, 1994).
7 Among the most recent works, note J.-L. Luc, *L'invention du jeune enfant au XIXe
  siècle. De la salle d'asile à l'école maternelle* (Paris, Belin, 1997); F. Jacquet-
  Francillon, *Instituteurs avant la République. La profession d'instituteur et ses*

représentations de la monarchie de juillet au Second Empire (Paris, Presses universitaires du Septentrion, 1999); J.-C. Caron, *A l'école de la violence. Châtiments et sévices dans l'institution scolaire au XIXe siècle* (Paris, Aubier, 1999).

8   C. Charle and J. Verger, *Histoire des universitiés*, p. 5.

9   *Atlas de la Révolution française* vol. 2: D. Julia (ed.), *L'enseignement 1760–1815* (Paris, Editions de l'EHESS, 1987), p. 75. See especially the maps and graphs with commentaries.

10   B. Lavillat, 'L'Université de Besançon au XVIIIe siècle (1691–1793)', *Institutions et vie universitaire dans l'Europe d'hier et d'aujourd'hui'* (Besançon, Annales littéraires de l'Université de Besançon/Les Belles Lettres, 1992), p. 71.

11   See *L'Université de Paris. La Sorbonne et la Révolution*. Exhibition catalogue for the celebration of the bicentenary of the French Revolution held at the Sorbonne in June–July 1989.

12   For the main dates relating to this legislation, see *Atlas de la Révolution française*, pp. 7–9.

13   See in particular *L'Ecole de santé de Strasbourg, 14 frimaire An III*. J. Héran, G. Livet and G. Vicente (eds), Proceedings of the Colloquium for the Bicentenary (Strasbourg, PUS, 1995); *Septième centenaire des universités de l'Académie de Montpellier 1889–1939* [1992], University of Montpellier I.

14   See Chapter 9.

15   Then called the *Ecole centrale de travaux publics*.

16   Title of a work published by Belin in 1987.

17   Cit. L. Liard, *L'Enseignement supérieur en France* (Paris, Colin, 1894), vol. 2, p. 431.

18   Ibid., p. 432.

19   Vol. 15 (1876), art. 'Université', p. 660.

20   The decree of 17 March thus invokes 'uniformity of education'.

21   Pius IX's encyclical of 15 May 1800, cit. *Université. Coup d'oeil sur cette institution* (date and place of publication not given), p. 21.

22   In 1810 France had 130 *départements*, 57 of which were in the conquered territories mainly adjacent to France's 1789 borders, in what is currently Belgium and the Netherlands, northern Germany as far as the mouth of the Elbe, the left bank of the Rhine, Savoy, the Ligurian and Italian coasts as far as Rome, part of Switzerland (le Valais) and in part of Austria known as the Illyrian provinces from Carinthia to Dalmatia.

23   Lavillat, p. 74. Besançon did not regain a Faculty of Medicine until 1967, one year before the creation of a Faculty of Law.

24   Burney, p. 63.

25   J. Minot, *Histoire des universités françaises* (Paris, PUF, 1991), pp. 37–8.

26   Liard, p. 145.

27   Numbering 20 in 1848 during the Vaulabelle ministry, then 16 in 1854 under the Fortoul ministry.

28   For these and other statistics, see J.-C. Caron, *La Jeunesse des Ecoles à Paris 1815–1848. Etude statistique, sociale et politique*. Doctoral thesis (University of Paris I, 1989), pp. 30 ff.

29   On this issue in the context of the ancien *régime*, see V. Frijhoff, 'Université et marché de l'emploi dans la République des Provinces-Unies' et R. Chartier, 'Espace social et imaginaire social: les intellectuels frustrés au XVIIe siècle', *Les Universités européennes du XVIe au XVIIIe siècle*, pp. 205–43, 245–60.

30 See J.-C. Caron, *Générations romantiques*, pp. 35 ff.

31 *Nouveaux Tableaux de Paris* (Paris, Pillé,1828), vol. 1, pp. 261–2.

32 F. Guizot, *Essais sur l'histoire et sur l'état actuel de l'instruction publique en France* (Paris, Maradan, 1816), pp. 2–3.

33 *L'Ere des révolutions (1789–1848)* (Paris, Fayard, 1970; reprint, Brussels, Complexe, 1988).

9
The New Paris Medical School and the Invention of the Clinic

Laurence Brockliss

On the signing of peace in 1802, the cream of Whig society flooded across the Channel to inspect the new France with which the British state had been at war for nearly ten years. While the majority of British visitors came in search of Revolutionary chic – and craved an interview with the First Consul – a small but significant group travelled to the continent specifically to view Revolutionary medicine. The London medical establishment was well aware that the Revolutionary decade had led to profound changes in the way that medicine was taught in France and also provided their Parisian colleagues with unprecedented opportunities for medical research. Only the year before a young anatomist, Marie-François-Xavier Bichat (1771–1802), had published an account of an entirely new conception of anatomical structure, based on the cell not the parts. The Treaty of Amiens offered British doctors the first chance to see for themselves the new developments.[1]

Medical reform had been on the agenda of the National Assembly from February 1790. In that month the Revolutionaries established the *comité de mendicité* whose brief included the regeneration of the country's medical services. Its activities were complemented in the following September with the establishment of a separate health committee, the *comité de salubrité*, under the presidency of the infamous Joseph-Ignace Guillotin (1738–1814), himself a graduate physician. Both committees were established on the assumption that contemporary medical practitioners were inadequately trained and their services too narrowly focused on the medical needs of the well to do. As Guillotin expressly commanded that interested individuals and medical corporations should send him suggestions for reform, the Committee was quickly inundated with plans for improving the nation's health.[2] The most important was presented in November 1790 on behalf of the *Société royale de médecine* by its permanent secretary, Félix Vicq d'Azyr (1748–94).[3] The Society had been set up by the crown in 1776 as primarily a licensing agency for new drugs. Much to the Paris faculty's disgust, however, it had rapidly laid claim to be the medical equivalent of the *Académie des sciences* and saw itself as the official promoter of medical policy and reform. Although close to the court – Vicq was the Queen's physician – the Society's voice commanded respect with many Revolutionaries thanks to its earlier tussles with the Paris faculty, its hatred of charlatanism (its victims included Franz-Anton Mesmer), and its progressive discourse.[4]

In the early years of the Revolution nothing came of these initiatives. Plans for medical reform were included in the general educational package Talleyrand placed before the Assembly in 1791 but this and subsequent proposals were never turned into legislation.[5] For all their good intentions, the Revolutionaries, especially once France became embroiled in war from the spring of 1792, had neither the time nor the resources to pay much attention to welfare projects. It was to be the war, however, that eventually acted as the catalyst for the specific reform of medical education. In 1789 institutionalised training in medicine was provided by a bewildering number of medical faculties, surgical colleges and army hospitals. Under the threat of the reforming axe, these institutions soldiered on until they were summarily abolished in September 1793. At this point the annual flow of certificated entrants to the French medical community abruptly came to a halt, if medical students continued to receive informal training. This 'stop' soon had an alarming effect on the army's medical corps. Given the high mortality rate of conscripted medical personnel, the army was fast running out of physicians and surgeons by late 1794, consequently forcing the Thermidorian regime to re-establish a system of medical education as soon as possible.[6]

On 7 frimaire Year III the chemist, Antoine-François Fourcroy (1755–1809), another graduate physician, proposed to the Convention the creation of the Paris *Ecole de santé*, and boasted that a new era had dawned. Employing the greatest medical talents in the Republic, the school would revivify medical science, rescue the French people from charlatanism, and provide 'an education superior to any other of this kind known in Europe'.[7] Located in the buildings of the former *Ecole de chirurgie* [College of Surgeons], erected only two decades earlier by the royal architect, Jacques Gondoin, it would occupy appropriately one of the finest and most majestic buildings in the city. Provided with proper dissecting and experimental facilities, and endowed with books and collections from a variety of defunct institutions (including the *Académie des sciences* and the *Société royale de médecine*), the new school was clearly intended to be a wonder of the world. Seven days later Fourcroy announced the establishment of two further medical schools at Montpellier and Strasbourg, but it was Paris that always enjoyed the lion's share of the resources and the attention. By 1800 it was attended by 1000 medical students, by the 1820s by 2000, while the largest *ancien régime* faculty – Montpellier – had had fewer than 250.[8] Understandably, it was the Paris school that the British medical establishment wanted to view.

The school that the British and other foreign visitors encountered was very different from the traditional medical faculty. In the first place, physicians and surgeons were taught together. In early modern Europe licensed medical practitioners were usually divided into three categories: physicians, surgeons and apothecaries. The physicians, by dint of the fact that they were university graduates and limited their activities to diagnosing disease and prescribing remedies, were deemed superior to the other two who were originally seen as manual operatives. Theoretically, in towns possessing physicians, the surgeons and apothecaries had to work under their orders. In the eighteenth century admittedly the status of surgeons had improved greatly, partly in recognition of their growing operative dexterity. But in France, especially, the traditional boundaries remained. Although French surgeons from 1772 no longer had to be apprentices and they were expected, just like physicians, to receive rigorous institutionalised education, their training was always kept separate, and many physicians continued to view even their most skilful colleagues as inferiors. The Paris school by deliberately integrating the education of the two branches of the profession clearly intimated that the old status divisions were dead and confirmed the victory of the surgical élite in their long-standing campaign for equality.[9]

According to Fourcroy when proposing the new school, medicine and surgery were by nature inseparable and their quarrels unedifying. Reunited, both would benefit: 'To study them separately is to abandon theory to the frenzy of the imagination and practice to a permanently blind routine.'[10] Much the same point was made eight years later by his colleague, Michel-Augustin Thouret (1748–1810), Dean of the new Paris *Ecole*. In a speech introducing the law of 19 Ventôse Year XI, which reconstituted the medical profession *tout court*, the division of physic and surgery was declared to have no historical warranty and to be the worst aspect of the *ancien-régime* medical system.[11] Henceforth, therefore, practitioners were to be divided into two new groups: graduate *médecins* who had trained in one of the three *écoles de médecine* (as they were now dubbed) and could practise anywhere, and *officiers de santé*, who had trained in a local hospital, and in consequence could only practise in the local *département*. Graduate *médecins* could take a doctorate in either physic or surgery and neither took precedence.[12]

In the second place, the Paris school provided a much more practically orientated and hands-on medical education. Although the surgical colleges may have been relatively hands-on institutions, there can be no doubt that the *ancien régime* faculties were pedagogically staid and out of step with Enlightenment views of learning. Professors principally lectured *ex cathedra* on the five parts of theoretical medicine: physiology, hygiene, semiotics, pathology and therapeutics. For the first part of the lecture they dictated from a *cahier*, for the rest of the hour they developed their thoughts off the cuff; visual aids were unknown. Lectures were also given on anatomy and other practical medical subjects, including chemistry, but they were seldom properly integrated into the curriculum and frequently cancelled – even at Montpellier anatomies could be postponed for lack of bodies. Moreover, practical subjects were generally taught in poor facilities by junior professors and the students seldom examined. In consequence, if students wanted high-quality training in the practical medical arts or hands-on experience in patient care, they had to seek extra-curricular instruction. Both Paris and Montpellier were important centres of private medical training throughout the century. Commercially minded anatomists had their own private amphitheatres where they instructed students in the art of dissection; hospital physicians and surgeons charged tyros a fee to walk the wards with them on their rounds.[13]

The Paris school quickly became renowned for offering a much more dynamic curriculum in accordance with Fourcroy's insistence that simply listening to lectures was of limited value: 'A little reading, much seeing and much doing: this will be the basis of the new teaching.'[14] Put at its simplest, the Paris professors of the early nineteenth century aimed to inform through entertainment: they turned the theoretical lecture into a *pièce de théâtre*. Eschewing the monotonous *dictée* of their predecessors, they expatiated on a theme verbatim, which they amply supported with experiments and visual aids. The Montpellier naturalist-physician, Pierre-Joseph Amoreux (1741–1820), first came to Paris for extra-curricular study in the 1760s after taking his degree in the southern faculty. Thirty-five years later he came back to the capital in 1800 to taste the delights of the new dispensation. In his autobiography he has left brief pen portraits of most of the serving professors. He was particularly impressed by Alphonse-Vincent-Louis-Antoine Le Roy (died 1816), who ostensibly held the obstetrics chair, but who was lecturing on 21 and 23

Fructidor on the physiological basis of a healthy mind and body. The man, Amoreux declared, was a genius. A great, one might say extravagant, declaimer, Le Roy illustrated his lectures, Hamlet-like, with reference to five human brains placed before him.[15]

More importantly, the Paris school showed its originality by integrating anatomy properly into the course for the first time by linking its teaching with physiology. From the beginning, the two subjects were joined together under the one professor, François Chaussier (1746–1828) of Dijon. The new school also offered novel opportunities for those who wanted to become expert anatomists with the foundation of the *Ecole pratique de dissection* in 1797. Modelled on a much smaller school attached to the old Paris *Ecole de chirurgie*, the *Ecole pratique* offered three years' free training in dissection to 40 new pupils a year, chosen on the basis of a competitive examination.[16]

However, the crowning glory of the new school was the opportunity that it gave students for clinical study, the section of the curriculum described by Fourcroy as: 'the most immediately useful part of their apprenticeship, the complement of all the others'.[17] Of the twelve chairs, three were specifically allocated for bedside teaching in Paris hospitals: one for internal diseases, one for external, and a third for rare conditions. So popular were these courses that by 1800 two further internal and external clinics had been established, plus others instituted for vaccination (a new fad), syphilis (a permanent problem) and obstetrics.[18] From 1802 furthermore the very best students had the opportunity to gain a much fuller acquaintance of patient care with the foundation of the competitive positions of extern and intern in the Paris hospitals. Whereas in *ancien-régime* France tyro physicians had to pay for the privilege of walking the wards, it was henceforth possible to win the right in a competition. Students first competed for the position of extern which merely brought the right to follow the hospital doctor on his rounds. Then, after a year, students were permitted to compete for an internship. This was a coveted position for the holder became the doctor's assistant for a 4-year term, was given 500 francs as an annual gratuity, and provided with free board and lodging during his *jours de garde*. François-Louis Poumiès de Siboutie who became an intern at the Salpetrière (a female prison hospital) in November 1812 described the post as: 'the marshal's baton for a student of medicine'.[19]

A good account of the life of an intern has been left by a surgeon called Caron, who served at the Hôtel-Dieu between 1808 and 1812. When he first entered the hospital, he was entrusted only with minor surgical operations. His journal recalls that he delivered a woman in labour, set broken bones and performed minor amputations, including a crushed thumb. He also treated patients suffering from venereal disease. By the end of his stay, however, Caron was performing quite complex operations and many autopsies. In particular, he noted a successful operation on a fistula, using the La Forest method.[20]

In the third place, the Paris school's reputation stemmed from the fact that it was a centre of original medical research as much as a centre of medical teaching. Professors in the old faculties and surgical colleges had not been expected to advance medical science, and few ever did, with the notable exception of the Montpellier nosologist, François Boissier de Sauvages (1706–67), and his vitalist successor, Paul-Joseph Barthez (1734–1806). The most innovative physiological work in eighteenth-century France was performed outside the faculties by figures such as René-Antoine Ferchault de Réaumur (1683–1757, not even a physician) or Théophile de Bordeu (1722–76).[21] Fourcroy intended in contrast that the professors in all three of the new *écoles* should be active medical scientists.

> The function of the new medical schools is not simply limited to teaching what is known; their remit also extends to the most detailed research into all the branches of the art of healing; their aim is the advancement of all the sciences which can enlighten physiology [literally, animal physics].[22]

The Convention, he insisted, expected that the French, the most industrious and enlightened people in the universe (Fourcroy's words!), would become the leading nation in Europe for medical science. By setting up the new schools, the legislature sent out its order: 'to French genius to surpass every nation in this aspect of human knowledge, as it already surpasses them in so great a number of others'. In the future, professors must be properly paid so that they were totally dedicated teachers and researchers.[23]

In the coming years, through a wise choice of the School's founding fathers and the continual promotion of original minds, Fourcroy's expectations were stunningly fulfilled in the capital. For the first three decades of the nineteenth century, Paris was unquestionably at the heart of European medical research in the particular fields of morbid anatomy and clinical pathology. An interest in identifying the relationship between a set of external symptoms and particular internal lesions can be traced to the work of Giovanni-Battista Morgagni (1682–1771) at Padua in the second quarter of the eighteenth century. Its growing popularity as an area of medical research across Europe in the decades before the Revolution reflected contemporary Enlightenment disenchantment with the rationalist fairy tales of traditional pathology which seldom had any empirical content.[24] According to Foucault, however, the first practitioners of the new pathology were primarily interested in confirming existing supposition rather than creating new knowledge. It was only with the establishment of the Paris School that the new pathology became a positive investigative science. The Paris professors brought to their research a novel imaginative *regard* or gaze that allowed them to describe symptoms and identify internal lesions much more accurately while giving much greater weight to the singularity of the individual experience of disease.[25]

While it is possible that Foucault exaggerates the conservativeness of pre-Revolutionary pathological anatomy, there can be no doubting the fecundity of the Paris School in this respect. In the space of 25 years professors and students such as Jean-Nicolas Corvisart-Desmaret (1755–1821), Gaspard-Laurent Bayle (1774–1816), François-Joseph-Victor Broussais (1803–47) and René-Théophile-Hyacinthe Laënnec (1781–1826) revolutionised understanding of heart disease, tuberculosis and typhoid. In particular they developed the diagnostic techniques that allowed them to discern the internal lesions in the living patient, thus allowing them to interpret the cluster of visible symptoms more successfully and offer a more solid prognosis. *Pace* Foucault, the professors' diagnostic skill derived from their ability to bring other senses to bear besides sight. To a certain extent physicians had always palpitated the bodies of their patients looking for internal signs of disease, if only in taking the pulse. The Paris professors, however, turned the habit into an art form. More importantly, they learnt to listen to patients' bodies as well as touch them. Auscultation as a diagnostic technique was initially developed by Corvisart in his study of heart disease. In the 1820s it became peculiarly associated with Laënnec, physician at the Charité hospital, who invented the stethoscope, a discovery announced to the world in 1819.[26]

The medical researchers of the Paris School, it must be stressed, did not form a homogeneous group. Not only did they have very different political and religious views – Broussais was a materialist and atheist, Laënnec a Catholic royalist – but they also had conflicting views about the nature and purpose of medical science. Some were hard-nosed researchers who did not make great claims for the therapeutic value of their discoveries. Corvisart, for instance, believed that diet and exercise could reduce the likelihood of a heart attack but that longevity had little point if it was purchased at the expense of life's pleasures.[27] Others were therapeutic nihilists arguing that there was little they could do for their patients: traditional remedies were useless and the physicians' best recourse was waiting on nature.[28] A few, on the other hand, were gung-ho optimists, most notably Broussais, who was a professor at the Paris military hospital of Val-de-Grâce. Following in the footsteps of Bichat, Broussais was a systematiser in a School that was generally suspicious of medical systems.[29] In 1816 he published a vicious attack on one of the founding fathers of the School, the nosologist Philippe Pinel (1745–1826), in which he argued that attempts to identify and study specific diseases symptomatically was flawed. Virtually all diseases had a common cause in internal inflammation, especially of the gastrointestinal tract, and should be treated by antiphlogistic remedies, that is, local bleeding.[30] Broussais' reductionism and arrogance split the medical community in two, but his positive and simplistic therapeutics proved very appealing to medical students who were understandably enticed by the thought of being able to offer their patients a successful cure. In 1823 France imported 320 000 leeches; by 1834 the figure had risen to 21 885 465.[31]

What united the researchers of the Paris School, then, was a particular investigative methodology which proved compatible with a variety of medical worldviews. What made their research possible, however, was the peculiar Revolutionary context. It was not just that Fourcroy had demanded the School become a centre of research. Rather, the Revolution had provided the conditions in which a school of clinical pathology could be successfully developed. In the pre-Revolutionary era the development of the new pathology had been held back in France by the difficulty of using the country's hospitals as centres of research. Although France had some 2000 hospitals for the sick poor, only the handful of military hospitals were really in the control of medical practitioners. Civilian hospitals were usually run by the Church and staffed by members of the regular orders who objected to their charges being used as objects of scientific enquiry. In particular, post-mortems were frowned upon.[32] The Revolution completely changed the hospital landscape. Hospital property was nationalised, the institutions put under State control, and the medical profession given *carte blanche* to treat the inmates as medical guinea-pigs. At the same time, it was made quite clear to the poor who entered a hospital's portals that they were now citizen-patients whose bodies belonged to the nation in return for their care. Ultimately, the fame of the Paris medical school was built on the peculiar access that the Revolution afforded medical men to the city's many hospitals. In 1788, the city boasted 48 hospitals with over 20 000 patients: in the name of progress (and the amelioration of the health of the Revolutionary bourgeoisie who could only benefit from therapeutic experimentation on the sick poor), these beneficiaries of charity were turned into medical statistics.[33]

The number of British doctors able to view the new Paris School at close quarters following the Peace of Amiens was obviously small. Hostilities were resumed too quickly for all but the most Francophile and go-ahead to make the trip. Once peace was permanently made in 1815, however, the British returned, this time to visit a School whose reputation had been dramatically enhanced in the interim through the published research of its leading lights. For the next twenty years, it became commonplace for British physicians, and an increasing number of Americans too, to spend several months receiving clinico-pathological instruction in the French capital.[34] Several, on their return, committed their thoughts on the new School to print, often, like the Edinburgh surgeon, John Thomson, deliberately inflating the positive value of their experience in order to play up the deficiencies of medical training at home.[35] In consequence, on this side of the Channel in particular, a myth of the originality and significance of the Paris School was quickly created which proved tenacious. It received its literary embodiment as late as 1872 in George Eliot's *Middlemarch*. When Eliot wanted to give the reforming physician Tertius Lydgate the right radical credentials to cause alarm and despondency among the Tory medical establishment of pre-reform Coventry, she made him a Paris graduate who had sat at the feet of Broussais.

Like all myths, however, the reality was always a little different from the glowing encomia contained in the reports of admiring foreigners. To begin with, when the medical changes that occurred in France through the reforms of 1794 to 1803 are assessed in the light of Vicq d'Azyr's original *Nouveau plan*, it is clear that the medical Revolution was incomplete. Much of Vicq's reform plan was adopted. Had he lived (he died in 1794) he would only have applauded the establishment of the new medical schools with their emphasis on clinical training and the integration of medicine and surgery. However, Vicq dreamed of making 'scientific' medical care open to all. He anticipated the division of the medical profession into graduate *médecins* and departmental *officiers de santé*, but he expected the latter to be state employees who would provide free medical treatment for the sick poor as much as possible in their own homes. He would not have approved of the establishment of a completely independent private liberal profession drawing its income from fees.[36] He would have been equally unhappy about some of the organizational features of the new schools. It was his intention that they should be physically located in suitable hospitals, not merely provide their clinical teaching there. He also wanted a course that would take six years to complete rather than the three that became the standard.[37] Above all, he would have found fault with the examination system.

In the *ancien-régime* faculties the students had been tested by *viva voce* examination and the oral defence of two or more medical dissertations, usually composed by the professor. Vicq believed that the system produced rhetoricians not learned doctors and demanded that the new schools introduce a completely new form of examination. Henceforth, he suggested students should be tested by eight days of written examinations, where they would be made to sit all day answering set questions in French. They would then spend a day performing manual operations on a corpse and finish by passing three days on the clinical ward. Here, they would be shown a number of specific cases, asked to make their examination, and then be required to retire to write about them.[38] In the event, the method of examination was scarcely changed from the system operating under the *ancien régime*. At the end of the 3-year course students had to undergo five public *viva voce* examinations (two in Latin) whose content matched the different parts of the official course. After this they had to sustain a public dissertation, written in either Latin or French.[39] Noticeably, there was no practical element. Given the number of degrees bestowed – some 300 per annum in the 1820s – the *viva voce* examinations were inevitably perfunctory, lasting seldom more than 25 to 30 minutes each. Had they lasted longer, the 12 professors and their understudies would have been examining all year. The dissertations, too, were probably highly derivative. Initially, in the years before 1803, when graduation was not compulsory for medical practitioners, only the most committed students sustained a thesis at the end of their studies, and the quality was high: many students even demonstrated some signs of independent research. Thereafter, however, it is difficult to see how this level was maintained among the ever-growing mass of graduands.[40] The Paris medical school, then, may have provided a state-of-the-art medical education, but there was no way of telling whether the doctor it sent out into the world was Balzac's Benassis or a Rastignac.[41]

In fact, the value of the education was also occasionally called into question. A commission set up by Louis XVIII on his accession to investigate the state of medical studies revealed a number of minor abuses and a great deal of dissatisfaction among surgeons. In the report drawn up for the King by the secretary, Jean-Baptiste-François Léveillé (1769–1829), it was suggested that the unification of the two careers far from enhancing surgery had sold the science short.

> Since the length of the course and the cost of matriculation, examination and graduation are the same for the physician and the surgeon, and since the practice of medicine is easier, more pleasant and generally elicits greater social esteem, it is to be observed that all the students have graduated as doctors of medicine and disdained surgery.[42]

As a result, of the 2153 doctoral promotions in Paris between 1803 and 1815 only 72 had been in surgery. In consequence, many top surgical appointments were going to physicians. The solution favoured by the majority of the committee was that the two professions should once again be separated and three surgical faculties created at Paris, Lyons and Toulouse.[43] Writing a few years later, the surgeon, Jean-Charles-Félix Caron (1745–1824, not to be confused with the young intern mentioned above), agreed wholeheartedly with this conclusion and urged the government to act on the advice. In Caron's view surgery and physic were as chalk and cheese. Physic was a useless and uncertain science, continually shown up by surgery's achievements and only kept alive by the gullibility of women: 'Perhaps, but for the nerves of our wives, [physic] would no longer exist.' In demanding to unite the two disciplines, Vicq d'Azyr had acted as surgery's enemy, out to destroy it.[44]

The physicians, too, were not always satisfied with the teaching, especially the quality of the clinical courses. In March 1815 one of the great old men of French medical reform, Nicolas Chambon de Montaux (1748–1826), produced his own lengthy memorandum on the current state of medical studies. A former member of the *Société royale de médecine*, an electro-therapist, a pioneer in private clinical teaching at the Salpetrière in the 1780s and mayor of Paris in the early days of the Republic, Chambon de Montaux was the authentic representative of the Vicq generation.[45] His judgement on the value of the clinical teaching of the Paris school after 20 years of existence was caustic.

Three clinical chairs are insufficient in France [read Paris] for the instruction of students. Those frequenting Paris are too numerous to profit from the lessons. Piled up around each bed, even if their number is small, only a few see the patient's face and recognise the signs of the morbid affection singled out in the professor's remarks. Moreover, the next day, these few are elbowed away from the bedside by their friends; it is thus impossible for them to experience sufficient observational continuity to obtain a precise idea of even a single example of a disease.[46]

In another memorandum from about the same date Chambon also complained that the conduct of the clinical class left a lot to be desired. There were, he claimed, three forms of clinical teaching current in early nineteenth-century Europe. The students might simply follow the professor around the ward and watch what he did, receiving no formal instruction. There again, formal instruction might be given but purely in the form of a professorial lecture, which might be given at the bedside, or after the visit, in a separate *salle*. Finally, the professor might let the students do the work, entrusting them with the task of interrogating the patient, making a diagnosis and prescribing a cure. The third 'hands-on' method was undoubtedly the best. Christened by Chambon the 'German way', it was the method that he himself had developed at the Salpetrière before the Revolution. It was not a method, though, that the French had adopted in the new medical school.[47]

Assuming that Chambon de Montaux was right, then the Parisian clinical course placed a premium on 'looking' rather than 'doing'. It may have been only with the clinic given by Auguste-François Chomel at the Charité from 1817 that a more sophisticated form of teaching was developed. Chomel split his clinic into three: the visit, where he interrogated and investigated the patient in front of the students, the lesson in a room apart, where he discussed the case, and the conference, where senior students offered their own diagnosis and prognosis of cases entrusted to them by the professor. Of course, whether students availed themselves of the opportunity to take part in the conference section is another question. The notes taken by Allen Thompson, future professor of anatomy at Glasgow, of Chomel's clinic, suggest that he for one primarily only attended the visit.[48]

Finally, the originality and dynamism of the Paris School should not be exaggerated. As its members well understood, a number of medical faculties in other countries had introduced institutionalised clinical teaching in the last decades of the eighteenth century. The reforms of

1794 may have created official clinical courses in French medical schools for the first time, but the development had been already anticipated elsewhere. When Chambon de Montaux gave his preference to the 'German' method of teaching these courses, he also acknowledged that Germany had been in advance of France: 'for many years in clinical teaching'.[49] More importantly, Paris was not the only centre of active research into clinical pathology at the dawn of the nineteenth century. In London, leading physicians and surgeons had established private medical schools both within and outside the city's seven hospitals in the second half of the eighteenth century, and prominent teachers, such as Matthew Baillie (1761–1823), were now engaged in innovative research into morbid anatomy. In Vienna, too, faculty professors were pursuing independent clinical study with the foundation of the new General Hospital in 1784 and the military Academy of Medicine in 1786, the second sheltering 1200 patients. In the annals of clinical pathology the names of Stoll and Skoda are as hallowed as those of Bayle and Laënnec. In other words, the new clinical pathology was not the property of the Revolution: similar developments were occurring in the capitals of the Revolution's bitterest enemies. Indeed, chronologically speaking, *pace* Foucault, the clinic was born on the Thames and the Danube, not on the Seine.[50]

The Paris School furthermore became so locked into a particular form of clinical pathology that it eventually lost its competitive edge. From 1840, if not before, it began to be overtaken by the leading German faculties, such as Berlin, that had also embraced the research ethic in the aftermath of the Napoleonic wars but had moved medical science in a different direction.[51] The German medical schools after 1820 focused their research activity increasingly on the chemistry of the human body and placed a premium on technological sophistication, using the microscope in particular to enhance their observational capacity. The Parisians, in contrast, remained wedded to their attempt to pinpoint the lesions of the solids associated with a particular cluster of symptoms using the naked eye. Although they were not so hostile in the second quarter of the nineteenth century to microscopy as has usually been thought, they certainly showed a limited interest in its value as a diagnostic tool, except in skin diseases.[52] As a result, the Parisian school, while still attracting foreign pupils to its clinics, intellectually stagnated. France was to be at the forefront of medical research again in the second half of the century through its contribution to bacteriology. The germ theory of disease, however, and the discovery of protective vaccines was not the work of physicians but of a group of chemists. Pasteur and his colleagues were associated with the *Ecole Normale*, not the Paris faculty, and their discoveries met initially with a sceptical reception in the medical world.[53]

It is essential therefore to distinguish the myth of the Paris School from the reality. The Revolution created the conditions in which the new clinical pathology could thrive. The war required the establishment of a new medical school. Successive Revolutionary regimes after the fall of Robespierre believed that the humanitarian and ethical goals of the new state demanded that it patronise science.[54] Above all, the influence of the utilitarian and progressive *Idéologues* in government circles, at least until Napoleon became emperor, ensured that medical research would be particularly privileged for its potential contribution to human happiness.[55] On the other hand, the Revolution did not invent the clinic: nor did its medical protégé have a monopoly over creative research. Foreigners flocked to Paris in the two decades after 1815 for various reasons. They were attracted by the fame of the professors; they valued the wide variety of clinical training available in the French capital; they wanted to experience a hospital system where the medics were really in charge; many Protestants probably simply wanted to spend a few months on the razzle in a decadent foreign city. But few foreign medical students can have gone to Paris to encounter an entirely novel medical culture.[56] Like the Revolution, the clinic belonged to the world. The clinical sun that rose over Paris in 1794 was destined to shine brightly for nearly four decades, but the same clinical dawn was already breaking in other cities The vagaries of the political weather would ensure that no other city would enjoy such ideal conditions for the maturation of clinical pathology, but the Paris School basked in the sun too long and ignored the gathering storm clouds over the Rhine.

On the eve of the opening of the new Paris School, however, its supporters understandably entertained no thought of transience. The large majority was in no doubt that theirs was an original and permanent enterprise that would bring untold benefits to mankind. One of the School's most enthusiastic champions, the physician and *Idéologue*, Pierre-Jean-Georges Cabanis (1757–1808), was convinced, *pace* Corvisart, that if medical science were to be established on a proper methodological footing, the art of healing would be transformed. A revivified medicine founded on observation and stringent analysis would be able to cure virtually every disease.[57] Inspired by the thought of the imminent medical Revolution that the new School would generate, Cabanis penned a lengthy account of the history of medical science to date. Arguably the first socio-cultural historian of medicine, Cabanis insisted that developments in medical science were intimately connected with changes in the wider intellectual and political environment. The fecundity of contemporary French science, illustrated above all in the field of chemistry and the foundation of the citizen's republic provided the conditions for the creation of new and truly useful medical science, if only its practitioners would seize the day:

> The present epoch is one of the great periods of history, to which posterity will often look back and eternally call to account those who could have caused mankind to march more rapidly and more certainly down the roads to improvement. Only a few favoured geniuses can exert a really profound influence; but given the state of the arts and sciences today, there is no one, broadly speaking, who cannot contribute to their progress. . . . Let us unite together, then, in our efforts: let us take on board the study and practice of our art, that superior philosophy and reason, without which, far from offering useful succour, it most often becomes a public scourge: let us dare to attach it by new ties to the other parts of human knowledge. Thereby they (our study and practice) will receive fresh and the purest enlightenment. In consequence, at the moment when the French nation is about to consolidate its republican existence, medicine, its dignity restored, may itself begin a new era, equally rich in glory and fertile in benefits.[58]

Notes

1   The two classic studies of the French medical Revolution are Michel Foucault, *La Naissance de la clinique* (Paris, PUF, 1963; Eng. trans. London, Tavistock Publications, 1973), and Erwin H. Ackerknecht, *Medicine at the Paris Hospital, 1794–1848* (Baltimore, Johns Hopkins Press, 1967). Ackerknecht's account in particular has been recently heavily criticised in Caroline Hannaway and Ann La Berge (eds), *Constructing Paris Medicine* (*Clio Medica*, 50: Amsterdam–Atlanta, Rodopi, 1998). Bichat is usually seen as the pre-eminent founding father of the new Paris school. His *Anatomie générale appliquée à la physiologie et à la médecine*, 3 vols (Paris, Brosson and Gabon, 1801) went on sale in August 1801. For a recent study of Bichat's significance, see Elizabeth Haigh, *Xavier Bichat and the Medical Theory of the Eighteenth Century* (*Medical History*, supplement 4: London, Wellcome Institute for the History of Medicine, 1984), esp. chs 4–7.

2 H. Ingrand, *Le Comité de Salubrité de l'Assemblée nationale constituante (1790–1791) : Un essai de réforme de l'enseignement médical, des services d'hygiène, et de protection de la santé publique* (Paris, Libriarie médicale, Marcel Vigne, 1934).

3 'Nouveau Plan de constitution pour la médecine en France', in *Histoire et mémoires de la Société royale de médecine*, 9 (1787–88 [Paris, Librairie médicale Marcel Vigne, 1790]), 1–201. Analysed in Caroline Hannaway, 'Caring for the Constitution: Medical Planning in Revolutionary France', *Transactions and Studies of the College of Physicians of Philadelphia*, ser. 5, 14: 2 (1992), 147–66.

4 Laurence Brockliss and Colin Jones, *The Medical World of Early Modern France* (Oxford, Clarendon Press, 1997), ch. 12.

5 Charles-Maurice de Talleyrand-Périgord, 'Rapport sur l'instruction publique, fait au nom du comité de la constitution de l'Assemblée nationale' (1791), reprinted in C. Hippeau (ed.), *L'Instruction publique en France pendant la Révolution* (Paris, Didier, 1881), esp. pp. 81–5.

6 Jacques Léonard, *Les Médecins de l'ouest au XIXe siècle* (reproduced doctoral dissertation: 3 vols, Lille, Université de Lille, 1978), vol. i, ch. 3; Jean-Charles Sournia, *La Médecine révolutionnaire* (Paris, Payot, 1989).

7 A.-F. Fourcroy, *Rapport et projet de décret sur l'établissement d'une Ecole centrale de santé à Paris* (Paris, Imprimerie nationale, 1794), p. 6.

8 Ackerknecht, *Paris Hospital*, p. 36; R. Chartier, M.-M. Compère and D. Julia, *L'Education en France du XVIe au XVIIIe siècle* (Paris, Sedes, 1976), p. 274.

9 Brockliss and Jones, *Medical World*, ch. 8. The best study of surgical education in eighteenth-century France is Toby Gelfand, *Professionalizing Modern Medicine. Paris Surgeons and Medical Science and Institutions in the Eighteenth Century* (Westport, CT, Greenwood Press, 1980).

10 Fourcroy, *Rapport*, pp. 11–12.

11 M.-A. Thouret, *Rapport fait au nom de la section de l'intérieur... sur le projet de loi relatif à l'exercice de la médecine*, 16 ventôse an XI (Paris, Imprimerie nationale, 1803). Cf. also the views of Vicq d'Azyr, 'Plan', pp. 5–7.

12 The full text of the *loi du 19 ventôse* [10 March 1803] is published *inter alia* in *Recueil des loix et règlements concernant l'éducation publique, depuis l'édit de Henri IV en 1598 jusqu'à ce jour. Publié par ordre de son excellence le Grand-Maître de l'Université de Paris*, 8 vols (Paris, 1814–22), ii. 344–53.

13 Brockliss and Jones, *Medical World*, pp. 499–516; Laurence Brockliss, 'Medicine and the Small Universities in Eighteenth-Century France', in G. P. Brizzi and J. Verger (eds), *Le università minori in Europa (secoli XV–XIX)* (Soveria Mannelli, Rubbettino, 1998), pp. 239–72. A good account of one physician's extracurricular studies is given in A. Rouxeau, *Un étudiant en médecine quimpérois (Guillaume-François Laënnec) aux derniers jours de l'ancien régime* (Nantes and Rennes, Imprimerie du 'Nouvelliste', 1926).

14 Fourcroy, *Rapport*, pp. 8–9.

15 Bibliothèque Municipal Avignon, MS 1269, pp. 127–8.

16 Standard account: Marie-José Imbault-Huart, *L'Ecole pratique de dissection de Paris ou l'influence du concept de médecine pratique et de médecine d'observation dans l'enseignement médico-chirurgical au XVIIIe siècle et au début du XIXe siècle* (reproduced doctoral dissertation: Lille, Université de Lille, 1975).

17 Fourcroy, *Rapport*, pp. 8–9.

18 Ibid., Ackerknecht, *Paris Hospital*, p. 38.

19 F.-L. Poumiès de Siboutie, in A. Branche and L. Degoury (eds), *Souvenirs d'un médecin de Paris* (Paris, Plan-Nourrit, 1870), pp. 107–8. Previously in the year 1811–12 he had been an intern at the Paris hospital of Saint-Louis which specialised in venereal diseases.

20 Bibliothèque de la Faculté de Médecine de Paris, MS 5061, 'Journal de chirurgie de Caron'. The account of this operation is not paginated.

21 The best general introduction to eighteenth-century French medical science is François Duchesneau, *La Physiologie des lumières: empirisme, modèles et théories* (The Hague, Nijhoff, 1982). See also, Haigh, *Bichat*, ch. 2.

22 A-F. Fourcroy, *Rapport et décret de la Convention nationale sur les Ecoles de santé de Paris, Montpellier et Strasbourg* [14 frimaire, an III] (Paris, Imprimerie du comité de salut public, 1794), pp. 17–18.

23 Fourcroy, *Rapport... sur l'établissement d'une Ecole... de Paris* [7 frimaire, an III], pp. 10–11.

24 Brockliss and Jones, *Medical World*, ch. 7, sect. C. Morgagni was the author of *De sedibus et causis morborum per anatomen indagatis* (2 vols.; Venice, ex typographia Remondiniana, 1761).

25 Foucault, *Naissance de la clinique*, esp. ch. 4.

26 *De l'auscultation médiate, ou traité du diagnostic des maladies des poumons et du coeur* (Paris, J.-A. Brosson and J.-S. Chaudé, 1819). The most recent studies of the achievements of the Paris School are Russell Maulitz, *Morbid Appearances: the Anatomy of Pathology in the Early Nineteenth Century* (Cambridge, Cambridge University Press, 1987), and J.E. Lesch, *Science and Medicine in France: the Emergence of Experimental Physiology, 1790–1855* (Cambridge, MA, Harvard University Press, 1984).

27 J.-N. Corvisart-Desmaret, *Essai sur les maladies et lésions du coeur et des gros vaisseaux* (Paris, Migneret, 1806); discussed in Imbault-Huart, *L'Ecole pratique*, pp. 164–9.

28 Ackerknecht, *Paris Hospital*, ch. xi.

29 Medical systematisation was more highly favoured at Montpellier where vitalism remained a strong influence: see Elizabeth Williams, *The Physical and the Moral: Anthropology, Physiology and Philosophical Medicine in France, 1750–1850* (Cambridge, Cambridge University Press, 1994).

30 F.-V. Broussais, *Examen de la doctrine médicale généralement adoptée...* (Paris, Gabon, 1816). On Broussais, see Jean-François Braunstein, *Broussais et le matérialisme: médecine et philosophie au XIXe siècle* (Paris, Meridiens Klincksieck, 1986). Pinel's nosology is discussed in Haigh, *Bichat*, pp. 83–6.

31 Ackerknecht, *Paris Hospital*, p. 62. By 1830 the Paris School had accepted some of Broussais's critique, in particular his rejection of the independent existence of many fever states.

32 Brockliss and Jones, *Medical World*, ch. xi.

33 Dora B. Weiner, *The Citizen Patient in Revolutionary Imperial Paris* (Baltimore, MA, and London, Johns Hopkins Press, 1993). Admittedly, even after the Revolution, medical practitioners did not always get their own way: see Colin Jones, 'Professionalizing Modern Medicine in French Hospitals', *Medical History*, 26 (1982), 348–9.

34 Russell C. Maulitz, 'Channel Crossing: the Lure of French Pathology for English Medical Students', *Bulletin of the History of Medicine*, 55 (1981), 475–96; John Harley Warner, 'The Selective Transport of Medical Knowledge:

Antebellum American Physicians and Parisian Medical Therapeutics', *Bulletin of the History of Medicine*, 59 (1985), 213–31.

35 John Thomson, *Additional Hints respecting the Improvement of the System of Medical Instruction followed in the University of Edinburgh* (Edinburgh, P. Neill, 1826). The most measured and detailed British account of study in Paris is John Green Crosse, *Sketches of the Medical Schools of Paris* (London, J. Callow, 1815), based on letters home to a friend. For a good example of an American's experience, see Russell M. Jones (ed.), *The Parisian Education of an American Surgeon: Letters of Jonathan Mason Warner, 1832–5* (Philadelphia, PA, American Philosophical Society, 1978).

36 Vicq d'Azyr, 'Plan', pp. 68–75. He accepted that pharmacy should remain separate from medicine.

37 Ibid., pp. 56–7, 41–5.

38 Ibid., pp. 45–55. At this date, written examinations were virtually unknown in Europe, though used in the Paris *agrégation* set up in 1766 to provide a pool of competent professors for the city's *collèges de plein exercice* (which taught the Latin and Greek humanities and philosophy). In *ancien-régime* France only the Paris faculty demanded its graduates took a practical surgical exam. See Brockliss, 'Medicine and the Small Universities', pp. 248–56.

39 Loi du 19 ventôse an XI, clauses 6 and 7: *Recueil des loix et règlements*, ii. 335.

40 Roselyne Rey, 'L'Ecole de santé de Paris sous la Révolution : transformation et innovation', *Histoire de l'Education*, 57 (1993), 23–57. Rey's study is based on the pre-1803 theses. No one admittedly has yet done a detailed study after that date. Pre-1789 theses sustained in one faculty were frequently sustained in the same form in another.

41 Benassis is the idealistic hero of *Le Médecin de la campagne*; Rastignac in *Père Goriot* becomes a cynical social climber after witnessing Goriot's humiliation and neglect at the hands of his daughters.

42 J.-B.-F. Léveillé, *Mémoire sur l'état actuel de l'enseignement de la médecine et de la chirurgie en France et sur les modifications dont il est susceptible* (Paris, J.-G. Dentu, 1816), p. 19.

43 Ibid., pp. 13, 20–24.

44 J.-C.-F. Caron, *Démonstration rigoreuse du peu d'utilité de l'Ecole de méde-cine... (du grand avantage que l'on a retiré, et que l'on retirera toujours du réta-blissement du Collège de chirurgie)* (Paris, Pillet aîné, 1818), pp. 23, 25. The intern Caron is probably Jean-Baptiste-François, author of *Nouvelle Doctrine des maladies vénériennes* (Paris, Croullebois, 1811).

45 He was also the author of *Moyens de rendre les hôpitaux plus utiles à la nation* (Paris, Rue et Hôtel de Serpente, 1787); he was Brissot's doctor.

46 Nicolas Chambon de Montaux, 'Projet de réforme dans l'enseignement de la médecine' (March, 1815), fo. 2r, in Bibliothèque de la Faculté de Médecine, MS 5143, collection of separately foliated memos. Chambon de Montaux was also incensed by the moral deficiencies of the professoriate, the laziness and decadence of the student body, and the ease with which degrees were given (fos 6v–11v).

47 Ibid. '*Remarques sur le mode de l'enseignement de la médecine clinique*' (fos 8r–10v). Incorporated in an undated memo, entitled '*Considérations générales sur l'enseignement de la médecine en Espagne*'.

48   L.S. Jacyna, 'Au lit des malades: A. F. Chomel's clinic at the Charité, 1828–9', *Medical History*, 33 (1989), 420–49. Chomel took over Laënnec's clinic in 1827 but had been conducting a private clinic for ten years. Chomel warned his students against discussing the diagnosis or prognosis in the patient's hearing (p. 425). Other Paris professors were less sensitive. Chambon de Montaux thought it did not matter because the patient would not understand the terms ('Remarques', fo. 8r). For a contemporary French account of the state of the Paris clinic in the late 1820s, see F.S. Ratier, 'Coup d'oeil sur les cliniques médicales de la Faculté de médecine et des hôpitaux civils de Paris', *Archives générales de médecine*, 13–14 (1827–28), pp. 321–4, 161–85, 559–86.

49   See above, note 47. The best survey of eighteenth-century clinical medicine is Othmar Keel, 'The Politics of Health and the Institutionalisation of Clinical Practice in Europe in the Second Half of the Eighteenth Century', in W.F. Bynum and Roy Porter (eds), *William Hunter and the Eighteenth-Century Medical World* (Cambridge, Cambridge University Press, 1985), pp. 207–56. A study of the development in one particular faculty is Guenther B. Risse, *Hospital Life in Enlightenment Scotland: Care and Teaching at the Royal Infirmary of Scotland* (Cambridge, Cambridge University Press, 1986). For the short-lived attempt to establish a pathological clinic at Strasbourg in the mid-eighteenth century, see E. Wickersheimer, 'La Clinique de l'hôpital de Strasbourg au XVIIIe siècle' *Archives internationales d'histoire des sciences*, 16 (1963), 253–76.

50   Susan C. Lawrence, *Charitable Knowledge. Hospital Pupils and Practitioners in Eighteenth-Century London* (Cambridge, Cambridge University Press, 1996), esp. ch. 8; Othmar Keel, 'Cabanis et la généalogie épistélologique de la médecine clinique', 2 vols, doctoral diss. McGill Univ., 1977, esp. chs 10–11. Baillie was the author of *Morbid Anatomy of Some of the Most Important Parts of the Human Body* (London, J. Johnson and G. Nicol, 1793).

51   The first important centres of German medical research emerged at the beginning of the nineteenth century: see T.H. Broman, *The Transformation of German Academic Medicine, 1750–1820 Medical Science* (Cambridge, Cambridge University Press, 1996), ch. 6.

52   William Coleman and Frederick L. Holmes (eds), *The Investigative Enterprise: Experimental Physiology in Nineteenth-Century Medicine* (Los Angeles, CA, University of California Press, 1988); E. Ackerknecht, *Rudolf Virchow: Doctor, Statesman, Anthropologist* (Madison, WN, Wisconsin University Press) [on one of the great figures of German experimental pathology]; Ann La Berge, 'Medical Microscopy in Paris, 1830–1855', in Ann La Berge and Mordechai Feingold (eds), *French Medical Culture in the Nineteenth Century* (Amsterdam, Rodopi, 1994), ch. 9.

53   Claire Salomon-Bayet, *Pasteur et la médecine parisienne* (Paris, Payot, 1985); Bruno Latour, *Pasteur. Une science, un style, un siècle* (Paris, Perrin, 1984); Gerald Geison, *The Private Science of Louis Pasteur* (Princeton, NJ, Princeton University Press, 1995); Anne Marie Moulin, 'Bacteriological Research and Medical Practice in and out of the Pastorian School', in La Berge and Feingold (eds), *French Medical Culture*, ch. 10.

54   There is a lengthy literature on the Revolution's love-affair with science: for example, Maurice P. Crosland, *The Society of Arcueil: a View of French Science at the Time of Napoleon 1* (London, Heinemann, 1967); Joseph Ben-David, 'The

Rise and Decline of France as a Scientific Centre', '*Minerva*, 8 (1970), 160–79; Robert Fox, 'The Rise and Decline of Laplacian Physics', *Historical Studies in the Physical Sciences*, 4 (1975), 89–136; Dorinda Outram, 'Politics and Vocation: French Science, 1793–1830', *The British Journal for the History of Science*, 13 (1980), 37–43; Nicole Dhombres, *Naissance d'un pouvoir: science et savants en France, 1793–1824* (Paris, Payot, 1989).

55 On Idéologie and its general influence, see esp. S. Moravia, *Il pensiero degli Idéologues* (Florence, La Nuova Italia, 1974), and François Azouvi, *L'Institution de la raison: la révolution culturelle des Idéologues* (Paris, J. Vrin, 1992).

56 A point made forcibly in John Harley Warner, 'Paradym Lost or Paradise Declining? American Physicians and the "Dead End" of the Paris Clinical School': see Hannaway and La Berge (eds), *Constructing Paris Medicine*, ch. 9.

57 P.-J.-G. Cabanis, 'Du degré de certitude de la médecine' (an VI), in *Oeuvres complètes* (5 vols; Paris, Bossanges frères, 1828), vol. i, pp. 400–531 (esp. pp. 459–74). A good recent study of his life and work is Martin S. Staum, *Cabanis, Enlightenment and Medical Philosophy in the French Revolution* (Princeton, NJ, Princeton University Press, 1980).

58 P.-J.-G. Cabanis, 'Coup d'oeil sur les révolutions et sur la réforme de la médecine', in Claude Lehec and Jean Cazaneuve (eds), *Oeuvres philosophiques* (2 vols, Paris, PUF, 1956), ii. 253–4. The text was written in the winter of Year III (ibid., p. 66, 'avertissement'), but not published until 1804 because Cabanis hoped to append to his history an account of the new medical methodology. For a recent analysis of this work, see Ludmilla Jordanova, 'Reflections on Medical Reform. Cabanis's *Coup d'oeil*', in Porter (ed.), *Medicine in the Enlightenment*, ch. 6. Keel, 'Cabanis', passim, argues that the *Idéologue* played no part in articulating an ideology of the anatomo-clinical method because he placed total emphasis on bedside learning and showed little interest in autoptic investigation: this is true, but Cabanis certainly helped to promote public awareness of the potential benefits of medical research.

10

Lefèvre's *Méthode de Clarinette* (1802): the Paris Conservatoire at Work

Colin Lawson

From Paris the name and fame of a man of real talent resounds throughout the whole world. There the nobility treat men of genius with the greatest deference, esteem and courtesy; there you will see a refined manner of life, which forms an astonishing contrast to the coarseness of our German courtiers and their ladies...[1]

This was the impression of Mozart's father Leopold during their stay in Paris in 1778. Mozart himself found the Parisian public somewhat unpredictable, though his 'Paris Symphony' K297 shows that he was able to respond to their taste in orchestral music. It was premièred at the *Concert spirituel* on 18 June after just one (disastrous) rehearsal. In composing the symphony Mozart was keen to please his audience and, having decided, against his original judgement, to attend the concert after all, he wrote: 'I prayed to God that it might go well... Right in the middle of the first *Allegro* was a passage that I knew they would like; the whole audience was thrilled by it and there was a tremendous burst of applause; but as I knew when I wrote it what kind of effect it would produce, I repeated it again at the end – when there were shouts of 'Da Capo'. The *Andante* also found favour, but particularly the last *Allegro* because, having observed that here [that is, in Paris] all final as well as first allegros begin with all the instruments playing together and generally *unisono*, I began mine with the two violins only, piano for the first eight bars – followed instantly by a *forte*; the audience, as I expected, said 'Shh!' at the soft beginning, and then, as soon as they heard the *forte* that followed, immediately began to clap their hands'.[2] This account offers insights not only into Mozart's creative mind but also indicates the potential impact of new music in a musical climate very different from our own. An interesting postscript to the history of the première of K297 is that although the concert's director Joseph le Gros greatly admired the symphony as a whole, he reckoned that the *Andante* was too long and full of modulations. Mozart did not agree, but nevertheless proceeded to compose an alternative slow movement, which was substituted in a performance of 15 August. In the same year, Mozart declined a permanent position as organist at Versailles, despite the amount of time it would have left him for composition.[3]

Notwithstanding Mozart's reservations, Paris really was at that time the capital of the musical world. Gluck had rejuvenated serious French opera in the 1770s, the *opéra comique* continued to flourish and Italian opera also found a permanent home. To complement all this activity, the *Concert spirituel* gave choral and instrumental concerts on religious holidays, while at the *Concerts de la loge olympique*, founded in 1781, famous guests were invited to appear. For example, Haydn performed his symphonies 82 to 87 there during the season 1785–86. In the last decade before the Revolution, music could be found in the Royal Palace, in the salons of the aristocracy, in the modest homes of the bourgeoisie, in the cafés and public gardens, on the boulevards and on the streets. There was great demand for new music and an enhanced appreciation of the power of instrumental as well as vocal works.[4]

With the Revolution, centuries of musical culture and tradition collapsed, notably with the abolition of the church-sponsored music schools. There had been almost four hundred of these *maîtrises* throughout the country, with a small staff of musicians and from 12 to 20 boy pupils studying plainchant, counterpoint, some composition, a little French, much Latin and some arithmetic. About four thousand pupils per year proceeded to theological seminaries or to lives as singers or organists. But teaching methods were antiquated and instrumental music neglected.

Educational developments in the wake of the Revolution have been well documented. In September 1789, Bernard Sarrette, a 23-year-old captain of the National Guard, assembled a military wind band of 45 musicians, who performed at all civic festivals and demonstrations. Soon the band had a permanent home in Paris, with the celebrated composer Gossec as musical director. In 1792 a school was attached to it, the *Ecole gratuite de musique de la Garde nationale parisienne*. Instruction was free, with only the obligation to buy a uniform, instrument and music paper. This was the principal (but not the sole) forerunner of the *Conservatoire de musique*, founded in 1795 on the new democratic principle of free education for the qualified, irrespective of social status.[5] Its development was the result of careful planning, artistic vision and astute political action. The staff were to serve both as performers and teachers; students of both sexes, admitted between the ages of eight and 13, were to be chosen from each geographical area by means of competitive examination. There would be prizes at the end of each school year. And in this way, many features of institutional musical life today were set in train, with consequences which remain subject to vigorous debate.

The Revolutionary leaders immediately recognised the power of music, which now became a civic act, a moral force in the service of the country as a whole. A composer's task was no longer to express individual emotion, but to speak the collective language of the people. The national festivals, for which the Conservatoire initially provided the music, were mass propaganda on a hitherto unknown scale. Everyone was expected to participate, including artists, writers, poets, painters and musicians. As Boris Schwarz has remarked, '... Torn from the shelter of the court, the chapels and the aristocratic salons, musicians were faced with a mass of impassioned, undisciplined and largely uneducated humanity'.[6] A new accessible musical style was required, with clear lines, strong rhythm, easy melody, simple harmony and brilliant orchestral colour painted with broad brush strokes. This was to be music of action, not reflection. Just after the declaration of war in 1792 was composed the *Marseillaise*, which embodied the prevailing mood of defiance and patriotic fervour. For the national festivals composers prepared special music for the bands, including overtures and marches, as well as vocal hymns, odes and chants. After Napoleon seized power, the festivals were rationalised to celebrate only the anniversaries of the Taking of the Bastille on 14 July and the Proclamation of the Republic on 22 September. The monumental musical events subsequently composed for these occasions were undoubtedly a direct inspiration for the large-scale works of Berlioz a generation or so later.

As opera and concert life became re-established, the Conservatoire students began to set new performing standards in orchestral music. Already in 1800 the critic of the *Décade philosophique* could write; '... A numerous orchestra, consisting entirely of young people, performed with unity, precision and firmness, using intelligence and discretion in the accompaniments, which is even more difficult...'.[7] Later, especially under the direction of the violinist François Habeneck, the unified and disciplined bowing of the string players won particular praise. In 1814 the *Journal de Paris* was captivated by the youthful fervour of the players and their sheer love of the music. Three years previously, an observer in the *Allgemeine musikalische Zeitung* drew some interesting comparisons between France and Germany, noting that the piano was not especially popular and that the French preferred the violin, flute, cello and harp. Significantly, he was surprised at the extent to which educated amateurs in France were happy to invest in the purchase of full scores of their favourite pieces. These included Austro-German composers such as Haydn, and to an increasing degree Mozart, whose posthumous reputation in France took a little more time to gather momentum.

The role of the Conservatoire in performances of Beethoven was a celebrated part of its early history. After the Eroica Symphony was played in 1811, a reviewer in the *Courrier de l'Europe et des spectacles* showed an equal measure of understanding and horror:

> The Symphony in E flat...is the most beautiful [Beethoven] has composed, aside from a few harsh Germanisms which he used by force of habit. All the rest offers a sensible and correct plan, though filled with vehemence; graceful episodes are artfully connected with the principal ideas, and his singing phrases have a freshness of colouring quite their own.[8]

It need hardly be added that Beethoven's talent dwarfed anything that developed in France during the period, however influenced he may have been by the music of native French composers and by political events in France. The influence of Cherubini on Beethoven has been well characterised by Winton Dean:

> It would scarcely be too much to say that Beethoven's entire instrumental style, in the symphonies as well as Fidelio, is a transformation of Cherubini's, with its balance of structural masses, its combination of a rhetorical melodic thrust, with seething orchestral textures, its sharply contrasted dynamics and intense rhythmic energy.[9]

The Conservatoire was the first truly modern institution for music education, organised on a national basis, free from charitable aims and with an entirely secular, indeed anti-clerical background. Because of its initial function of providing ceremonial music, many of its teaching staff specialised in wind instruments, with a particular emphasis on the clarinet and bassoon. But the teaching curriculum catered for all the usual instruments, together with singing and keyboard skills, as well as the theory of music. Examinations were introduced on a regular basis. The staff included many distinguished composers, including Gossec, Méhul, Cherubini and Boieldieu. Importantly, the concept of a state conservatory for music soon spread throughout Europe, to Prague (1811), Graz

(1815) and Vienna (1817), as well as London's Royal Academy of Music (1822). The Regio Conservatorio di Musica at Milan was established in 1824, with a curriculum which modified that of Paris and with students recruited partly on a fee-paying basis and partly by state subvention. Somewhat later, the conservatory at Leipzig proved a huge influence from its inception in 1843, with a staff which included Mendelssohn and Schumann. Other German cities soon followed suit and there were later foundations in Italy, Russia and the USA, as well as further developments in Britain resulting in the Royal College of Music and the Guildhall School. As a footnote we may add that conservatoires by their very nature attracted rebels. In his youth Berlioz encountered a conservatism which has always been a characteristic of institutional life and his early career was blighted by Cherubini, the Paris Conservatoire's director.[10]

From the outset, teaching was taken very seriously at the Conservatoire. In the words of the composer Méhul, France's leading operatic composer in the 1790s: 'To perpetuate oneself through numerous students of distinguished merit means to crown with dignity a long and honourable career; it means to discharge the indebtedness of one's talent toward his country.'[11] And as Schwarz has observed, the Conservatoire elevated the teaching profession to a position of unprecedented dignity and importance; the *professeur de musique*, formerly a call boy for the nobleman, became a pillar of musical culture and tradition.[12] But, as with many such situations, not everything was as rigorous as the syllabus might imply. In 1798 the 23-year-old François-Adrien Boieldieu from Rouen was appointed to the piano faculty and was described in the following way by one of his pupils, François-Joseph Fétis:

> Too occupied with his career as a dramatic composer to take interest in lessons of instrumental technique, Boieldieu was a rather bad piano teacher; but his conversation was studded with very fine remarks on his art, full of interest for his students and not without profit for their studies.[13]

During the time Fétis studied with Boieldieu around 1800 the master was occupied with the composition of his opera *Le Caliphe de Bagdad* and Fétis noted that: 'he often consulted us with charming modesty, and the piano lesson was spent while we grouped around him to sing the ensemble numbers of his latest opera'.[14]

Was there a price to be paid for this new musical accessibility? The Revolution brought in its wake the most far-reaching attempt to make music intelligible to all, by means of a fundamental simplification of musical means and expression. In the eighteenth century an understanding of musical language had been an integral part of learning an instrument, but the Conservatoire published tutors which replaced verbal description with pictorial elements. This production of faculty-based treatises, offering systematic courses of technical and interpretative instruction for aspiring professionals, incorporated exercises and studies for advanced players. But this was at the expense of philosophy about musical rhetoric and the communication of emotion. Institutions were bound to encourage competition, and virtuosity was an element that could easily be measured and encouraged. The German violinist-composer Louis Spohr arrived in Paris at the end of 1820 and was received with great kindness by his French colleagues, whose music he knew well. Yet in his autobiography he wrote:

> It is very singular how all here, young and old, strive only to shine by mechanical execution ... Everyone produces his own showpiece: you hear nothing but *airs variés, rondos favoris, nocturnes* ... and from the singers romances and little duets ... Poor in such pretty trifles, with my earnest German music I am ill at ease in such musical parties.[15]

After one of Spohr's first concerts in Paris the *Courrier des spectacles* ventured to suggest that if he would remain in Paris for some time he could perfect his taste and then return to mould that of the good Germans. Spohr commented: 'if only the good man knew what the "good Germans" think of the musical taste of the French!'[16] Mendelssohn too was appalled by the superficiality of taste he encountered, noting in 1825 that no-one knew a note of Beethoven's *Fidelio* and believed Bach to be: 'nothing but an old-fashioned wig stuffed with learning'.[17] By the time Chopin arrived in 1831, he was appalled by the sheer numbers of empty virtuosi, the very type of executant that eighteenth-century writers had repeatedly warned against. French training cannot take sole responsibility for this empty virtuosity, which extended to other cities in Europe, notably London and Vienna. Yet Paris was the centre of technical schooling, if not its utilisation for musical ends.

It is a salutary exercise to compare the syllabus of the newly founded Conservatoire with what was regarded as an appropriate education by one of Mozart's closest associates in Vienna. It so happens that in the autumn of 1799 the clarinettist Anton Stadler was invited by Count Georg Festetics to draw up a plan for the foundation of a music school in Hungary on what is now Lake Balaton. In addition to theory, performance and composition, every student would be required to sing, whatever the quality of the individual voice. Stadler continues:

> Education, therefore, and literature are necessary for the true musician, if he wants to become great, because if he is entirely without all other knowledge he becomes a half-thing...Whoever wants to understand music must know the whole of worldly wisdom and mathematics, poetry, elocution, art, and many languages.[18]

On the Conservatoire syllabus there was of course no opportunity to study 'the whole of worldly wisdom'.

Indeed, Nikolaus Harnoncourt has recently argued that developments in France after the Revolution marked the beginning of a shift from music's position as one of life's moving forces to a mere adornment.[19] From the Middle Ages music had been one of the foundations of cultural life and the understanding of music formed part of a general education. Harnoncourt remarks that people nowadays find a car or aeroplane more valuable than a violin, the circuitry of a computer more important than a symphony. When music was actually a living language and continually re-created, there was a belief that one's very being could actually be changed by it. He deduces that at the end of the twentieth century a reduction to what is merely beautiful and universally appreciated affects not just listeners but performers themselves. Our own current debate about the role and value of commercial classical radio stations revolves around this very question of whether music needs to be understood or merely absorbed by the listener. It is undoubtedly true that music used to have its own vocabulary and syntax which gave it an incredible power over the body and soul of man, whereas now only the aesthetic and emotional aspects are portrayed. It can indeed be argued that we are completely unaware of what has been lost, because the dramatic elements in music have been forgotten and rhetorical links buried under long sweeping melodic lines, which mask the small-scale phrasing of classical composers. Our listening exhausts itself by comparisons of minor differences in interpretation and thus our sense of music has been reduced to a ridiculously primitive stage. One sympathises with Harnoncourt's regret at the passing of a more élitist age, though the Paris Conservatoire simply cannot be identified as the sole villain of the piece. Musical styles would certainly have been subject to change without its influence, and Wagner's scene-painting and conducting of Beethoven in his own image were other contributory factors later in the nineteenth century.

What of the Conservatoire's musical legacy? It must be admitted that the organisation of professional study coincided with a relatively undistinguished period of French composition. Throughout the nineteenth century there developed a dry academicism about much French music, above which only an isolated genius such as Berlioz could rise. In 1796 Jean-Baptiste Leclerc, a member of the Council of Five Hundred, published an ideological plan for a national musical education, in which the so-called *genre hymnique* would engage the citizenry. It would replace the old devotion to opera and would substitute for religious ceremony. Music would be composed in simple forms with simple harmonisations, promoting the unification of the limited performance abilities and understanding of the people in small villages with the more grandiose displays of civic sentiment in larger cities. Leclerc wrote:

> As for harmony, we think it will be necessary to turn the clock back a few years. As it is important to keep it within limits that it should never exceed, we must look for the epoch when its practice best agreed with a simple and somewhat legislative theory. The system of basso continuo, despite its imperfections, is the one that best meets this objective, and we adopt it the more willingly because it unites fecundity with wisdom, and because it offers the man of genius sufficient resources to produce all the effects that can reasonably be expected from music.[20]

With the falling off of the Festivals, musical style could only be enforced through theory and in 1801 the Conservatoire adopted Charles-Simon Catel's *Traité d'harmonie* as its didactic method, thus hoping to remain in control through its pedagogical programme. Catel had composed at least 25 Revolutionary hymns, marches and military symphonies during the period 1792 to 1797. His treatise was a manual of the basic principles and rules of harmonic practice, rather than a theoretical tract in the tradition of Rameau. His purpose was to simplify and codify the elements of good harmonic writing and his approach was logical, precise and systematic, essentially describing eight chords from which all others could be said to arise. The book remained a standard text for many years and became popular in translation in Germany, Italy and England. Catel provided a way of understanding existing compositions through an analytical method which is not limiting, allowing for a flexible interpretation of linear and vertical elements. Thus the works of contemporary French composers such as Gossec, Le Sueur, Méhul and Cherubini could be analysed within a consistent framework of harmonic terminology and national compositional techniques communicated to aspiring student composers. But the maintenance of a distinct musical style through the association of theory and education was perhaps an unattainable goal. This was already recognised in 1810, when Choron and Fayolle's *Dictionaire historique des musiciens* remarked:

> If the Italians were the innovators in all areas of musical art and perfected almost everything, and if the Germans brought to perfection what the Italians had left imperfect, one wonders what the French have done, and what right they have to be represented as a school after these people who seem to have accomplished everything?[21]

Yet in French opera of the 1790s, theatre, its Revolutionary rhetoric, and the communal will bonded together with fruitful results. Operas could be quickly written and revised, reflecting actual events and containing forward-looking compositional features such as substantial choruses, advanced use of harmonic dissonance and use of novel techniques of orchestration. The traditional French love of spectacle was allied to hymns and marches, reflecting contemporary themes in the new libretti. This is an area where Beethoven's debt to the French is palpable. But even in the sphere of instrumental music, much of it as yet unperformed in modern times, it is difficult to agree wholeheartedly with Anthony Lewis that: 'The importance of this music of the French Revolution lies not so much in its intrinsic value, as in the role it plays in a great social movement.'[22] The danger here is that this repertory be judged solely in terms of Austro-German principles and that its lack of emphasis on counterpoint and the development of material be regarded as such negative features as to blight perceptions of the whole. It is inevitable, perhaps, that the towering figures of Haydn, Mozart, Beethoven and Schubert should encourage the proposition that the entire Classical style is totally encompassed within their music.

The instrumental tutors published by the Conservatoire offer considerable insight into technical practices of the period, many of which soon spread throughout Europe. By 1805 the bassoon, cello, clarinet, flute, piano and violin had newly written manuals for them. Jean-Louis Adam's *Méthode de piano* remained in use for many years. Significantly, in 1826 it was translated into German by Beethoven's pupil Carl Czerny. Adam's advice on pedalling is important; he advises that: 'the large [damper] pedal is to be employed only during consonant harmonies, when the music is very slow, and where the harmonies do not change'.[23]

He recommends it only for pure, harmonious pieces, as for example, in pastorales and musettes, in tender and melancholy airs, romances, religious pieces, and so forth. Adam's comments indeed reflect Beethoven's notation in his piano sonatas and were reiterated by German theorists in the 1820s. Czerny's later recollection that Beethoven pedalled much more frequently than indicated in his music may well reflect practice as it had developed by the 1840s. Adam's piano method has further significance in its redefining of the trill as a structural rather than ornamental device; he is among the first writers to indicate that there are numerous contexts in which the trill should start on its principal, rather than the upper note.

For the violin the Conservatoire published a multi-authored work by Baillot, Rode and Kreutzer, which set out the performer's chief expressive means as sound quality, movement, style, taste, genius of execution and precision. It is highly significant that flexibility of tempo was regarded as an essential musical effect, especially as this remains one of the most difficult aspects of performance to describe in words. The tutor as a whole emphasises musical taste at least as much as technique, and certainly cannot be accused of advocating mere virtuosity. It advises:

> In order to succeed, the head must be accustomed early to moderate the liveliness of the senses and to regulate those passions which must move the performer; if he allows himself to be carried away by them, there will no longer be any sense of the beat, nuances, nor pleasing effects; if he is too reserved, his performance will be cold; art consists in maintaining a balance between the feelings that carry you away and those which hold you back; as one can see, this is a different kind of precision from that which aims solely at the exact division of the beat and the bar; it is the result as much of good practice as of maturity and talent.[24]

Characteristically, wind tutors offered fewer hints as to musical taste, though Etienne Ozi's bassoon method has some useful practical advice about the articulation of staccato notes and also about extempore ornamentation, which was still widely practised. Ozi states specifically that bassoonists (like other woodwind players) were expected to add phrasing to unmarked sequences of notes. This remark was soon translated in German tutors and has important resonances for the wind music of both Mozart and Beethoven.

The author of the *Méthode de clarinette*, Jean Xavier Lefèvre, was born in Lausanne in 1763, but moved to Paris in his youth. He made his first concert appearance there just before the Revolution and afterwards joined the orchestra of the Opéra, eventually being promoted to a select group of players which was required only on special occasions. At a meeting at the Conservatoire on 12 June 1801 the format of the clarinet method was discussed and Lefèvre was charged with its implementation. The ensuing work was hugely influential and translated into other European languages, with reprints as recently as the 1930s. Lefèvre discusses various different aspects of the clarinet and clarinet playing in a total of 14 articles, together with studies, exercises and sonatas.

The clarinet had been developed in Germany around 1700, its tone-quality reflected in its name, which denotes a small clarino or trumpet. It was furnished with a single reed and mouthpiece, its bore was cylindrical and its mechanism restricted to two keys at the top of the instrument. Initially the clarinet was played by oboists and this is reflected in 1753 in what must be one of the shortest (and most inaccurate) articles in the *Encyclopédie* of Diderot and d'Alembert. The entry simply reads 'sorte de hautbois'.[25] The illustration associated with the article indeed showed a conical shape more characteristic of an oboe than a truly cylindrical clarinet. Around the same time, in 1751, Rameau made some important use of the clarinet in his opera *Acante et Céphise*. By now, it was acquiring a more vocal character and becoming more technically versatile. In 1764 the German clarinettist Valentin Roeser published in Paris an essay for the use of composers writing for the clarinet and the horn. Roeser emphasises in particular his relationship with the Mannheim composer Johann Stamitz, who visited Paris and included the clarinet in his symphonies in the 1750s, besides writing a Concerto for the instrument. In 1776 the writer of a now much-expanded article in the *Encyclopédie supplément* described a clarinet with four keys, but added that a player had just passed through Berlin with a six-keyed clarinet and what a difficult instrument this must be to play. Additional mechanism was at that time still regarded with great suspicion. There were one or two other French tutors before Lefèvre, notably that by Amand Vanderhagen, circa 1785. By now, five keys were the clarinet's normal configuration, and it was beginning to assume a prominent place in ensemble music. In Vienna, Mozart was drawn to it in the 1780s and it began to exert a supremacy over the oboe in various contexts. For the new Revolutionary bands in France, its expressive power would prove ideal; indeed, Lefèvre describes it as equally suitable for battle hymns and shepherds' songs, capable of encompassing a vast range of musical genres.

Notwithstanding the overall importance of eighteenth-century Austro-German clarinet repertory, didactic sources from those countries barely exist during the period between the 1730s and the tutor written by the Nuremberg clarinettist Heinrich Backofen circa 1803. Meanwhile, the eighteenth-century dominance of the flute is illustrated by important philosophical tracts by Quantz (1752) and Tromlitz (1791), both significant sources not just for an understanding of style but also for information on what it actually meant to be a working musician in their respective lifetimes.[26] We may add by way of a footnote that English sources, though plentiful, address a primarily amateur market in a somewhat naïve manner.

The commission which received Lefèvre's work drew attention to the clarinet's ability to sing, reminding students that they should aim to move the listener, rather than merely surprise him. This declared aim of a performer to move an audience had been a recurrent theme in eighteenth-century German sources, notably Quantz and C.P.E. Bach. In general, Lefèvre's text dilutes an old-style philosophical approach with sound practical advice. His illustrations and fingering charts show that the clarinet was still played in France with the reed against the top lip, a technique officially abandoned at the Conservatoire only in 1831, but probably already used in Vienna during Mozart's lifetime. Lefèvre's practical applications include instruction on posture, holding the clarinet and finger placement. To modern readers the correct positioning of fingers upon the instrument appears to be dealt with in painstaking if not laborious fashion; fingers were to be bent and their phalanges allowed to fall horizontally on to the holes, like hammers. Reassuringly, Lefèvre found good cane for clarinet reeds difficult to acquire; he reckoned that cane tended to be cut too green or too dry. Green cane is spongy and muffles the sound, he says, whereas dry cane is too hard to produce the necessary resonance. We may nowadays be surprised that Lefèvre discusses the clarinet mechanism at great length, with a detailed description of each key. But as we have noted, at that time each extra key brought with it a real risk of malfunction, which needed to be weighed against any potential artistic benefit.

Lefèvre's detailed list of the clarinet's out-of-tune notes, which needed correcting by means of the embouchure, is important evidence in today's ongoing debate about the intonation of classical wind players. He seems all too realistic about the clarinet's shortcomings and perhaps over-optimistic about the manner in which they might be overcome. His comments contrast radically with those of the Leipzig flautist Tromlitz, who as late as 1791 was discussing different sizes of semitone within the scale and the use of unequal temperaments in flute repertory. This radically different approach can only be in part a reflection of the flute's superiority in terms of tonal flexibility. In relation to articulation, Lefèvre describes a much smaller range of options than Tromlitz, whilst advising use of the tongue rather than the throat or chest, techniques which had previously also been in vogue. Melodic ornaments too were reduced to a relatively small group of grace-note, trill and turn.

Artistic aspects of clarinet playing attracted special attention in the tutor and are still highly relevant to modern players. Reflecting eighteenth-century principles, Lefèvre states that performance becomes monotonous without attention to nuance of sound and articulation. He warns that it is not sufficient merely to read the music and play the notes, but that its character must be truly assimilated. A coldness and monotony often ascribed to the clarinet is in fact the responsibility of the performer, whose armoury must include a good knowledge of harmony and sound musical taste. His advice on the correct manner of playing an *Allegro* and an *Adagio* also recalls eighteenth-century sources in referring players to listen to the finest singers. Characterisation of the music is paramount, with slow pieces a particular challenge. An *Adagio* is always noble and expressive and the player must enter into the spirit of the music. Lefèvre comes close to echoing C.P.E. Bach's advice that a player must be moved himself in order to affect an audience, and on this evidence he too cannot be charged with unduly advancing the cause of virtuosity at the expense of artistry. Indeed his studies for the beginner are based on the practice of long notes and control of clarinet sound. The exercises in the latter stages of his book include scales and arpeggios but also simple cantabile melodies accompanied by a straightforward bass line.

Aspects of the clarinet which we now take for granted, such as its status as a transposing instrument, are discussed in very considerable detail. In particular, the handling of the clarinet's five-keyed mechanism is analysed to a generous degree and there is information for composers on what is idiomatic for the instrument and what is best avoided. In addition, Lefèvre recommends the addition of a sixth key to make available an otherwise non-existent semitone. His 12 progressive sonatas are well suited to his instrument, contrasted in mood yet direct in utterance. Originally accompanied only by a bass line (probably for the cello), they reflect the stylistic outlook of their time, attractive melodically yet developing the musical material to only a limited degree. Lefèvre's tutor provides sufficient technical groundwork for the performance of most Austro-German music written by the generation of Mozart, although Beethoven was soon radically to expand the horizons of what was demanded of all his principal wind players in the orchestra; a knowledge of Lefèvre would not, for example, be quite sufficient to equip a principal clarinet for the extreme demands of Beethoven's Eighth Symphony. Furthermore, as Beethoven expanded the range of tonality in his music, Lefèvre's technical boundaries would be soon breached and the range of tonalities pushed way beyond what he regarded as idiomatic for the clarinet.

Beethoven's progressive approach to composition was soon to be matched by instrument manufacturers throughout Europe. In 1812, a new 13-keyed clarinet was submitted to the Conservatoire by Iwan Müller, an Estonian clarinettist of German parentage. Müller rather rashly claimed that his instrument had no restrictions and could play in any tonality. Together with the composers Cherubini and Méhul, Lefèvre was on the panel which rejected it on behalf of the Conservatoire, not wishing to jettison the different tone-qualities of the various sizes of clarinet then in use.[27] Perhaps Lefèvre had some vested interest in preserving the six-keyed clarinet for which his tutor had been written. But in fact, Müller's clarinet made considerable headway outside the Conservatoire and proved highly influential throughout the nineteenth century. The scene was now set for Berlioz's love affair with the clarinet. In his celebrated orchestration treatise of 1843 he describes it as: 'an epic instrument... the voice of heroic love'.[28]

Notes

1   *The Letters of Mozart and his Family*, trans. Emily Anderson (2nd edn, London and New York, Macmillan, 1966), vol. 1, p. 478.
2   Ibid., vol. II, p. 539.
3   Ibid., vol. II, p. 558.
4   See Boris Schwarz, *French Instrumental Music between the Revolutions* (New York, Da Capo, 1987), pp. 3–9.
5   During the late sixteenth century music had become the principal activity in certain charitable organisations in Venice and Naples. Fees were paid by some pupils and specialist teachers began to be employed, notably Antonio Vivaldi from 1704 at the Ospedale della Pietà in Venice. The subsequent influence of these conservatories was responsible for the domination of Italian musicians throughout Europe, though during the second half of the eighteenth century they were already in decline.
6   Schwarz, *French Instrumental Music*, p. 13.
7   Cited in C. Pierre, *Le Conservatoire nationale de musique et de déclamation* (Paris, Imprimerie nationale, 1900), p. 461.

8   Cited in J.-G. Prod'homme, *Les symphonies de Beethoven* (Paris, Libraire Dela-grave, 1906/*R*1977), p. 121.

9   W. Dean, 'German Opera', in G. Abraham (ed.), *The Age of Beethoven, 1790–1830 (The New Oxford History of Music, viii)* (Oxford, OUP, 1982), p. 472.

10 We may note in passing that some half a century later, Debussy's composition report for 1879 would describe him as 'a pupil with a considerable gift for harmony, but desperately careless'. See S. Sadie (ed.), *The New Grove Dictionary of Music and Musicians*, London, Macmillan, 1980, vol. 5, p. 307.

11 E. Méhul, *Eloge* on Gossec (1808), quoted in A. Lavignac and L. de la Laurencie (eds), *Encyclopédie de la musique et dictionnaire du Conservatoire* (Paris, C. Dela-grave, 1931), Part I, vol. III, p. 1639.

12 Schwarz, *French Instrumental Music*, p. 44.

13 F.J. Fétis, *Biographie universelle des musiciens* (2nd edn, Paris, Didot Frères, 1860–65), vol. II, p. 3.

14 Ibid.

15 L. Spohr, *Autobiography* (Eng. transl., London, Reeves and Turner, 1878/*R*1969), vol. II, p. 114.

16 Ibid., p. 123.

17 S. Hensel, *Die Familie Mendelssohn* (Berlin, B. Behr, 1879), vol. I, p. 174.

18 See P.L. Poulin, 'A View of Eighteenth-Century Musical Life and Training: Anton Stadler's "Musick Plan"', *Music and Letters*, 71, (1990), p. 219.

19 N. Harnoncourt, *Musik als Klangrede* (Residenz Verlag, Salzburg and Vienna), Eng. transl. as *Baroque Music Today: Music as Speech* (Portland, Amadeus Press, 1982), pp. 22–7.

20 J.-B. Leclerc, *Essai sur la propagation de la musique en France, sa consomption, et ses rapports avec le gouvernement* (Paris, prairial an IV/May-June 1796), pp. 35–6.

21 A.-E. Choron and J. Fayolle (eds), *Dictionnaire historique des musiciens, artistes et amateurs, morts ou vivants* (Paris, Valade, 1810/*R*1971), p. lxxvii.

22 A. Lewis, 'Choral Music' in *The Age of Beethoven*, p. 657.

23 J.-L. Adam, *Méthode de piano du Conservatoire* (Paris, Magasin de Musique de Conservatoire Royal, 1804), p. 219.

24 Cited from R. Stowell, *Violin Technique and Performance Practice in the Late Eighteenth and Early Nineteenth Centuries* (Cambridge, CUP, 1985), p. 273.

25 D. Diderot and J. Le R. D'Alembert (eds), *Encyclopédie, ou Dictionnaire Raisonné des Sciences, des Arts et des Métiers par une Société de Gens de Lettres* (17 vols Paris, Briasson, David, Le Breton, 1751–65), vol. III, p. 505.

26 J.J. Quantz, *Versuch einer Anweisung die Flöte traversiere zu spielen* (Berlin, J.F. Voss, 1752); J.G. Tromlitz, *Ausführlicher und gründlicher Unterricht die Flöte zu spielen* (Leipzig, A.F. Böhme, 1791)

27 See Lawson (ed.), *The Cambridge Companion to the Clarinet* (Cambridge, CUP, 1995), p. 34; see also p. 40 for a facsimile of the opening movement of Lefèvre's first sonata; pp. 134–49 for illustrations and discussion of the tutor as a whole.

28 H. Berlioz, *Grand traité de l'instrumentation et d'orchestration modernes Op. 10* (Paris, 1843), Eng. trans. (2nd edn, rev. J. Bennett, London, Novello, Ewer & Co., 1904), p. 108.

11

Bonnes lectures: Improving Women and Society through Literature in Post-Revolutionary France

Denise Z. Davidson

In an essay first published in 1819, *De la Politesse, ouvrage critique, moral et philosophique*, Louis-Damien Emeric made the following generalisation: 'Social bonds, order, and general prosperity depend on the behaviour of women.'[1] Many members of the French intellectual community, and no doubt others who left fewer traces, agreed with Emeric. Literally hundreds of books by and about women appeared in the first decades of the nineteenth century because of such assumptions. In the context of post-Revolutionary uncertainties about the future of French society, women's behaviour emerged as a matter of extreme urgency, one with potentially dire consequences if not addressed promptly.

Much of this work represented a continuation of pre-Revolutionary and Revolutionary interests in delineating and circumscribing women's place in society. Building on Rousseau's influential writings on education and family life, *Emile* and *Julie, ou la nouvelle Héloïse*, many early nineteenth-century writers devoted themselves to depicting the benefits of leading an honest, simple lifestyle. Telling women to avoid *le monde* and its frivolous pleasures, they instructed them in domestic pursuits and child-rearing, and tried to convince them of the benefits they would reap from opting for this quieter existence.[2] French writers consistently assumed that while English women led domestic lives, French women did not. Demonstrating her familiarity with these ideas, Germaine de Staël argued against the view that French women needed to emulate British ones. If French women became more like English women, she explained, French men would lose the intellectual companionship they had grown accustomed to in their wives and the other women in their families.[3] Although the Revolution may appear to have made certain women lose their 'public' roles, it did not relegate them into a purely 'private' existence either. Post-Revolutionary prescriptions that women should focus on the home emerged precisely because so many women were *not* leading domestic lifestyles.[4] Social theorists and other writers debated with great intensity the issue of women's proper roles in part because of the strong female presence in countless aspects of life and society.

This chapter focuses on widely read works by and for women, as well as on reading practices themselves. Most of the sources were cheaply produced volumes written to instruct and entertain women and children. Children are included because so much prescriptive literature was created to help mothers in the upbringing of their daughters, and occasionally their sons. Reading, particularly novel-reading, had long been viewed as dangerous for women. In the post-Revolutionary period, many authors, especially female ones, attempted to address this problem by creating literature that they believed would be beneficial rather than detrimental to women, and thus to society at large.[5]

The size, shape and format of the sources used can be as informative as their contents. Most are multi-volume works. Ostensibly written to instruct while entertaining their readers, children's books and lowbrow fiction gained their worth in part by sheer number of pages. In these cases, quantity often seemed to matter more than quality.[6] To make them appear longer, the books were small in size (*duodecimo* [in-12°], *sextodecimo* [in-16°], and even *vicesimo-quarto* [in-24°]); their pages had wide margins and large print. Most books published for women tended to be small-format, as though they were made to fit better into delicate, feminine hands. These small, multi-volume works were easily portable and affordable. The books thus suited female forms of sociability as women gathered in one another's homes to read the latest publications. Literate women of all classes had a variety of reading material available to them. While few specific data on women's literacy exist, urban male literacy rates at the end of the eighteenth century were as high as 80 per cent. As women's literacy rates tended to be significantly lower than men's, a conservative estimate suggests that well over half of women in large cities were literate in 1800.[7] Those numbers increased steadily over the course of the nineteenth century. Publishers and writers in turn worked to satisfy the demand for books. Popular fiction circulated widely thanks to travelling book peddlers, *cabinets littéraires* that lent books to subscribers for a small fee, and the new practice of publishing novels serially in newspapers.[8]

As this chapter is particularly concerned with readers, great use has been made of forewords and other places where authors addressed their audience. In fact, as is the case for the theatre,[9] prefaces often proved as informative as the works they were introducing, if not more so, because they give an indication of how the books were meant to be utilised. Of course, this information is not problem-free; authors and editors cannot always predict how a book will be received, and to whom it will most appeal. Lacking readers' direct testimony, however, extensive use has been made of these introductory remarks as the only available source of information on readers. Occasional references to readers and reading that appear in the midst of plot and character development in novels themselves provide further insight. Women read for a variety of reasons including instruction, piety, and entertainment. While 'good' literature was always available, much of the material produced at the time, that particular to the period, would not have been characterised as such. Novels and prescriptive literature tended to be extremely formulaic: even the titles could be redundant. Among novels, dozens followed the model set by Jacques-Henri Bernardin de Saint-Pierre in *Paul et Virginie*. Throughout the first few decades of the nineteenth century, countless works appeared under titles with two first names. Like Bernardin de Saint-Pierre's work, these novels told moralistic tales about young love, fidelity, and the rewards of virtue. Guides to child-rearing and running a household resemble novels, though they took a more concrete approach as they extolled the values of a well-run household and economical lifestyles. Much of the source material belongs in a category somewhere between these two main classifications. These are stories and anecdotes meant for girls and young women in which virtuous behaviour leads to happiness while misbehaviour leads to ruin.

Neither historians nor critics of literature have paid much attention to the texts analysed in this chapter. Historians have increasingly recognised the value of popular literature as a source of information about tastes and behaviour, especially for the early modern period.[10] In literary studies as well, non-canonical texts are only just receiving their rightful due as critics begin to analyse genres previously deemed unworthy.[11] Two general studies of reading in modern France provide important background for a more narrow focus: James Smith Allen's *In the Public Eye* and Martyn Lyons's *Le Triomphe du Livre*.[12] As both trace the explosion of reading over the course of the nineteenth century, their focus is on change over time looking ahead to ever-expanding literacy rates and enlarged circulation rates. Similarly, the long time-span covered by Mona Ozouf in *Les Mots des Femmes* helps to position the literature of the post-Revolutionary period in a larger context.[13] Unlike those of Allen and Lyons, however, Ozouf's analysis places more emphasis on continuity rather than change over time as she examines the place of writing in women's lives.

In her intellectual history of post-Revolutionary discourse pertaining to women, the philosopher Geneviève Fraisse analyses many works from the same period discussed here. She argues in part that the obsession with defining women's roles resulted from fears of confusion between the two sexes in the post-Revolutionary period.[14] Like other forms of social distinction, gender differences justifying men's dominant place in the hierarchy of the sexes had been destabilised by the Revolution. According to Fraisse, two perspectives emerged in the debate about women's roles: one argued for women's exclusion from the world of politics and intellectual endeavours; the other hoped to enlarge their influence in those spheres. Though far less intellectual than the works cited by Fraisse, the literature examined takes on many of the same issues Fraisse found in more sophisticated texts. They differ more in form than in content.

The authors of women's literature wrote with what they saw as particularly female concerns in mind. In the preface to the novel *Emile et Rosalie*, Mme C ***[15] explained her motivation for writing:

> Women are subjected to great constraints; so little that interests them is permitted to them ... the more their interest is stimulated, the more they must repress it so that, living entire years in society, they really have less than an hour there.

The boring, inauthentic language of high society replaced: 'the touching expressions of nature's sweet sentiments', she continued. 'To compensate for these oppressive conventions, and the boredom of living with these *personnages circulaires*, most [women] create imaginary beings; that is my succour; like the sensitive and unfortunate J.-J. [Jean-Jacques (Rousseau)], I like to populate my solitude with these beings formed according to my heart; I like to give them the activity, the force of thought that we call exaltation.'[16] Writing a novel, like reading one, allowed women to create fulfilling lives for themselves within the constraints that society placed upon them.[17] In the preface to her 1811 publication, *De l'Influence des femmes sur la littérature française*, Madame de Genlis wrote:

> It is not sedentary tastes that can distract women from their duties; let them write, if they sacrifice for this amusement the theatre, games of chance, balls, and unnecessary visits. Now these are the dangerous

distractions that impede them from raising their children and that ruin families.[18]

De Genlis saw many of women's activities as far more threatening than literary pursuits would be. While reading had often been portrayed as inherently dangerous for women, an effort to produce reading material that could counteract those dangerous effects emerged in the post-Revolutionary period.[19] Much of what was published for women readers in the early nineteenth century under the guise of fiction was inherently prescriptive. Novels and short stories broadcast explicitly moralistic messages, while manuals and guidebooks resembled fiction because they presented their prescriptions through characters invented by the authors. Women wrote much of this literature.[20]

Madame Cottin, Madame Dufrénoy, the Comtesse d'Hautpoul, Madame de Chastenay, Madame Babois, and Fanny de Beauharnais were the writers that an early twentieth-century historian, Alfred Marquiset, chose to describe as '*les bas-bleus du Premier Empire*'.[21] Forgotten already in his day, many of these women are no longer familiar even to those who specialise in nineteenth-century French literature. Yet their novels and other writings represented the best-sellers of their day. Prolific, influential, and successful, these women wrote primarily for other women. The simple act of writing, and more specifically publishing, which necessarily brought the author to public attention, qualified these women to be labelled 'bluestockings' from the perspective of a man writing a century later. From our own perspective, however, these works seem anything but progressive as regards women. By recounting tales that, on the surface at least, reinforced prevailing notions that women should focus on 'domestic' pursuits, the books written by these women seem reactionary by current standards. Who is right? Were these female authors radical 'proto-feminists' deserving of the appellation of 'bluestockings'? Or, were they conservative women who had accepted the argument that women's mingling in the 'public' world had caused the downfall of French society before and during the Revolution? In fact, both these seemingly contradictory conclusions have validity. The messages presented by these works were conservative with regard to women's roles: most argued that women should limit their participation in the 'public' world. Nonetheless, the fact that women were writing these books was in itself fairly radical; it represented an immediate and visible contradiction to their explicit messages. In addition, reading itself, particularly novel-reading, was an activity that contradicted the prescriptions in these books. Thus both the creation and the consumption of the novels and other types of literature discussed here represented a rejection of the prescriptions articulated by the works themselves.

The works of the best-known women writers of the period are not discussed because that has been done elsewhere. Madame de Staël and Madame Campan, for example, have received significant amounts of attention from literary scholars and historians, as has Madame de Duras more recently.[22] In addition, these authors wrote what can be termed 'good literature', literature that has withstood the test of time, something which was more or less understood when they were alive. Unlike those sophisticated texts, the literature discussed here filled a niche particular to this period, and it was quickly left aside as worthless. These books appealed to readers only quite briefly, and it is precisely this historical specificity that makes them valuable indicators of early nine-teenth-century mentalities. Most of the 'bluestockings' discussed by Marquiset were aristocrats who wrote out of financial necessity. Madame Dufrénoy was in that situation. Her husband had gone blind, and she was the breadwinner for her entire family. Many were also *salonnières* who loved *la vie mondaine*. Madame d'Hautpoul, one of the founders of the short-lived periodical *L'Athenée des dames*, was friends with Madame de Genlis and Madame Récamier.[23] She held *salons* throughout the Empire and the Restoration. Madame de Chastenay, whom one historian described as an ingenious yet sincere moralist, was a liberal aristocrat who welcomed the Revolution, played an active role in the Napoleonic court, and then celebrated the returned Bourbons. She published several philosophical works and attended Parisian salons, including Talleyrand's.[24]

One of the most popular novelists of the period was not an aristocrat, though her novels arguably continued aristocratic traditions. Sophie Cottin wrote five novels: *Claire D'Albe* appeared in 1799; *Malvina, Amélie Mansfield, Mathilde*, and *Elisabeth* then followed in quick succession. She published anonymously at first, but eventually signed her name to her work.[25] All followed similar models; plot development generally took place through letters written by the characters. Like much popular lit-erature, most of these novels received a cold reception from critics and those who believed that they knew good literature. De Genlis believed that Cottin was altogether without talent, for example. Cottin's books nonetheless sold quite well. Within a year after the appearance of *Malvina*, her next novel was ready and her publisher offered her 4000 francs for the manuscript.[26] Her works were even translated into five languages. These quickly written love stories made little effort at intellectual sophistication, but their straightforward tales suited many readers' tastes. Among the most successful of her novels, *Claire d'Albe* was reprinted seven times between 1816 and 1831.[27] The novel presents the dangers of adultery: its main character dies as a direct result of her love for her elderly husband's adoptive son.[28] The formulaic nature of their plots as well as their widely varied settings give these works certain similarities to modern-day popular literature, especially romance novels.[29] Innocent young women were seduced, taken advantage of, and could be quickly turned on to the wrong path by choosing to mingle with the wrong people. Highly prone to outside influences, young women's characters were shaped by those who surrounded them, the education they received, and the atmospheres of the places they frequented. Many of the novels recount the tale of a woman's entire life to make this point. Otherwise 'pure' women fall victim to circumstances beyond their control; once in love, they are willing to sacrifice everything, even their lives, for their love; then, the characters either live happily ever after, or they die, thus presumably allowing their love to live on in spirit or in the afterlife. Formulaic, moralistic, and simplistic, novels portrayed women as highly sensitive creatures with a natural tendency towards virtuous behaviour, but who were easily led astray.

Many of the works that were explicitly addressed to women took the form of collections of anecdotes rather than one long narrative, a genre defined at the time as the *roman anecdotique*.[30] These novels recounted numerous separate stories told by the characters over the course of the main plot. First published in 1825, Bayle-Mouillard's *La Sortie de pension* was published in two volumes in *duodecimo* format (in-12°). Produced as inexpensively as possible, the cover is simply green paper and on the back of the book is a list of other recent publications dealing with 'the instruction and edification of youth'. The contents are primarily stories recounted in the process of carrying on the main plot. Claire, a 15-year-old girl, has just left her *pension*. The book focuses on how her aunt deals with the final stages of her education. Wanting to show her niece that . . . 'the pleasures of the capital are bland without some knowledge', . . . the aunt takes her ward to the Louvre to make her recognise her ignorance of art and of history. Later, the older woman explains that 'the first goal of an education is to save us from the weight of boredom, [and] from the efforts of passion'.[31] Clearly, reading was both the means and the potential outcome of such a moral education.

The anecdotal format suited women readers' needs. It allowed them to read at shorter intervals and demanded lower levels of concentration, which meant that frequent interruptions were less bothersome than they would have been with a longer story. While these collections were meant to be entertaining, most were also instructive. Félicité de Choiseul-Meuse's *Récréations morales et amusantes* is an early example. As the title suggests, amusing while instructing was her goal. She wished to provide stories suitable for an age she believed was too often neglected: adolescence. This was a period when 'a vague disquiet of mind and heart upsets their noisy games of childhood [and] when the idea of the world and of pleasure begins to fill their imaginations'. The stories she included, which she modestly refers to as 'écrites sans art', were meant to make girls recognise the difficulties and dangers that came with the end of their studies. To accomplish this, they emphasised 'the disastrous results that the slightest indiscretion could bring, [and] the danger of coquetry'.[32] Girls needed to have morally uplifting, yet entertaining, reading material available to them to distract them from the large amount of literature that was seen as licentious. A prevalent belief in these books was that a person's character, once formed, was inflexible. It was thus important that girls receive proper education early in their lives. This conviction explains the indistinct boundary separating novels from prescriptive literature. Madame Gacon-Dufour's *Manuel complet de la maîtresse de maison* presented just such an argument:

> Mothers, believe me when I tell you that your daughters' happiness depends on the first principles you give them and the care that you take, when they arrive at the age of reason, to make them follow these principles exactly. Then they will be in a position to raise their own daughters, and to inspire in them all the virtues without which women cannot be happy.[33]

Convinced that women and girls needed to be properly instructed both to lead satisfying lives and to ensure the happiness of everyone around them, Gacon-Dufour wrote books like this one to help them on the path towards this greater good. 'Virtues are the children of a good education', she wrote just after the passage cited above.

In her *roman anecdotique*, *Les Dangers de la prévention*, Madame Gacon-Dufour explained that: 'a good education gives the means of supporting the pains with which human life is sown'.[34] The moral of the stories contained in this collection was simple: no one could count on anything, except virtuous behaviour and knowledge; one needed to be prepared for any possible turn of events. It was best if women learned all the skills necessary to run a household, either because they would definitely make use of them, or because they might find themselves forced to use them in the case of financial ruin. The Revolution had placed doubts in people's minds about the future; they had to prepare for limitless possibilities. Earlier, women could be fairly certain that their social position was guaranteed by birth. Now, even aristocratic women should know the fundamentals of running a household, down to the smallest detail. Then, such a woman hoped she would only use those skills to ensure that her domestics were performing their tasks properly. If necessary, however, she could take on household tasks herself.

Unsurprisingly, Madame de Genlis, a liberal aristocrat and the former governess of the children of the Duc d'Orléans, also discussed education at great length. In the course of a woman's education, she argued: 'all personal ambition in her must be destroyed, though it is desirable that she possess a noble ambition for her husband and her children. Similarly, a vibrant and delicate sensitivity that utterly destroys all selfishness must be cultivated in her.'[35] It was nonetheless necessary, she continued, 'for her to be given a thorough education so that once she became a mother, she would be able to educate her daughters and run a household with wise economy'. A proper education was the only sure method of creating virtuous women who would in turn guarantee social order on a larger scale. They were the cornerstones upon which everything else lay. De Genlis assumed that her central argument pertained only to women of means. The limited nature of her analysis is clear when, later in the same work, she took on the subject of proper education for the lower classes, which needed to be instructed to follow the laws of society. 'To enlighten *un peuple* is to teach them ... to appreciate morals and decency, knowledge of the dignity of his status and of their obligations.'[36] She thus expressed a form of aristocratic paternalism. As in her argument for women's education, de Genlis desired that each member of society recognise and appreciate his or her particular place in society. Everyone, rich or poor, male or female, child or parent, had to accept and live up to the obligations that accompanied their social positions.

The moral quality of reading matter could be even more important for the lower classes. In her 1828 collection of stories entitled *Le La Bruyère des domestiques*, de Genlis explained that:

'*Les mauvaises lectures* are dangerous to youth in general; but at least among the classes above the *peuple*, education, accepted decorum, conversations [held] by cultivated, reasonable people, in short, social customs [*l'usage du monde*], always temper the ill effects; while for the *peuple*, this horrible danger is completely uncontrolled; and today it is more awful than ever: one can tell from the dreadful number of domestic thefts, brigands, and prostitutes. These *mauvaises lectures* produced all of this havoc.[37]

De Genlis argued that bad reading material caused problems not only on an individual level, but also on a much wider scale. It made sense to create good reading material to counteract the effect of the bad; this was one of this experienced educator's outright goals. She went on to explain that this particular book was meant to be read by domestic servants and was specifically designed for them. 'Domestic servants cannot read large amounts, which is all the more reason that what they read be good in order to profit as much as possible from the little time they can devote to reading each day.' She hoped that they would find the stories in her book enjoyable and that they would pass it around among their peers. It was, she explained, 'very useful to man-servants and *femmes de chambres* to know how to read aloud'.[38] This interest in the reading practices of those lower down on the social scale was a post-Revolutionary phenomenon, one no doubt linked to both the Revolutionary experience itself as well as the expansion of literacy and new types of reading matter.

Félicité de Choiseul-Meuse demonstrated a similar interest:

> Walk past [some] humble boutiques, . . . stroll along the *boulevards populaires* where young merchants carry their ambulant commerce, and at every step you will find a novel. The *peuple* knows how to read and wants to read.[39]

She wrote the collection of stories called *L'Ecole des jeunes filles* for such an audience. In it, Choiseul-Meuse tells the story of a 'young girl, gifted with all the graces of youth and beauty, who prefers the illusions of vain ambition to a solid establishment suitable to her condition'. Naturally, her story ends tragically: she dies of chagrin after her husband spends his entire fortune.[40] Another story focuses on Aurore, a virtuous young woman who refused to allow her co-workers, most of whom acted like *grisettes*, to influence her. Aurore is rewarded for her steadfast morals in the face of adversity: a wealthy man finds her a job away from these bad seeds, and then marries her.[41] Choiseul-Meuse presented clear morals to her readers: virtuous behaviour and living honourably in the position to which you were born would lead to happiness.

An altogether different sort of book also brings up the issue of lower-class reading practices. *Les Cabarets de Paris* by J.-P.-R. Cuisin, a writer of many borderline-pornographic, or at least quite licentious publications about Parisian life, includes an anecdote about a barmaid who was a voracious reader. Cuisin's wish to create humorous anecdotes about life in Paris no doubt inspired this story. What is significant for our purposes is the fact that a commentary about a working woman's reading practices seemed the best way to do so. Despite its dubious veracity, the passage merits being quoted at length:

> She is a girl with a lot of spirit; subscribed at 1 fr. 50 per month to a *cabinet de lecture*, she knows by heart all the novels of Ducray-Duminin, Carnaval and d'Angélique and Jeanneton; she gives her opinion on many works, and says curiously, without effort, that Madame de Staël is unintelligible; but, in contrast, that Peau d'Ane, is a delicious work and above all she prefers the literature of the Pont-Neuf, about which she revels: 'How I love this passage', ... while showing you a chapter from *l'Enfant du Mystère*!, 'one cannot stop oneself from crying'. But at the moment when she reads the sentimental piece to you, in the style of the declamation of the boulevards, the waiter cries: 'a half a litre at 16 and five glasses'! It is thus necessary for the sensitive priestess of the altars of Bacchus to rush down to the cellar.[42]

While serious critics may have dismissed this woman's choices of reading material as base and non-literary, the books she read spoke to her. Pigault-Lebrun's *L'Enfant du carnaval*, for example, told an exciting, rags-to-riches, often violent story to which the lower classes could relate much more readily than the more intellectual love stories contained in the works of Madame de Staël.[43] The fiction this woman enjoyed paralleled the dramatic plot-lines of Boulevard theatre: this was culture created expressly to appeal to the 'masses'.

Suzanne Volquin, a working-class woman who wrote her memoirs later in life after having been a prominent Saint-Simonian, makes similar distinctions when she mentions the books that filled her life. After the death of her mother in 1821, reading became the only distraction that interested her. She pointed to Rousseau's *Emile,* but especially *Julie, ou la nouvelle Héloïse,* as a book that affected her deeply.

> I did not feel I was the same person after reading this book. I still sought out my same old reliable authors, but I was forced to admit to myself my preference for works of romance because they spoke to my imagination. Madame Cottin and Madame de Genlis, the charming storytellers of that period were my favourites. As for the learned Madame de Staël, I took pleasure in reading her books ... These various works, all celebrating love, colluded with nature

itself in sharply stirring my imagination and filling my heart with unknown desires.[44]

Madame de Staël was 'learned,' but this young reader's favourite authors, Cottin and Genlis, were simple storytellers. Linking all these authors, Volquin found that novel-reading stirred up her emotions, a perception which parallels concerns articulated by many contemporary moralists.

Prescriptive literature published in the post-Revolutionary period often addressed the implications of women's reading practices, too. Reading could be good for women if they read the right things, but it could also be highly dangerous. Madame de Genlis, for example, argued that school libraries should contain 'no literature, no novels, a little history, a lot of moral discipline, [and] some travel tales'.[45] In Dr Gregory's 'Advice to Women', which was published in the collection edited by Madame Dufrénoy and Madame Tastu, *Le Livre des femmes*, the author maintained that women often damaged their health by reading: 'Those with great intelligence and refinement very often have a fragility analogous to the complexion of the body they neglect too often. Their passion for reading and late nights are injurious to both health and beauty.'[46] Reading carried a dual risk: it could itself be a 'passion' while at the same time it often inspired other passions that could be far worse. Even in fiction, novel reading consistently appears as a dangerous way to pass one's time.[47] In *Le La Bruyère des domestiques*, Madame de Genlis included a story about a young, virtuous woman named Sophie who was hired as a domestic servant because of her ability to read out loud. Three weeks after Sophie began work, her employer, the Marquise de R***, became ill and, handing Sophie a book, asked her to read aloud:

> As soon as she opened it Sophie saw by the title that it was a novel and placing it on her knees, she said in a respectful tone, that she did not realise that there were novels that could be read without any danger.

As she had made a solemn promise to herself never to read one, she begged the Marquise never to make her read anything but 'books of piety, morals, history, and certain plays from the *Théâtre Français*'. The Marquise responded by firing her, but before leaving, Sophie noted down the title of the book, which turned out to be 'an infamous novel filled with impieties and licentious details!' In the end, of course, Sophie was rewarded for her virtuous behaviour; she was hired by a countess who treated her well and helped her to improve her reading skills.[48]

The primary dichotomy used in these prescriptions and proscriptions for women was the depiction of the good woman versus the bad woman. Good women were selfless, domestic creatures who avoided the public eye. Bad women enjoyed being at the centre of attention and were egotistical, selfish *coquettes*. Both, however, shared common female traits. Tending to be irrational, sentimental and emotional, women could either learn to curb their natural leanings toward excess and develop their stronger characteristics, or they could lose themselves in the frivolity of *le monde*, a place that encouraged them to lose track of the best female traits, especially those that involved caring for others. The underlying assumption in all of these texts was that, depending on their behaviour, women's influence in society could be detrimental or beneficial. One way or the other, women would determine the current and future health of French society. As readers, they received messages about how they should behave, namely that women should focus on domestic pursuits and avoid attention in public. Yet the fact that women needed to be convinced of the value of domesticity suggests that many were not actually leading such lives. The sheer number of references to women who made the mistake of instilling a love of luxury in their daughters and then saw them ruined later in life, makes it clear that many opted for the excitement and draw of fashionable society over a sedentary lifestyle. Broader social and economic changes may have eventually caused French women to behave more like their English counterparts supposedly did, but this transition was slow, and it was never completely accepted.

In fact, the very act of reading, and even more so writing, could be a form of rebellion against such prescriptions. The authors whose works have been examined here were contributing to a post-Revolutionary effort to write novels that would be good for women, to replace those that were licentious or simply morally lax. Not unlike the actress-philosopher Marie Madeleine Jodin, these authors were writing as women for women. They most likely believed that they were aiding the plight of women by working to convince their sex to lead lives that would be more fulfilling and satisfying than if they had chosen to fill their hours with frivolous pleasures. Literature, these writers had decided, could help to create a stable social order filled with moral, virtuous men and women.

Notes

1 L.-D.Éméric, *De la Politesse, ouvrage critique, moral et philosophique* (Paris, Delauney, 1819), p. 43.

2 On connections between Rousseau and early nineteenth-century women writers, see Clarissa Cambell Orr, 'A Republican Answers back: Jean-Jacques Rousseau, Albertine Necker de Saussure, and forcing little girls to be free' in Clarissa Cambell Orr (ed), *Wollstonecraft's Daughters: Womanhood in England and France 1780–1920* (Manchester, Manchester University Press, 1996), pp. 61–78.

3 Madame de Staël, 'Des Femmes qui cultivent les lettres' in her *De la Littérature considérée dans ses rapports avec les institutions sociales*, vol. 2 ([1800] Genève, Droz and Paris, Minard, 1959), p. 336. In 'Women are Made not Born: Making Bourgeois Girls into Women, France 1830–1870' (Ph.D. thesis, Rutgers University, 1981). Ann Alter emphasises differences between French and English women's ideal roles and behaviour.

4 See Joan Landes, *Women in the Public Sphere in the Age of the French Revolution* (Ithaca, Cornell University Press, 1988) for the best known argument about the Revolution's forcing women out of the public sphere. On domesticity, see M. Darrow, 'French Women and the New Domesticity, 1750–1850', *Feminist Studies* 5 (1979), 41–65; B.G. Smith, *Ladies of the Leisure Class: the Bourgeoises of Northern France in the Nineteenth Century* (Princeton, Princeton University Press, 1981); and M. Ozouf, *Les Mots des femmes* (Paris, Fayard, 1995), pp. 124–6 (on Madame de Staël) and *Essai sur la singularité française*.

5 On similar trends in the American context during the early-national period, see C. Davidson, *Revolution and the Word: the Rise of the Novel in America* (New York, Oxford University Press, 1986), pp. 110–50. Thanks to S. Garfinkel for bringing this book to the author's attention.

6 According to one early twentieth-century scholar, most of these books were overly verbose: 'Novels always unfortunately counted three or four volumes.' A. Marquiset, *Les Bas-bleus du Premier Empire* (Paris, Librairie Ancienne Honoré Champion, 1914), p. 8.

7 On literacy rates, see F. Furet and M. Ozouf, *Reading and Writing: Literacy in France from Calvin to Jules Ferry* (Cambridge, Cambridge University Press, 1982). Based on Maggiolo's 1877 study of literacy rates, 54.5 per cent of men and 34.7 per cent of women nationally could sign their marriage contracts in 1816–20. Rural literacy rates tended to be much lower than urban ones.

8 See J.-C. Vareille, *Le Roman populaire français (1789–1914): Idéologies et pratiques* (Paris, Pulim/Nuit Blanche, 1994).

9 See Cooper, ch. 14.

10 Some *ancien-régime* practices for the circulation of popular literature continued to be relevant. See R. Chartier, *The Cultural Uses of Print in Early Modern France* (Princeton, Princeton University Press, 1987), especially ch. 6, 'Urban Reading Practices, 1660–1780'; G. Bollème, 'Littérature populaire et littérature de colportage au 18ème siècle' in *Livre et société dans la France du XVIIIe siècle* (Paris, Mouton & Co., 1965); R. Mandrou, *De la Culture populaire aux 17e et 18e siècles* (Paris, Stock, 1964); R. Muchembled, *Culture populaire et culture des élites dans la France moderne, XVe–XVIIIe siècles* (Paris, Flammarion, 1978); and

R. Darnton, 'Readers Respond to Rousseau' in *The Great Cat Massacre and Other Episodes in French Cultural History* (New York, Vintage, 1984), pp. 215–56.

11 One important contribution is J. Radway, *Reading the Romance: Women, Patriarchy, and Popular Literature* (1984; 2nd edition; Chapel Hill, University of North Carolina Press, 1991).

12 J.S. Allen, *In the Public Eye: a History of Reading in Modern France, 1800–1940* (Princeton, Princeton University Press, 1991) and M. Lyons, *Le Triomphe du livre: une histoire sociologique de la lecture dans la France du XIXe siècle* (Paris, Promodis, 1987).

13 Ozouf, *Les Mots des femmes*.

14 G. Fraisse, *Muse de la raison: la démocratie exclusive et la différence des sexes* (Aix-en-Provence, Alinea, 1989), p. 197.

15 Madame C*** stood for Elisabeth Celnart, the pseudonym of Elisabeth-Félicie Bayle-Mouillard, née Canard.

16 *Emile et Rosalie, ou les Epoux amans* par Madame Elisabeth C*** (Paris, 1820), pp. 2–3.

17 Radway found that romance writers were often romance readers first. They then found that they enjoyed writing novels as much or more than reading them. *Reading the Romance*, pp. 68–9. Bayle-Mouillard's feelings about writing were strikingly similar.

18 Madame de Genlis, *De l'Influence des femmes sur la littérature française, comme protectrices des lettres et comme auteurs, ou précis de l'histoire des femmes françaises les plus célèbres* (2 vols, Paris, Maradan, 1811), vol. 1, pp. xxxv–xxxvi.

19 For a discussion of debates about women readers, see Fraisse, *Muse de la Raison*, pp. 22–3 and 39–43.

20 In fact, the success of female authors inspired one male writer, Boissy de Faverolles, to take a feminine pseudonym: Madame Guénard de Méré. Lyons, *Triomphe du livre*, p. 107.

21 Marquiset, *Les Bas-bleus*.

22 Two recent examples are M. Gutwirth *et al.* (eds), *Germaine de Staël: Crossing the Borders* (New Brunswick, NJ, Rutgers University Press, 1991); and G. Besser, *Germaine de Staël Revisited* (New York, Maxwell Macmillan, 1994). R. Rogers, *Les Demoiselles de la Légion d'honneur* (Paris, Plon, 1992) devotes significant attention to Madame Campan. Some of the female authors of the period have been receiving more attention recently, especially Claire de Durfort Duras whose best-known novel has been republished: R. Little (ed.), *Ourika* (Exeter, Exeter University Press, 1993), also J. DeJean (ed.), *Ourika: the Original French Text* (New York, MLA Press, 1994). See also, Madame de Genlis, *Mademoiselle de Clermont* and Madame de Duras, *Edouard* (Paris, Editions Autrement, 1994).

23 Marquiset, *Les Bas-bleus*, pp. 73–83, 121–33. On *L'Athenée des dames*, see Evelyne Sullerot, *Histoire de la presse féminine en France des origines à 1848* (Paris, Armand Colin, 1966), pp. 115–23; and Fraisse, *Muse de la Raison*, pp. 65–7.

24 G. Chaussinand-Nogaret, 'Introduction' to Madame de Chastenay, *Mémoires, 1771–1815* (Paris, Perrin, 1987), pp. 1–14.

25 Lyons analyses Madame Cottin's novels under the rubric of 'le roman royaliste'. See *Triomphe du livre*, pp. 107–10.

26 Ibid., pp. 43–4. *Claire d'Albe*, de Genlis argued, was the first novel of the '*"genre personae"*' . . . but it had the sad honour of forming a new school of

novelists'. De Genlis, *De l'Influence des femmes,* vol. 2, p. 242. Madame Cottin's life and work are also discussed in Dufrénoy, *Biographie des jeunes demoiselles, ou vies des femmes célèbres depuis les Hébreux* (2 vols. Paris, A. Eymery, 1816), vol. 2, pp. 567–70. A few scholars have begun to pay attention to Cottin's works. All preface their discussions by mentioning how she has been ignored despite the great popularity of her novels when they appeared. These include M.J. Call, 'Measuring Up: Infertility and "Plénitude" in Sophie Cottin's *Claire d'Albe', Eighteenth-Century Fiction* 7 (1995), 185–201; S.I. Spencer, ' "Reading in Pairs": La Nouvelle Héloïse and Claire d'Albe', *Modern Languages Annual* 7 (1995), 166–72; and Spencer, 'The French Revolution and the Early Nineteenth-Century French Novel: the Case of Sophie Cottin', *Proceedings of the Annual Meeting of the Western Society for French History* 18 (1991), 498–504.

27   Lyons, *Triomphe du livre,* pp. 107–8.

28   L. Hunt discusses *Claire d'Albe* in *The Family Romance of the French Revolution* (Berkeley, University of California Press, 1992), pp. 169–71.

29   See Radway, *Reading the Romance,* especially p. 29.

30   Marie-Armande-Jeanne d'Humières Gacon-Dufour, *Les Dangers de la prévention* (Paris, Buisson, 1806) is described in this way on its title page.

31   Madame Elisabeth Celnart (pseudonym of Bayle-Mouillard), *La Sortie du Pension* (Paris, Boiste fils ainé, 1825), pp. 25 and 33. Ozouf discusses the issue of boredom as a particularly feminine problem in her *Les Mots des femmes,* p. 40.

32   Félicité de Choiseul-Meuse, *Récréations morales et amusantes à l'usage des jeunes demoiselles qui entrent dans le monde* (Paris, Blanchard, 1810), pp. 5–7. Her novel *Entre chien et loup* ([1808] Brussels, Maheu, 1894) also takes an anecdotal form. Unlike her *Récréations morales,* this earlier publication could not be defined as 'moral' and was actually banned from French reading rooms in 1825. On the novel and its reception, see Beth Ann Glessner, 'Libertinism and Gender in Five Late-Enlightenment Novels by Morency, Cottin and Choiseul-Meuse' (Ph.D. thesis, Pennsylvania State University, 1994), pp. 45–6, 58, 178–81.

33   Gacon-Dufour, *Manuel complet de la maîtresse de maison et de la parfaite ménagère ou Guide pratique pour la gestion d'une maison à la ville et à la campagne* (Paris, Roret, 1826), p. 39.

34   Gacon-Dufour, *Les Dangers de la prévention,* p. 35.

35   De Genlis, *Discours moraux sur divers sujets, et particulièrement sur l'éducation* (Paris, Maradan, an X [1802]), p. 144. A good biography is G. de Broglie, *Madame de Genlis* (Paris, Perrin, 1985). De Genlis's theories formed part of an important movement of this period: that of the *mère éducatrice.*

36   De Genlis, *Discours moraux,* pp. 209–10.

37   De Genlis, *Le La Bruyère des domestiques* (Paris, V. Thiercelin, 1828), pp. 2–3.

38   De Genlis, *Le La Bruyère,* p. 7.

39   Félicité de Choiseul-Meuse, *L'École des jeunes filles* (3 vols, Paris, A. Eymery, 1822), vol. 1, p. i.

40   Ibid., vol. 1, pp. iii and 145.

41   Ibid., vol. 2, pp. 145–97. On the image of the *grisette,* see J-C Caron, *Générations romantiques: les étudiants de Paris et le quartier latin* (1814–1851) (Paris, Armand Colin, 1991), pp. 205–6 and D. Davidson, 'Constructing Order in Post-Revolutionary France: Women's Identities and Cultural Practices, 1800–

1830' (Ph.D. Thesis, University of Pennsylvania, 1997), pp. 36–7. The novel *La Grisette* by August Ricard was published in Paris in 1827.

42 J.-P.-R. Cuisin, *Les Cabarets de Paris, ou l'homme peint d'après nature* (Paris, Delongchamps, 1821), 14–16. Cuisin's works include: *Les Bains de Paris et des principales villes des quatres parties du monde, ou le Neptune des dames, avec anecdotes, galanteries décentes, etc.* (Paris, 1821); *Clémentine orpheline et andro-gyne, ou les caprices de la nature et de la fortune* (Paris, 1819); and *Le Guide des épouseurs pour 1825, ou le Conjugalisme : Etrennes aux futures par un homme qui s'est marié sept fois* (Paris, 1824).

43 Pigault-Lebrun, *L'Enfant du carnaval : Histoire remarquable et surtout véritable* (Paris, Barba, an VIII [1799]). The novel was reprinted several times during the Empire and the Restoration. For a discussion of this novel's and its connection to the Revolution, see Hunt, *Family Romance*, pp. 174–5.

44 Suzanne Volquin, 'A Daughter of the People' in M. Traugott (ed. and transl.), *The French Worker: Autobiographies from the Early Industrial Era* (Berkeley, University of California Press, 1993), p. 108.

45 De Genlis, *Discours moraux*, p. 335.

46 Gregory 'Avis aux femmes' in Dufrenoy and Amable Tastu, *Le Livre des femmes, choix de morceaux extraits des meilleurs écrivains français sur le caractère, les mœurs et l'esprit des femmes* (2 vols, Paris, Gand, 1823), vol. 2, p. 186. 'Dr Gregory' is probably Dr John Gregory whose publications included *A Father's Legacy to His Daughters*, which was published repeatedly in England at the end of the eighteenth century and the beginning of the nineteenth. Thanks to Felicia Gordon for the reference.

47 These prohibitions existed already in the eighteenth century. See G. May, *Le Dilemme du roman au XVIIIe siècle* (New Haven, Yale University Press; and Paris, Presses Universitaires de France, 1963) and J. DeJean, *Tender Geographies: Women and the Origins of the Novel in France* (New York, Columbia University Press, 1991).

48 De Genlis, *Le La Bruyère*, pp. 9–12.

12
From Mobilisation to Normalisation: Scientific Networks and Practices for War (1792–1824)[1]

Patrice Bret

One day people will wonder how a nation, at war with all Europe, cut off from other nations, torn internally by civil strife, could raise its industry up to the level it actually attained....It was in the most difficult circumstances that all these changes occurred; *the government, given the urgency of the situation, took a number of scientists one after another from their research laboratories to place them in plants* [my emphasis] where in a very short time most of them performed wonders.'[2]

Twenty-five years after the event, Jean-Antoine Chaptal, Count of Chanteloup and a peer of France, a chemist and a member of the Academy of Science, made the scientists' role in the victory of the *Montagnard* Republic in 1794 the starting point for the modernisation of French industry. No doubt this is an exaggeration, for under Louis XVIII, the nation's industry was still aspiring to taking up the British challenge of the industrial revolution.[3] On the other hand, beyond the world of industry, the mobilisation of scientists in Year II contributed enormously to the reconfiguration of relationships between science and politics by establishing scientific networks and practices for war, drawing on the Colbertist tradition, of which Jacobinism and the continental blockade in a way represent the high point.[4] The international context explains easily why the move from mobilisation to normalisation can be seen clearly in the field of scientific research and military engineering. It is this first stage that we will examine here.

The Revolutionary event to which Chaptal refers is important insofar as it gave a 'national' and republican legitimacy to a science which until then had been characterised by its strong links with absolute monarchy through the Royal Academy of Science. On the other hand, this 'national' legitimacy very soon turned the mobilisation of scientists into an archetypal crisis out of which a real republican myth has been constructed.[5] Celebrated as early as 1803 by the physicist Jean-Baptiste Biot,[6] despite his opposition to the *Montagnards*, this event was presented explicitly as a model by scientists and inventors in the face of the allied invasion in 1814 and during the Hundred Days in the following Spring.[7] The *Commission scientifique de la défense de Paris*, of which the chemist Berthelot was president, resuscitated it during the Franco-Prussian war in 1870–71,[8] and the *Commission supérieure d'examen des inventions intéressant la défense nationale* did the same thing during the First World War, under the presidency of the mathematicians, Appell and Painlevé.[9] The national myth of the role of scientists in defence of the endangered homeland is thus revived whenever there is a threat from a foreign power. Even better, it is an intrinsic part of republican practice, especially in times of reconstruction. The very fact that the chemists Guyton-Morveau, Fourcroy, Chaptal, Dumas and Bertholot, or the mathematicians Monge, Carnot, Laplace and Painlevé were part of the governments of the First Republic, of the Consulate and of the Second and Third Republics is enough to illustrate the tenacious relationship between scientists and politics.

The collective appropriation of the myth is filtered through republican imagery and popular literature which invest it with heroic-symbolic qualities that complement each other as one crisis follows another: Coutelle's balloon at Fleurus, Gambetta's flight out of Paris, the aces of aviation, Chappe's telegraph machine, carrier pigeons (and microphotography), wireless telegraphy. But the historians are not left behind. After the 1871 defeat, Georges Pouchet echoed all this in an article reprinted by James Guillaume in the centenary years of the Revolution at the time of the great push for revenge following the Franco-Russian Alliance in 1890.[10] The very phrase 'mobilisation of scientists in Year II' was thought up by Albert Mathiez in December 1917, and with this he gave historical legitimacy to the contemporary war effort which had just been shaken by a world conflict that had got bogged down, the Russian Revolution and mutiny on the western front.[11] Immediately after the Great War, mobilisation during the Revolution was studied in detail by Camille Richard in a model positivist-historical thesis.[12]

This juxtaposition of circumstances between the historian *in situ* and his historical subject reveals how this perspective, tightly linked in a specific political and military context, deserves reassessment in the light of recent research in the field of the history of science and engineering. Furthermore, the years 1792 to 1824 correspond precisely to the key dates of the birth of modern state research in France, that is to say: the first decree by the Committee of Public Safety of 9 April 1793, under the presidency of Guyton, a chemist who mobilised scientists by establishing a 'committee of four citizens, experts in chemistry and engineering, appointed with a specific mission to research and test new defence methods', and the creation by Louis XVIII on 19 May 1824 of the *Ecole centrale de pyrotechnie* in Metz, which brought the normalisation process to an end.

To approach the question from a cultural perspective would take into account the mirror effect between the invention of politics and the politics of invention. The French Revolution was vital not only in terms of the development of a typically French political culture, but also in terms of the parallel emergence of a scientific and technical culture, no doubt still in its early stages, but one firmly rooted in middle-class élites, the professional classes and certain artisan industries. For this cultural revolution, the events of the Revolution were a means to gain access to the corridors of power. It thus gave birth to the first modern form of research policy, characterised by state initiative, rationalisation of aims and methods, exploration of solutions to be found outside the prevailing technological system, strong links with basic research and teaching, joint research arising from the move from the collective practice of specialist committees to that of the laboratory.[13] A comparative study of Great Britain, Austria and Denmark in the same period, comparing in particular certain French innovations (the military aerostation) with British ones (the war rocket), clearly demonstrate the originality of the French. The influence of this model is easily found in other countries after 1815, especially in America, Russia, Poland and Sweden.[14] Two concepts prove to be particularly useful to the understanding of this phenomenon, that of *networks* at the crossroads between science and politics, and that of academic *practices* now applied to engineering expertise. A few pertinent examples throw light on the strategy and approach adopted by members of the Academy of Science during the Revolution in order to retain through mobilisation the power they had before, on the shift from temporary revolutionary structures to permanent structures during the Directorial and Consular Republics, the Empire then the Monarchy, and lastly on the inherent dynamic of the research programmes that led to normalisation.

If the procedures for mobilising scientists marked a total break with the *ancien régime*, the principle of having recourse to scientists coincides perfectly with the traditions of the relationship between the monarchy and the Royal Academy of Science. This apparent paradox requires an understanding of how members of the Academy of Science, who under the Monarchy had the monopoly of knowledge, and functioned like a tribunal for science and technology, adapted to democratisation, and managed to gain access to political power and to the new authorities. The answer is to be found first of all in the strategy that was deployed in the face of the democratisation of knowledge and expertise, that is to say, in the face of the proliferation of learned societies and societies of inventors which began to take place as early as 1788 with the *Société philomathique*. One of the first issues at stake in 1791 was that of membership of the *Bureau de consultation des arts et métiers*, charged with the allocation to deserving inventors of the national awards created by the constituent *Assemblée nationale*.[15] The members of the Academy of Science understood its significance immediately.

The struggle for power began in the corridors of the Assembly. The initial proposal concerning membership and the terms of reference of the Bureau, as presented by the *Comité d'agriculture et de commerce*, allocated to each learned society an equal number of seats. But soon the *Comité de commerce*, as well as the spokesman Boufflers, found themselves facing ever-growing difficulties, with more and more obstacles to slow down their progress. All the tricks of academic intrigue were studied in turn and used consistently.[16] In the end, yielding to pressure, the Legislative Assembly granted 15 seats to the Academy of Science, and a total of 15 to the other 12 societies.[17] Thus, two years after the Third Estate had gained equal representation to that of the two privileged orders in the Estates General – a first step towards democracy – the Academy managed to scoop up half of the seats on the Bureau de consultation – a victory of official science over the young societies which, like the press, blossomed in a climate of freedom, and sought to give science democratic legitimacy.

Robbed of their expectations, the societies came together in November to petition the Assembly. In vain. The *Journal des sciences, arts et métiers* picked up the baton, clamouring against 'claims made by a venerable and distinguished public body, whose hidden underground roots are to this very day still strenuously stopping the trunk from being torn up'. To the arrogant posturing of the Academy the journal opposed the virtuous simplicity of the *Société des inventions et découvertes* led by Servières, Trouville and Leblanc, a society which 'does not claim, like these public academic bodies, to have the exclusive privilege of thought'.[18] This severe, but not unjustified, attack nine months before the dissolution of the Academy, was not isolated. Marat had already condemned 'academic charlatanism', and soon the *Lycée des arts*, founded in August 1792 immediately after the King's fall from power, claimed to be the 'first free assembly of artists...distancing itself totally from the academic aristocracy'.[19] For the supporters of *sans-culottes* science the academic establishment was indeed the obstacle to overcome. The *Bureau de consultation* was the ideal arena for this battle. In this affair the Home Secretary, Roland, clearly sided with the members of the Academy, going as far as to question the quality of the representatives from the other societies, 'who perhaps do not have the level of academic expertise or objectivity which the public has a right to expect'.[20] His successor, Garat, followed his lead. In fact, by legitimising the links between political power and knowledge, and by refocusing the assessment of the 'useful arts' on inventions relating only to arts and crafts, it was for them simply a question of emphasising ministerial authority over an institution that was rather too independent.[21]

In a way, these ministerial attacks led to a tightening of links between the members of the Advisory Bureau. More firmly united under the presidency of Berthollet in the Spring of 1793, the Bureau was backed by the Convention's *Comité d'instruction publique,* and one year later, the dissolution of the ministries put a timely end to the debate. One must not of course overstate the conflict between the academicians, scientists and artists who had all been cheated of official recognition.[22] A compromise was reached on acceptable working procedures, but directly inspired by the ones used by academic commissions which, like the *Jury des armes,* soon prevailed in other proceedings to make decisions on the question of weapons. In fact, an analysis of the actual business of the new institutions during the Revolution shows that the academicians were able to retain, indeed increase, their power, even at the cost of the abolition of the Academy itself. Their leaders occupied posts of even greater strategic importance. Leaving aside revolutionary rhetoric, the primacy of 'talent' or knowledge over 'civic merit' or ideology was officially recognised. This hierarchy is particularly obvious in the field of arms and gunpowder manufacture, and in the training of engineers (at the *Ecole polytechnique,* for example).

Political choices are only one aspect of the problem. Behind the ideology-based criterion for the selection of members, one can detect some networks with old roots at the scientific as well as the political level. These networks, sometimes based on geographical location, sometimes more on institutions, were centred on a few well-known figures, and often intersected. The first sprang directly from the Arsenal group, which for ten years had been taking part in the chemical revolution led by Lavoisier.[23] This included scientists, regrouped within the *Section des armes et poudres,* who were collaborating directly with the Committee for Public Safety.[24] Despite its great importance at the heart of executive power and the fame of its members (although since the Revolution several had occupied administrative and political posts, and had been the source of secondary networks stemming from it), this group was only really activated by means of another network, one of the most clearly defined, and certainly the most important: the Burgundian network. This network was formed originally around one man (Guyton, a chemist and member of the Convention), one scientific institution (the Dijon Academy) and one political society (the Dijon *Club patriotique*), of which Guyton was the driving force.[25] Its operations covered key posts in politics and administration, as well as in engineering, and intermediate posts in research and training.

The Burgundian network gained access to executive power at the highest level. It placed the two 'technician' members of the great Committee for Public Safety, Lazare Carnot and Prieur de la Côte-d'Or, under the influence of Guyton, who had just left the Committee three weeks earlier, on 10 July 1793. A distant relative of Prieur de la Côte-d'Or, who had been one of his students, Guyton was Chancellor of the Dijon Academy in 1784 when it had rewarded Carnot for his *Eloge de Vauban*. The two men then worked together in the Legislative Assembly, and subsequently in the Convention's diplomatic committee. Having left the Committee for Public Safety, Guyton found in Carnot, and especially in Prieur, indispensable intermediaries enabling him to keep the ear of the Committee and pursue the policy of applied research which he had initiated that Spring. Thus, he became the power behind the Committee with regard to weapons and munitions, and in consequence even with regard to the chemical industry. Many minutes relating to decrees, written in Guyton's hand and presented by Prieur to the Committee, provide ample proof of this secret role which emerges clearly in the correspondence between the two men. Moreover, Guyton acknowledged receipt of documents in the name of the Committee, signing letters on behalf of it when he was no longer a member.[26] This indicates the closeness of the links between the Committee for Public Safety and the cluster of scientists around it.

The second circle of the network could be found at the level of administrative posts in the offices of the Committee, and in the executive commissions. The Burgundian Chabeuf, who had been Chief Clerk at the Tax Office, headed the offices of the Committee's *Section des armes et poudres*. The *Commission de l'organisation et du mouvement des armées de terre* was headed by General Pille, a former journalist and colleague of Guyton in the Dijon Military Committee. Working under the orders of one and then the other, the future pedagogue from Dijon, Jean-Joseph Jacotot – who had taught mathematics before serving as an officer in a volunteer artillery corps – was assigned to the Committee's *Bureau des poudres et salpêtres* in the winter of 1793–94, before becoming Pille's secretary at the Commission after 9 Thermidor.[27] The influence of the network extended in particular to administrative responsibilities linked directly to production, especially in the gunpowder industry. In December 1792, Guyton had his friend and associate Champy, the commissioner for gunpowder in Dijon, appointed as head of the *Régie nationale des poudres et salpêtres* after the resignations of Lavoisier and Fourcroy.[28] Pierre Jacotot, a professor of physics in Dijon, was sent on a mission to Touraine with Vauquelin, and was then given responsibility for one of the eight saltpetre *Inspectorats*. The Dijon-born apothecary, Jacques Tartelin, received another.[29] The *Commissariat des épreuves secrètes de Meudon* was under the control of the Committee's agent, Jean Borthon, an artillery officer and one of Prieur's cousins. Finally, a third, more loosely organised, circle was formed from among Burgundian craftsmen and engineers who had settled in Paris before the Revolution, like Edme Régnier, an arms manufacturer at the Paris Arsenal, or Mégnié, a manufacturer of scientific instruments at the *Atelier de perfectionnement des armes portatives*. They also helped in the control of war materials.

Thus, in Year II, the Guyton network controlled in fact the majority of key posts in military affairs on the Committee and in its executive commissions, and between a quarter and a third of key posts in the gunpowder industry. But the Burgundians also gained power over the teaching of military engineering in the widest sense. Apart from Guyton and Monge, four were employed at the *Ecole centrale des travaux publics* (*Ecole polytechnique*): Barruel, a physicist and member of the interim commission for the arts, and Chaussier, a doctor and professor at the *Ecole de santé* in Paris and also at the *Ecole de Mars*, taught there, and the two Jacotots were employed there.[30] Guyton's Burgundian network was reinforced by private or family links as between Prieur and Guyton, or Prieur and Borthon, while professional links allowed it to extend beyond its regional bounds. Among the first to be nominated were two of Guyton's scientific partners in his industrial activities:[31] Champy, his associate in several ventures, and Carny, from Grenoble, who had been his associate, just before the Revolution, in a project to establish a soda works.[32] The part played by Guyton in the recruitment of these two figures is beyond dispute. Thus he was an important member of the Convention, soon to be chairman of the *Comité de la défense générale* (January–March 1793), and of the Committee for Public Safety

(April–July). He was the only one, in the scientific entourage of the temporary Executive Council, to be familiar with Champy's professional skills and to know about the soundness of his political views, when the latter was appointed Director for gunpowder manufacture in December 1792. He was the only one on the first Committee for Public Safety to know Carny, who in April 1793 was asked to supervise the production of potassium nitrate to manufacture a new gunpowder. Similarly, no one else in Paris had sufficient knowledge of the Dijon scientists to find politically safe talents among them, like the two Jacotots in October 1793, or Tartelin in January 1794.

Often other links were added to, or overlapped with, these geographical and personal criteria. In short, the cradle of recruitment of the Burgundy scientists was to be found in the two Dijon institutions to which Guyton was central: the *Académie des sciences, arts et belles-lettres*, founded in 1740, and the *Club patriotique*, which he had founded himself after the Night of 4 August 1789, the night of the abolition of privileges. Most of the people mentioned above belonged to at least one of these institutions. Pille, Champy, Prieur, Chaussier, Jacotot, Tartelin and Borthon were all members of the *Club patriotique*, affiliated to the Friends of the Constitution. Some even occupied official posts, including the presidency of the club. Several entered the Dijon Academy when Guyton was Vice-Chancellor or Chancellor. This was so in the case of Chaussier (August 1776), Tartelin (August 1778), Champy (June 1780) and Pierre Jacotot (December 1785), who was the secretary of the Science Department, and even Prieur (July 1790). Other members who did not belong to the Dijon-based circle, but were Burgundians like Carnot (August 1784) or Monge (February 1788) also belonged to this Academy. Through them, and through Prieur, Guyton's scientific and political network was linked to another arising out of the teaching activities at the *Ecole du génie* at Mézières. Besides the many former pupils who had remained military engineers, or had entered civilian life, like Faipoult, this network included some of Monge's colleagues, teachers like Ferry, Clouet and Hachette, or 'craftsmen' like Savart and Adnès. Automatically part of the military engineering corps, the circle was equally active in administration, education and in the manufacture of war materials. Other, smaller networks can be detected around Berthollet and Chaptal, or behind Fourcroy.[33] The latter arranged appointments for his protégé Vauquelin, his cousin Laugier and his pupil Raymond, who stated in his memoirs:

I owe my appointment to the kindness and memory of my former professor, Faucroy, who was a member of the Committee for Public

Safety at the time, and it is not the only kindness for which I have to be grateful to him, as I had no job at the time other than the one at the saltpetre plant where I worked hard, but for little reward.[34]

Mobilisation was also a matter of appointments and salaries at a time when aristocratic patronage had disappeared, and when the education system had not yet been rebuilt. From 1795, the *Ecole polytechnique*, the *Ecole normale*, the medical schools, the secondary *Ecoles centrales*, and then the *lycées* and the universities, would offer jobs to the scientists mobilised in 1793–94. Pierre Jacotot, for example, would be a professor of physics at the *Ecole centrale*, at the Faculty of Sciences in Dijon, before becoming Rector of the new Academy of the imperial *Université*. Other posts and other salaries, often held simultaneously, would be offered by the advisory and research institutes, which would gradually be established on a more permanent basis.

Mobilisation, introduced as an emergency measure with temporary commissions born from academic practices, led to permanent institutions, commissions or committees.[35] This process certainly corresponded to an institutional dynamic relating to the political and military powers – that is to say, the various relevant bodies (firstly the *Artillerie* and the *Administration des poudres et salpêtres*, and secondly the engineering corps and the navy), which were to turn these vehicles of influence to their own advantage in the end. By virtue of their members, the succession of temporary commissions, with highly specialised tasks, tended to form a permanent structure, with broader areas of expertise, together with a transition from testing to research. This is particularly well exemplified by the commission of 9 April 1793, and the three subsequent commissions at the centre for secret testing in Meudon under the direct control of the Committee for Public Safety from 1793 to 1800.[36]

The main activity of the 9 April Commission involved research programmes which had been going on for a few weeks, such as the chloride powder programme in which one of the commissioners (Berthollet) was particularly involved, while his three colleagues were involved in other ventures.[37] Six weeks later, in fact, these programmes converged, and in daily routine the chemist worked with Fabre, an artillery officer, in charge of the programme on incendiary cannon-balls, and then, in July, with General Choderlos de Laclos, who was responsible for the programme on hollow cannon-balls or shells. Acknowledging the situation and the string of difficulties arising in these programmes, the Committee for Public Safety decided to restructure them. On 28 September, the Committee created a new commission for secret research. Only Berthollet belonged to both the new structure and the old, whose legacy he insured, but his new colleagues were in fact the people who had been working with him, Fabre and Laclos – apart from the latter's aide-de-camp and a civil engineer who had also worked with Montalembert. Rather than an advisory commission, it was a research and development laboratory. To avoid the gaze of the curious, and to minimise the risk of accidents, the commission established itself in a national estate in Meudon which offered all the opportunities and necessary guarantees needed for secret artillery tests. While obscuring the precise nature of its activities, the official title that it had been given of *Establissement national pour différentes épreuves, sous la surveillance du Comité du salut public* emphasised the political control and the political will governing this establishment.[38] However, the smooth running of the commission was soon to be made difficult by political radicalisation (Laclos was arrested in November 1793), and by the development of mobilisation itself (Berthollet, already very involved at the *Section des armes et poudres*, was charged with the provision of 'revolutionary courses' in February 1794).

Recognising these difficulties, the Committee for Public Safety then replaced the Commission after it had existed only six months. Although his many tasks prevented him from daily participation in the activities of the commission, Berthollet's role in the weapons section enabled him to keep an eye on these activities, and occasionally to take part in them. On the other hand, Fabre's presence continued to be indispensable to the continuation of programmes already under way, but stricter supervision appeared to be needed, and he was not particularly keen to return to his first post. These various factors were kept in mind when the members of the new commision were nominated. On 22 March 1794, the Committee for Public Safety created, under its direct authority, the *Commission des épreuves d'artillerie de Meudon* or the *Administration révolutionnaire des épreuves, sous la surveillance du Comité du salut public, établie à Meudon par son arrêté du 2 germinal*.[39] The three commissioners (or administrators) were appointed the following day. Fabre was joined by Welter, a young chemist who was part of the Arsenal group, and Pain, an inspector of students on the course on saltpetre.[40] This time, the commission worked diligently on programmes relating to incendiary cannon-balls, artillery shells and chloride powder. As the experiments commissioned by the weapons section and the Committee for Public Safety continued and came to fruition, there was a progression from experimental to mass production, explosive materials being made in the Meudon centre,[41] but with the casings and raw materials coming from other plants. The increased importance of the Centre called for stricter supervision. The Committee soon appointed to it the people's representative, Battelier, and then a private agent responsible for sending him a daily progress report. Prieur put his cousin Borthon, an artillery officer, in this position of trust.[42] Before this last appointment, the Committee had asked Hassenfratz to submit a report on the progress of the work undertaken in Meudon, and the measures needed to speed it up.[43] Its contents are not known, but it was most likely the reason for the important measures taken subsequently. One of these measures, probably underlining a firmer intention to institutionalise the venture, changed the official title of the commission and of the establishment to the *Commissariat des épreuves de Meudon;* another measure allocated 50 000 *livres* to programmes in progress.[44] After the fall of Robespierre, these programmes continued for another year and a half until the Spring of 1796. Not counting the shells used in the experiments at the developmental phase, more than 170 000 incendiary cannon-balls and hollow cannon-balls were manufactured, and sent to the ports.[45]

The destruction of the *château* following an explosion resulted in the disappearance of the *Commissariat*, whereas the neighbouring centre for aerostatics, remained. Fabre was then given another regiment, and Welter was appointed as a chemistry assistant at the *Ecole polytechnique.*[46] Pain, the administrative member, was the only one left. He was the link with the third, and last, Meudon Commission which, while still retaining part of the legacy, reverted to more traditional forms, functions and practices, testing once again taking over from research and development. More than a year after the suppression of the second one, this new commission, responsible for secret testing, was officially established by executive decree on 16 December 1797.[47] With the exception of the secretary-treasurer and of Fabre, the members of the last Meudon *Commission des épreuves* were once again scientists, members of the mathematics and physics class of the new *Institut National.* Under the presidency of Vice-Admiral Rosily (a future academician) former colleagues in the Revolutionary government's weapons section (Monge) sat with scientists who had been sidelined, or shielded as ex-aristocrats (Laplace and Borda) as well as with Andréossy, an artillery General and future academician.[48] When Andréossy and Monge left on the expedition to Egypt in 1798, other members were added: Deydier, an ex-member of the Convention, Gassendi, an artillery colonel, Burgues-Missiesy, a Rear-Admiral and Périer, a mechanical engineer from the *Institut National.*[49] However, the Commission's status was very different. On the one hand, once again attached to the Admiralty, which had kept the Meudon plant on as a mere supply depot, it was no longer under the direct supervision of the Executive. On the other hand, although it continued to have a particular interest in explosive materials, in the tradition of previous commissions, and to carry out experiments, it no longer really developed programmes of applied research.

The Meudon centre for research and development was thus no more than a test centre where trials were still taking place, but where only Pain still lived. However, the regular presence of a single commission, and the eminence of its members, made it a unique centre in comparison to those like Vincennes or La Fère which were the locations for specific trials conducted before special commissions. When the centre came under threat, this uniqueness was highlighted by Pain:

> The reason for this establishment's existence lies in the countless projects presented to the Government requiring commissioners to be appointed to examine them. But the latter rarely provided government departments with satisfactory information, and were thus a waste of time and money.[50]

The most interesting experiments, consolidating the link with previous commissions, were those under the direction of Fabre once again on behalf of the Commission, with the shells and incendiary cannon-balls he had been recently manufacturing.[51] General Bonaparte seemed highly interested in the experiments conducted by his colleagues at the *Institut* and his comrades in arms. Indeed, he took incendiary cannon-balls with him on the Egyptian expedition, using them, in vain, at Saint-Jean d'Acre in April 1799.[52] However, the disappearance of the direct link with central power, and the fact that the Commission was now attached to the Admiralty, was the cause of Meudon's decline, despite its key advantage of having a discreetly located plant which had some-times caused it to be preferred to the park at Vincennes, even though Vincennes was closer to Paris.[53] Despite the efforts of the president and of the secretary of the commission, succeeded by Deydier, a member of the Council of Five Hundred, Meudon could not survive competition from Vincennes, where the Artillery was conducting its own experi-ments. The closure of the centre and of the commission, first requested in June 1799, was approved in January 1800.[54] Presented as an economy measure, this barely concealed the return to power of the military over institutions created by central government and the heavy hand of the *Comité central de l'artillerie*, whose powers had been strengthened by the fact that the First Consul belonged to that branch of the army.[55] Therefore, despite the ways in which their nature had changed, the Meudon commissions emerge as the inheritors of the 9 April Commission, partly because of the spirit in which they had been created, partly because of their wish to maintain a mixed membership: first-class scientists and engineers, and partly through a certain continuity of membership, limited perhaps, but nonetheless important.

The profession of the commissioner ensuring that continuity indicates a major transition. This stable role was filled at first by a scientist (Berthollet), then an artillerist (Fabre) and finally the two latter and an administrator (Pain, secretary for almost six years from March 1794 to January 1800), an evolution reflecting a quest for a permanent structure. It indicates above all a turning away from the potential for revolutionary innovation of the first foundation. Although the Admiralty had been the original force behind the creation of the Meudon centre, the centre had immediately become directly dependent on the Committee for Public Safety until the re-establishment of the ministries. But, as in the case of the aerostation, the *Directoire* did not take up the baton of government supervision. Mobilisation was primarily the responsibility of the political powers; the administrative machinery and the logic of the corps were responsible for normalisation. However, that logic embraced the need to set up mixed institutions, including at least one scientist and a few members of a military corps, before the polytechnicians could provide officer-scientists themselves, some of whom would also be members, or corresponding members, of the Academy of Science. This logic was put into practice, for example, when the commission for the improvement of gunpowder was created in 1802, a distant heir to the revolutionary Essonnes commissions, with members coming from five different bodies (*Institut National, Artillerie, Artillerie de marine, Poudres et salpêtres, Mines*). It led to the establishment of the *Comité consultatif des poudres* in 1818, chaired by an academician: Gay-Lussac, his pupil Pelouze, and Pelouze's pupil Berthellot was a succession that lasted until the beginning of the twentieth century.

In the last analysis, the permanent establishment of the commissions was mainly about scientific expertise and application. It still remains to be seen how the research programmes, launched as emergency measures, had become the norm within permanent institutions. The early history of what was then the *Ecole centrale de pyrotechnie militaire*, officially founded in 1824, and destined to last for one and a half centuries, certainly provides the best example with which to pursue this issue. This school, which in the Restoration resumed the research on explosive materials and hollow cannon-balls undertaken at Meudon in the

Revolution, first inherited the military rocket programme, and is a clear illustration of the perpetuation of the Year II model during the Empire. Research on military rockets, still in its infancy in the Revolution, when it was encouraged rather than organised,[56] was launched by Napoleon in February 1810 in order to gain a long-range incendiary weapon adapted to siege warfare in Spain, thus taking up the British challenge represented by Congreve's invention.[57] On the same pattern as during the Revolution, the Emperor set up a mixed commission of scientists, administrators from the gunpowder department, and artillery officers. With Monge as its President, the Commission perfected a complete rocket system and circulated, in December, a directive to all artillery headquarters and ports in the Empire, from Flushing to Corfu and from Brest to Hamburg, as well as to the allied ports from Naples to Danzig. Courses were organised the following year in Vincennes, not just for the artillery corps, but also for the maritime artillery and artillerymen sent by the vassal kingdoms of Italy and Naples. At the same time, production facilities were set up in French military ports and in Spain.[58] Important developments in rocket technology in Denmark brought about the establishment by Brulard of a second system in Hamburg. Brulard was to resume his work in Vincennes during the Hundred Days.[59] If the research programmes undertaken between 1810 and 1815 had been a technical success, within the bounds of contemporary knowledge and materials, the actual deployment of rockets, if not their production, had been an obvious failure.[60] This was no doubt due to unfavourable circumstances, but also to structural flaws such as the lack of qualified personnel and the lack of an integrated scheme for training artificers, the prevailing one being totally inadequate. The need for a proper teaching programme in munitions was also felt at regimental level, but the Ministry responded only with expedients, namely occasional courses on explosives put on in the regimental artillery schools.[61] In order to meet temporary needs, generals for their part were sometimes forced to create local companies of artificers.

The *Comité central de l'artillerie* was fully aware of the deficiencies. During the Hundred Days, at a time when research on rockets had just been resumed in Vincennes, it requested from the Ministry 'that a company of artificers be set up on the foreign model, and in particular the British'.[62] It was decided to establish such a company on 4 May 1815. Captain Jacquier, who had commanded the Company of Artificers in Egypt in 1800, was appointed to lead it. He had been one of the key members of the 1810 Commission, and had obtained the best results at the rocket-manufacturing facilities established in Seville in 1811 for the siege of Cadiz. The new company, disbanded by a general edict on 16 July 1815, was reinstated six weeks later by special decree. The Company of Artificers had the dual mission to manufacture munitions to train 'men instructed in that branch of the service', but not to carry out research.[63] Nevertheless, it allowed expertise acquired during the Empire to be maintained by constructing each year about twenty rockets for training purposes.[64] This is how the French came to be in a position to use rockets – not very successfully, it must be said – at the capture of the Trocadero, in Cadiz, during the French military intervention in Spain in 1823.

Originally founded in Bourges, the Company was then transferred to the regimental artillery school in Toulouse in 1818. There the education programme was started up leading to the establishment of the *Ecole centrale de pyrotechnie militaire*. The *Comité central* was required to submit 'the draft of a course on the theory and practice of munitions manufacture, to be attended by this company whose role was to conduct the required experiments in a research programme pre-determined by the Committee'.[65] So the Company took the form of a munitions school, but the system was a closed one since the trainees remained within it afterwards. Thus 'knowledge remained concentrated within its extremely limited number of personnel, and did not spread throughout the corps where expertise in munitions is essential'.[66] Under the aegis of a *Commission d'artifices*, founded specifically at the request of the Minister in July 1818, training went on alongside a return to research, but only within the means available in Toulouse. Apart from the President (Lieutenant-Colonel Etchégoyen), the Commission was composed of six officers from the artillery regiments in Toulouse, four officers from the Company of Artificers and Carny the professor of mathematics at the regimental artillery school in Toulouse. It was organised in three sections: the first was responsible for 'the course on theoretical pyrotechnics', the second, made up of officers from the Company, headed by Jacquier, prepared the practical part of the course; the third, the largest, had the task of setting up 'a programme of experiments to be conducted at the *Ecole des artificiers* with the aim of improving specified military devices'.[67] However, as was generally the case for this type of military commission, the work was constantly hindered by petty details about duties, which led to the dissolution of the commission after only eight months, when its president was moved with his regiment. In his final report, he did not fail to point out the negative effects of this kind of working structure.[68] Thus the Toulouse period represents a relative failure to normalise and institutionalise munitions teaching and research.

The narrow scope of the training programme within a company that was too independent of its parent corps, and the difficulties encountered in the workings of a commission that was conversely too lacking in autonomy, revealed the limitations of this type of organisation.

The appointment of a polytechnician (Munier) to the command of the Company of Artificers,[69] its transfer to a location near the regimental artillery school in Metz,[70] its restructuring on a basis that was more open and more closely integrated with the artillery, and the reconstitution of the munitions commission, provided a fresh impetus from 1821. Indeed, the company's recruitment policy changed in August of that year, and from then on each artillery regiment sent four gunners to it for a two-year period. This rota system was to have two consequences, one internal and the other external: the unit was becoming clearly like a teaching establishment – a training council was even set up,[71] and secondly the teaching could then be spread across the regiments. In parallel, the *Commission des artifices de guerre* was reconstituted on 10 May 1821 near the regimental artillery school in Metz, with Colonel Aymar at its head. It included Jacquier and Munier, the professor of mathematics at the artillery school (Bergery), and two other officers who were polytechnicians.[72] Like the Toulouse commission, it concentrated first of all on the preparation of a course of instruction, but it also resumed experimental research along the lines of the Meudon programmes. Above all, it was responsible for setting up and carrying out programmes of experiments ordered by the King in 1822, and by the Ministry in the following year. However, it initially conducted experiments on the resistance of cast iron for hollow cannon-balls: the commissioned experiments were not conducted until 1825 within the improved structure that the new *Ecole centrale de pyrotechnie* would from now on provide.[73]

In fact, while the recruitment policy of the *Compagnie d'artificiers*, implemented in 1821, had been deemed 'beneficial as it provides the company with men capable of becoming good artificers, and the corps with non-commissioned officers trained in this branch of the service',[74] it had quickly become apparent that 'such an institution was not perfect, and that a totally isolated structure incapable of evolving was not guaranteed to last'.[75] Only the establishment of a real school could guarantee the stability needed. On 19 May 1824, Louis XVIII founded the *Ecole centrale de pyrotechnie militaire*, to be located near a regimental school.[76] Under the authority of the commanding officer of this regimental school, the Director had to be a field officer, assisted by a captain, two first lieutenants and four master-artificers,[77] while recruitment from the ranks of the artillery regiments, adapted to the system of instruction, was retained. The same regulation put an end to the *Compagnie d'artificiers*, now of no further use. Its officers provided the staff for the new school, starting with its commander, Munier, who became Deputy Director.[78] The main body of pupils (29 out of 35) during the first year came from the Company. The total prescribed number to be recruited in line with the new recruitment policy was not reached until the second year. The 18 September 1824 regulation added a third year, and soon only pupils in that year were authorised to become chief artificers. The exercise of the prerogative to recruit, so dear to the *Ecole polytechnique* and the subsequent higher engineering schools, was thus extended to elementary technical education. Above all, the 18 September 1824 regulation altered in a major way the aims of the school by giving it very explicitly a research and experimentation role, to be accentuated by practice. It was here that in subsequent years the Paixhans guns and shells, which were to revolutionise naval warfare, were developed, and also the new Bedford war rocket system. Bearing the legacy of the Revolution and Empire commissions, the *Ecole centrale de pyrotechnie* became the main centre for experimental research on the subject until the Franco-Prussian War of 1870–71, when it was transferred to Bourges where its predecessor, the 1815 *Compagnie d'artificiers*, had originated, and where it would continue to function for another century.

So, over and above the real and the symbolic importance of the mobilisation of scientists in Year II, and of its success in terms of national defence, it should be noted that this brief phenomenon not only lay behind the reorganisation of the teaching of science and engineering in France, as Biot had already emphasised in 1803 far more so than the modernisation of industry, but that it was a crucial moment in the establishment of a policy of invention and state-controlled research:

> The scientists who had brought about such great things enjoyed an enormous influence. It was a well-known fact that the Republic owed its safety and its existence to them. They took advantage of this favourable moment to provide France with this enlightened superiority which had enabled it to triumph over its enemies. This was the origin of the *Ecole polytechnique*. The facts were too obvious for the usefulness of science and engineering to be doubted.[79]

In part, having started from practical reforms, developed between the Seven Years' War and the Revolution, tried out as an emergency measure when the country was threatened, and during the mobilisation of Year II, this policy was still in its infancy when implemented and normalised by the successive governments and regimes that came to power between the Thermidorian Convention and the Restoration. No doubt losing force and conviction after the drama of the Revolution, it gained in terms of ordered structure (rather than in effectiveness) and became embedded in the complex of committees, laboratories and schools that made up the administrative identity of the French military scene in the nineteenth century. However if, in normal times, the image of the scientist as *deus ex machina* gave way in these more permanent institutions to the polytechnic officer-scientist responsible for the day-to-day management of research programmes, it remains nevertheless, as part of the tradition of the Republic, a necessary last resort in times of national crisis.

Notes

1 Jeanette Short and David Williams translated this chapter from French.
2 J.A. Chaptal, *De l'industrie française* (Paris, Renouard, 1819), in L. Bergeron (ed.), (Paris, Imprimerie nationale, 1993), pp. 267–9.
3 As a scientist, industrialist and politician, Chaptal knew the subject well. He himself participated in this mobilisation of Republican science before taking part in the normalisation process as a teacher and minister. In fact, as a chemistry professor in the Languedoc, and as a pioneer of the chemical industry in Montpellier in the last years of Louis XVI's reign and of the *ancien régime*, he was an Inspector for the collection of saltpetre in the Mediterranean departments under the Revolutionary government of Year II (despite being implicated with the Federalists), a national agent for saltpetre and gunpowder, and a professor at the *Ecole polytechnique* under the Thermidorian Convention in 1794–95, a Home Secretary between 1801 and 1804 under the Consulate, a member of the Senate between 1804 and 1814, under the Empire, then a minister of state in charge of agriculture, commerce and industry during the Hundred Days (1815).
4 N. et J. Dhombres, *Naissance d'un nouveau pouvoir: sciences et savants en France, 1793–1824* (Paris, Payot, 1989).
5 See P. Bret, *La Pratique révolutionnaire du progrès technique. De l'institution de la recherche militaire en France, 1775–1825.* (Doctoral thesis, University of Paris I/ Panthéon-Sorbonne, 1994).
6 J.-B. Biot, *Essai sur l'histoire générale des sciences pendant la Révolution française* (Paris. Duprat/Fuchs, An XI-1803).
7 J. Duhem, *Histoire de l'armée aérienne avant le moteur* (Paris, Nouvelles édition latines, 1964). pp. 252–5; P. Bret, 'L'oeuvre militaire du chimiste et conventionnel Guyton-Morveau: Ebauches d'une conception nouvelle de la recherche en matière d'armement', *Histoire militaire de la Révolution française* (Dijon-Auxonne colloquium, 1988); *Mémoires de la Société pour l'histoire du droit*

et des institutions des anciens pays bourguignons, comtois et romands, 49 (1992), 117–31 (p. 130).

8 M. Crosland, 'Science and the Franco-Prussian War', *Social Studies of Science* 6 (1976), 185–214 (p. 186). On the role of this committee in Berthelot's work, see J. Jacques, *Berthelot, 1827–1907. Autopsie d'un mythe* (Paris, Belin, 1987), pp. 123–45.

9 Y. Roussel, 'L'histoire d'une politique des inventions, 1887–1918', *Cahiers pour l'histoire du CNRS 1939–89* 3 (September 1988), 19–57.

10 G. Pouchet, 'Les sciences pendant la Terreur', *Philosophie positive* (November–December 1873), in J. Guillaume (ed.), *La Révolution française* 30 (1896), 251–77, 333–64.

11 A. Mathiez, 'La mobilisation des savants en l'an II', *Revue de Paris* (1 December 1917), 542–65.

12 C. Richard, *Le Comité du salut public et les fabrications de guerre sous la Terreur* (Paris, Rieder-Société de l'histoire de la Révolution française, 1921). Soon after, part of the memoirs of C.-A. Prieur de la Côte-d'Or was published outlining his relationship with the scientists in the *Section des armes et poudres* ('Révélations sur le Comité du salut public', *Revue bleue* 56 (1918), 76–80, 108–12).

13 See Bret, 'L'oeuvre militaire' and *La Pratique révolutionnaire*, esp. pp. 554–63.

14 Bret, *La Pratique révolutionnaire*, pp. 563–80.

15 Lavoisier's papers show in fact how he dealt with it. See P. Bret (ed.), *Oeuvres de Lavoisier: Correspondance* (Paris, Académie des Sciences, 1997), vol. 7 (1792–94).

16 *Journal des sciences, arts et métiers*. Cit. D. de Place, 'Le Bureau de consultation pour les arts. Paris 1791–1796', *History and Technology* 5 (1988), 139–78 (p. 140).

17 The following were nominated by the Academy of Science: Berthollet, Borda, Bossut (replaced in 1792 by Baumé (resigned 12 May 1794), Brisson, Coulomb, Desmarets (resigned 20 October 1793), Guillot-Duhamel (replaced by Fourcroy in 1792), Lagrange, Laplace, Lavoisier, Leroy, Meusnier (replaced by Pelletier in 1792), Périer, Rochon (replaced by Cousin in 1792), Vandermonde. The following were nominated by other societies: Bourru and Jumelin (Faculté de Médecine), Louis (Académie de Chirurgie: deceased and replaced by Desault, a doctor, in 1792), Hallé (Société Royale de Médecine), Parmentier (Société Royale d'Agriculture), Pelletier (Société royale d'histoire naturelle, replaced by Millin in 1792), Hassenfratz (Société des Annales de chimie), Silvestre (Société philomathique), Droz and Calippe (Société du Point Central) – irregular nomination, immediately replaced by Dumas, a doctor, and Desaudray (Lycée des Arts), Lucotte (Société des artistes réunis, his appointment was questioned and he was forced to withdraw in 1792), Servières, Trouville, Guiraut and Leblanc (Société des inventions et découvertes, known also as the Société des artistes inventeurs). *See* de Place, pp. 143–4.

18 *See* de Place, p. 141.

19 L. Scheler, *Lavoisier et la Révolution française* I: *Le Lycée des arts* (Paris, Hermann, 1957), pp. 13–14; N. and J. Dhombes, pp. 32–3, drew attention to Descremps' *Science sansculottisée*, published in Year II; claiming to deal with the problem

of the popularisation of science, this book is actually concerned with the problem of democratisation.

20 *See* de Place, p. 142.

21 The Bureau owed its survival to the artists who denounced Roland to the Convention as 'a man who thinks he is a walking encyclopaedia and is trying to destroy a public and legal institution'. The people's representatives decided in their favour and increased the Bureau's status.

22 The Bureau's attempt to have Lavoisier freed in the Spring of 1794 reveals a certain harmony between the two groups: the four ex-academicians (Borda, Coulomb, Lagrange, Leroy) are in a minority against the seven non-members of the suppressed Academy who had signed it (Desaudray, Dumas, Hallé, Jumelin, Servières, Silvestre and Trouville). The membership of the Bureau had been reduced by members of its left wing on missions for the revolutionary government (Berthollet, Hassenfratz, Pelletier, Périer, Vandermonde), by resignations (Lucotte, Desmarets, Baumé), by arrests (Lavoisier, Cousin, Guiraut, Millin) and the removal of the ex-aristocrats Borda and Trouville. *See* de Place, p. 145.

23 Lavoisier himself, nominated on 18 September 1793 by Garat, took part in the Commission on aerostatics and in the experiments which followed two weeks later. See J. Langins, 'Hydrogen Production for Ballooning during the French Revolution: an Early Example of Chemical Process Development', *Annals of Science* 40 (1983), 531–58; Bret, 'Recherche scientifique, innovation technique et conception tactique d'une arme nouvelle: l'aérostation militaire 1793–1799', in J.P. Charnay (ed.), *Lazare Carnot ou le savant citoyen* (Paris, Presses de l'Université de Paris-Sorbonne, 1990), pp. 429–51; 'La mise en place humaine et industrielle de l'aérostation militaire (1794–1796). Essai de géographie technologique d'une mobilisation', *Révolution française* (Paris, CTHS, 1991), pp. 439–66.

24 '[Prieur] gathered around himself several men of rare talent, almost all of them were either members of the Academy of Science or became members later on. They were first of all the celebrated Monge, Berthollet, Vandermonde, Fourcroy, Guyton-Morveau (the last two being members of the Convention), Hassenfratz, a mining engineer, and Adet, ambassador and (after August 1813) senior counsellor at the *Cour des comptes*, and other scientists and craftsmen, as needed. Within the Committee for Public Safety, they formed another committee, of which Prieur was the common factor, passing to the latter, the opinions and orders of the first, and reporting to the former on the latter's results and requests' (Prieur de la Côte-d'Or).

25 See L. Hugueney, *Les Clubs dijonnais sous la Révolution, leur rôle politique et économique* (Dijon 1905). For a preliminary analysis of this network see Bret, 'L'oeuvre militaire', pp. 121–5; *La Pratique révolutionnaire*, pp. 175–83.

26 For example, in August 1793, Guyton received the official report on the experiments conducted as part of an artillery programme, and in January 1794, on behalf of the Committee for Public Safety he invited Dizé, a chemist, to present a report to the committee on the method used in Franciade to produce soda artificially. *See* Bret, 'Une tentative d'exploitation militaire de la recherche en chimie: Berthollet et la poudre de muriate oxygéné de potasse 1787–1794', in M. Goupil (ed.), *Lavoisier et la Révolution chimique* (Palaiseau,

SABIX-Ecole polytechnique, 1992), pp. 195–238 (p. 207); A. Pillas and J.A.-F. Balland, *Le Chimiste Dizé, sa vie, ses travaux, 1764–1852* (Paris, 1906), p. 8.

27 L.-E. Missinne, 'Un pédagogue bourguignon: Joseph Jacotot, 1770–1840', *Annales de Bourgogne* 36 (1964), 5–43.

28 See below, note 32. 'Jacques-Pierre Champy (1744–1816), successeur de Lavoisier à la Régie des Poudres et salpêtres, membre de l'Institut de l'Egypte', *Scientifiques et sociétés pendant la Révolution et l'Empire* (Paris, CTHS, 1990), pp. 177–201.

29 Bret, 'The Organization of Gunpowder Production in France (1775–1830)', in B.J. Buchanan, (ed.), *Gunpowder. The History of an International Technology* (Bath, Bath University Press, 1996), pp. 261–74; P. Barbier, 'Pierre Jacotot (1756–1821), professeur de collège à Dijon, bibliothécaire de l'Ecole centrale des travaux publics', *SABIX. Bulletin de la Société des amis de la Bibliothèque de l'Ecole polytechnique* 20 (January 1999), 17–38; Bret, 'La conservation de l'utilité journalière du jardin botanique: l'apothicaire Jacques Tartelin (1748–1823) et le premier jardin de Dijon', in J.L. Fischer (ed.), *Le Jardin entre science et représentation* (Paris, CTHS, 1999), pp. 91–109.

30 See J. Langins, *La République avait besoin de savants. Les débuts de l'Ecole polytechnique: l'Ecole centrale des travaux publics et les cours révolutionnaires de l'an III* (Paris, Belin, 1987).

31 Chaussier also had professional links with Guyton as he was his assistant on the chemistry course in the Dijon Academy from 1781, and was his successor in 1790. Cf. W.A. Smeaton, 'Guyton de Morveau's course of chemistry in the Dijon Academy', *Ambix* 9 (1961), 53–69. Champy also deputised for Guyton in these lectures.

32 Guyton and Champy together ran a factory for the production of artificial nitrates outside Dijon, a coal mine and a glass works in Saint-Bérain-sur-Dheune. See Bret, 'Champy'; A.C. Déré and J. Dhombres, 'Economie portuaire, innovation technique et diffusion restreinte: les fabriques de soude artificielle dans la région nantaise (1777–1815)', *Sciences et techniques en perspective* 22 (1992), 1–176; E. Grison, 'Hassenfratz, Carny et Lavoisier dans la compétition pour la fabrication de la soude artificielle en 1790', *History and Technology* 10 (1993), 179–97.

33 Berthollet's influence is clear, or at least highly probable, in the appointments of Welter (see below, note 39), of Bonjour (his former assistant in the Duc d'Orléans' circle), who went from the Admiralty to the *Agence des poudres et salpêtres,* of Leblanc (another former protégé of the Duc d'Orléans, and the fourth Director of the Gunpowder Agency, and of Descroisilles (his counterpart in Rouen), another temporary Inspector for saltpetre. As for Chaptal, he was no doubt involved in recruiting Dorthès, Fournier and Lenormand from the Montpellier area who were responsible for the collection of saltpetre during the Revolution. All these key people in the networks (Guyton, Monge, Berthollet, Fourcroy) were either collaborating with the chemical revolution led by Lavoisier, at least from 1787, or its strong supporters (Chaptal), and regular contributors to the *Annales de chimie.*

34 J.-M. Raymond-Latour, *Souvenirs d'un oisif* (Lyon/Paris, 1836), vol. 1, p. 243. Raymond is wrong about the role of Fourcroy at the time of his appointment: Fourcroy then had a seat in the *Convention* and worked at the Weapons Section, but he did not join the Committee for Public Safety until 15 fructidor of Year II. A. Kuscinski, *Dictionnaire des Conventionnels* (Paris, Société de l'his-

toire de la Révolution française et Rieder, 1919), p. 267, also believes Fourcroy to be responsible for the conscription of Darcet and Chaptal in order to save them, although Chaptal only refers to letters received from Carnot, Prieur and Berthollet, see Chaptal, *Mes Souvenirs sur Napoléon* (Paris, Plon-Nourrit, 1893), p. 42.

35 On academic commissions, see Bret, 'La prise de décision académique: procédures et pratiques de choix et d'expertise à l'Académie Royale des Sciences', in E. Brian and C.D.-Douyère (eds), *Règlement, usages et science dans la France de l'absolutisme* (Colloque du tricentenaire du *Règlement, usages de 1699, June 1999*, Paris, Tec & Doc), forthcoming.

36 See Bret, 'Une tentative d'exploitation militaire'; C.C. Gillispie, 'Science and Secret Weapons Development in Revolutionary France 1792–1804: a documentary history', *Historical Studies in Physical Sciences* 23 (1992), 35–152; Bret, *La Pratique révolutionnaire*, pp. 149–60.

37 Particularly Lafitte-Clavé, a General Inspector for military engineering, and Fourcroy who replaced Marat in the Convention.

38 Decree of the 29th day of the first month Year II (Archives nationales, AF II 220, doss. 1896, n. 3).

39 Archives nationales, AF II, doss. 1896, n. 12 and n. 30.

40 Berthollet probably had a say in the choice of the latter two as he was certainly following the matter very closely. Several minutes of meetings recorded by him relate to the delivery of shells and the replacement of Pain. Berthollet knew Welter, who had already worked on bleaching with potassium chloride water which he himself had perfected, and had him appointed as a chemistry assistant at the *Ecole polytechnique*.

41 Welter's assistants were Bouvier, a chemist and Dubois, his laboratory assistant. Cf. Bret, 'Une tentative d'exploitation militaire', p. 234.

42 Decrees of 4 floréal and 29 prairial (Archives nationales, AF II 220, doss. 1896, n. 27 and n. 60). Battelier also supervised the nearby centre for aerostatics after Guyton's departure for the army at Sambre-et-Meuse.

43 Decree of 23 floréal (Archives nationales, AF II 220, doss. 1896, n. 36).

44 Archives nationales, AF II 220, doss. 1896, n. 46 and n. 37.

45 Fabre, 'Rapport sur les boulets incendiaires, présenté au général Marmont' (16 pluviôse Year XII). Service historique de l'armée de terre, Vincennes, Artillerie (henceforth SHAT/Artil.), 6.f.4 doss. Fabre.

46 The *Conseil d'instruction* ordered him to retrieve 'substances and data stored at Meudon' from the Keeper of the *cabinet de chimie*, Bouillon–Lagrange (Arch. Polytechnique, procès-verbaux du Conseil d'instruction, 28 floréal Year IV; Bret, 'Une tentative d'exploitation militaire', p. 213.

47 'Renseignements sur l'établissement à Meudon des épreuves de machines de guerre pour le service de terre et de mer', 8 nivôse [Year VIII] and the report to the Minister for War, messidor Year VII (SHAT/Artil., 4.h.1/7; 'procès-verbal des épreuves' (SHAT/Artil., 6.f.4, doss. Fabre).

48 Report to the Minister for War, messidor Year VII (SHAT/Artil., 4.h.1/7) and 'procès-verbal des épreuves' (SHAT/Artil., 6.f.4, doss. Fabre).

49 Minutes (SHAT/Artil., 6.f.4, doss. Fabre) and Rosily to Bernadotte, Paris, 21 messidor Year VII (SHAT/Artil., 4.h.1/7).

50 Pain to Rosily, Meudon 19 messidor Year VII (SHAT/Artil., a.147 and 4.h.1/7).

51   Rosily to Bernadotte, Paris 21 messidor Year VII (SHAT/Artil., 4.h.1/7 and 2.a.147). See Gillispie, 'Science and Secret Weapons Development'.

52   C. de La Jonquière, *L'Expédition d'Egypte, 1798–1801* (Paris, Lavauzelle, 1899–1907), vol. 1, p. 354; Bret, 'Une tentative d'exploitation militaire', p. 224.

53   This argument is closely documented in the case of the Chevalier incendiary rockets in 1798.

54   Report from Andréossy to Berthier, 15 nivôse Year VIII. The centre for aerostatics in Meudon, itself on the point of closure as Conté and Coutelle had left for Egypt, and as the companies had been suppressed a few months earlier, was also to disappear soon afterwards.

55   In his paper 'Organiser l'expertise: expérimenter, juger et jauger en matière d'artillerie', the author returns to the question of rivalry between the commissions and the committees in the corps at the colloquium on 'The Impossible Settlement: Problems of a New Order in post-Revolutionary France', organised by Judith A. Miller and Howard G. Brown at Emory University, Atlanta (12–13 November 1999).

56   Bret, *La Pratique révolutionnaire*, pp. 200–6.

57   On Napoleon's attitude, *see* Bret, 'Napoléon et les technologies militaires nouvelles: essai d'analyse à partir des exemples de l'aérostation et de la fusée de guerre', *Revue de l'Institut Napoléon* 148 (1987), 446–60.

58   For the French programme on war rockets, see Bret, *La Pratique révolutionnaire*, pp. 463–509; *La Fusée de guerre en France pendant la période révolutionnaire et impériale (1792–1815)*. Master's thesis for the University of Provence, Aix-en-Provence, 1971.

59   Ibid. After the bombing of Copenhagen (1807), Schumacher had developed a Danish system, and had been the first to equip the rockets with explosive charges. *See* also Bret, 'Imaginaire, espionnage, trahison et coopération: stratégies de conquête du secret dans la recherche militaire (1780–1850)', in A. Guillerme (ed.), *De La Diffusion des sciences à l'espionnage scientifique et industriel (XVIe-XXe siècles)* (Paris, ENS Editions-SFHST, 1999) *Cahiers d'histoire et de philosophie des sciences*, 47, pp. 53–66.

60   Mass production had been started in Toulon in 1811 for the war in Spain where plants were also set up in Seville and Tortosa, while others were set up in 1813 in Hamburg and Danzig. In fact, only a few rockets were fired against Cadiz and against the allied troops around Hamburg.

61   For example in Strasbourg in 1810 and 1813, *see* Bret, *La Pratique révolutionnaire*, pp. 525–6.

62   SHAT/Artil., register of Central Committee reports, 22 April 1815, p. 322. The report is transcribed in Bret, *La Fusée de guerre en France*, pp. 80–81. On the Company of Artificers, see Bret, *La Pratique révolutionnaire*, pp. 526–9.

63   SHAT/Artil., register of Central Committee reports, 22 April 1815, p. 322.

64   M. Susane, 'Les fusées de guerre', *Mémoires de l'Académie impériale de Metz (1862–1863)*, 44 (1864), 203–56 (p. 248); J. Challéat, *L'Artillerie de terre en France pendant un siècle. Histoire technique 1816–1919* (Paris, Lavauzelle, 1933), vol. 1, p. 88.

65   Evain to the President of the Committee, 14 April 1818 (SHAT/Artil., 2.b.2/34, doss. 1807).

66   Desmazières, 'Notice sur l'Ecole de Pyrotechnie militaire', Metz, 17 October 1846 (SHAT/Artil., 2.a.129/1).

67 'Rapport sur la situation des travaux de la Commission d'artifice créée par ordre du jour du 19 juillet 1818', Toulouse 13 March 1819 (SHAT/Artil., 2.b.2/ 34, doss. 1807). On the *Commission d'artifices, see* Bret, *La Pratique révolutionnaire*, pp. 529–31.

68 Nevertheless, Dussaussoy was made responsible for the experiments on war rocket shells set up by the third section.

69 Munier had already established, during the siege of Danzig in 1813, a production plant for war rockets, and had been in command of a temporary company of artificers.

70 Metz was the town in which the *Ecole d'application de l'artillerie et du génie* was located, which trained officers from the *Ecole polytechnique* and lower-level regimental schools such as those in Toulouse, Strasbourg and so on.

71 Under the supervision of the Commander General of the School of Artillery, the Training Council was made up of the four company officers and the non-commissioned officers responsible for the details of practical training (Colonel Desmazières, 'Notice sur l'Ecole de pyrotechnie militaire', Metz 17 October 1846 (SHAT/Artil., 2.a.129/1).

72 Composition in July 1823.

73 Munier, 'Rapport sur les expériences relatives aux projectiles creux faites en exécution des ordres de Son Excellence le Ministre de la Guerre', Metz, 1 February 1826 (SHAT/Artil., 4.d.19).

74 From the Minister to the Director of the *Ecole royale d'artillerie* in Strasbourg, Paris, 18 October 1823 (SHAT/Artil., 2.a.129/1).

75 Desmazières, 'Notice sur l'Ecole de pyrotechnie'.

76 The founding ordinance is reproduced in G.H. Cotty, *Supplément au Dictionnaire de l'artillerie* (Paris, Anselin, 1832), pp. 176–8. On this school, *see* Bret, *La Pratique révolutionnaire*, pp. 531–4 and 'La recherche expérimentale à l'Ecole de Metz', in B. Belhoste and A. Picon (eds), *L'Ecole d'application de l'artillerie et du génie de Metz (1802–1870). Enseignement et recherches* (Paris, Musée des Plans-reliefs, 1996), pp. 50–60.

77 It was possible for the Minister to send other 'supernumerary' lieutenants there. In 1825, Munier was the captain, the lieutenants attached to the *Ecole* were Lechevalier and Beausire, the 'supernumerary' lieutenants being Moreau, Jacques, Didion and Rodolphe. The latter replaced Beausire in the following year.

78 A second lieutenant was also left as a supernumerary officer at the school. The non-commissioned officers of the company had been allowed to compete with the Chief-Artificers from the regiments for the four posts of Master-Artificer provided for the new institution (art. 7). Cailly, 'Note sur l'Ecole centrale de pyrotechnie militaire', Metz, 2 February 1831 (SHAT/Artil., 2.a.129/1).

79 Biot, *Essai*, p. 58.

13
Avant-garde aristocrats? French Noblemen, Patents, and the Modernisation of France (1815–48)

Joël Felix

One of the most important consequences of Sieyès's political master-piece, *What is the Third Estate?* (1788) was to expel the nobility from the construction of the French nation and, as a corollary, from the history of modern France. It is true that the nobility, and especially its deputies to the Estates-General, did manage to ostracise itself and become the symbol of the opposition to the new citizenship and the principles that emerged in 1789. But despite these bitter disputes and whatever the material damage done to the privileged élite on the night of 4 August and thereafter, the concept of a nobility survived the law of 20 June 1790 which abolished noble and chivalric titles. This survival is not only a consequence of Napoleon's decision to distinguish an élite among the *notables* who were granted titles, nor of the Charter of 1814 which recognised the Empire's titles alongside those of the *ancien régime* and gave the King the power to create his own élite of new nobles and hereditary peers. In fact, as soon as titles were suppressed, a large majority of the noble deputies in the Constituent Assembly protested against this and expressed the view that in its very essence the nobility did not obey laws, not even the King's laws, but was a natural and hereditary distinction that could not be suppressed by the legislator.

This cultural definition of the nobility has been recently reinforced in two major studies of the nobility in nineteenth-century France. David Higgs defines the post-Revolutionary nobles as 'similar to an ethnic group' or 'a self-perceived group of people who hold in common a set of traditions not shared by the others with whom they are in contact'.[1] In her extensive study on the nobility of Franche-Comté, Claude-Isabelle Brelot concluded rather in the same way:

The aristocrats of Franche-Comté ... withstood the pressures of post-Revolutionary society by reinventing the idea of nobility. Forced to do so by the civil disappearance of the Second Estate ... they affirmed their symbolic worth of their family fortunes and sumptuous castles.[2]

This cultural approach to the nobility is obviously useful for it makes it possible to account for the coexistence in the nineteenth century of a 'pre-industrial and pre-bourgeois' society in which the noble family retains the 'complicity that lay behind hierarchical views' and the competing egalitarian values of a 'new urban society' that would not always reject the power of attraction of the noble's lifestyle. However, this view of a persisting *ancien régime* remains partly unsatisfactory because it creates a new species, the highly adaptable *homo nobilis,* which does not fully account for the individuals and their differences in terms of their family history, their wealth, their occupation, their religious and political beliefs in relation to the evolution of the society of their time.

The aim of this chapter is to argue that the nobility, as a small social group, provides a valuable basis not only for the understanding of the nobility in the nineteenth century, but for the evolution of French society as a whole. The chapter will study an aspect of the nobility which has been largely ignored and not systematically researched: the involvement of former *gentry* in the economic modernisation of France, and especially their role in the process of technical development between 1815 and 1848. By its power of destruction and innovation, the French Revolution was a fundamental turning-point in the field of technical inventions. On the one hand, the Revolution created new scientific establishments, such as the *Ecole polytechnique,* and with a new system of patents (7 and 25 May 1791) it organised a new legal framework, derived from the English model, which was to guarantee the rights of inventors to protect and take full advantage of their inventions. Yet, the statistics of patents suggest that the immediate consequences of Revolutionary wars were to put a halt to the development of new inventions, and to abandon the fierce competition with England. The number of patents taken out in 1791 and 1792 was about 30 per year. This figure dropped to five a year between 1793 and 1796. Only in the Year IX would the number of patents rise to the figure of 1791 to stabilise between 50 and 90 until 1815.[3]

This increase in new patents was partly the result of Napoleon's encouragement of the development of the French economy. Furthermore, if British travellers had taken advantage of the Peace of Amiens to see how France had changed since 1789, Frenchmen had also crossed the Channel to visit England and brought back with them the certainty of the 'economic backwardness' of their country. Whatever the impact of Napoleon's industrialising strategy, the peace of 1814–15 was a new dawn in the history of French modernisation. Peace afforded the opportunity to restore and develop the French economy in order to compete with England. This desire to boost the economic growth of France could be seen in many sectors. The most striking is probably again in the statistics of patents. In 1816, the number of patents had reached 100 for the first time; with 217 new inventions the number of patents had doubled in 1824. The figure rose to 452 patents in 1829, 800 in 1837 and more than 2000 in 1840. Of course, it should be said that a large proportion of new patents, such as a wire wig or *patins nageoires mobiles* [portable water roller skates] to walk on rivers, never entered the golden book of inventions or the history of techniques.[4] Furthermore, inventions were not always protected by a patent, but by secrecy. Yet, the amazing growth in new patents reflects the belief in the virtues of the industrial modernisation of France sustained somehow by the frenzy of inventors who hoped to become millionaires overnight. Balzac, who was one of them, had perfectly depicted in *César Birotteau* the story of such men who dreamed of making a fortune from selling magic potions to restore hair.

To many, the amazing movement of technical innovations – it surpassed the United Kingdom at the same time[5] – seemed to be a mystery: 'The number of patents for inventions and imports issued last year (1840) is greater than it has ever been; it has risen to 1305[6] whereas it was only 539 in 1839; there is no obvious explanation for this increasing proportion.'[7] Four years later, a specialist saw in this trend a good reason to resist the temptation to prohibit the introduction of foreign machinery in France:

> Isn't it immediately obvious that exports of French machines are increasing daily to such an extent that they have almost doubled in two years from 1840 to 1842, while foreign steam engine imports for the French market have diminished by 80 per cent in the same period...this two way process is manifest proof of the progress of our constructors and of the possibilities for them...to withstand competition beyond the home market.[8]

Official statistics revealed that the total exports of French machines had doubled in value between 1840 (2.9 million) and 1841 (4.5 million) and represented in 1842 90 per cent of all foreign machines imported into England. At the same time, the value of steam engines imported by France had dropped from 1.2 million francs in 1840 to 0.64 million francs by 1841 and 0.28 million francs in 1842. As a consequence, the balance of exports and imports became positive in 1841 and 1842.

From the Restoration, the nobility played a significant role in the process of the modernisation of France. Abandoned iron mills were rebuilt and extended with additional furnaces. The creation of Decazeville by Duc Decazes is probably the best example of the Restoration and new developments of the iron and steel industry from the 1820s. This movement of reconstruction, extension and modernisation can be easily analysed in many regions of France. The *département* of Haute-Saône is typical of the national trend. There the nobility owned 31 iron mills and over 51 furnaces and almost all the new buildings were constructed in the first half of the nineteenth century.[9] As a consequence, new mining concessions were sought after by the noble owners of iron mills or by landlords. The nobility also invested its money in the new joint-stock companies in a proportion that varied over the years but which was not less than 15 per cent of all the shares issued between 1815 and 1848. The involvement of the nobility in the capital of limited partnership companies is more difficult to evaluate. Detailed research in the archives of the *tribunaux de commerce* [trade courts] would show that the nobility was also very active in financing new companies. A study of limited partnership in the Côte d'Or revealed for instance that 24 per cent of all the money invested in new *sociétés en commandité* [limited partnerships] between 1830 and 1850 came from noble families.[10] Of course, not all nobles invested in industry for not every family was rich enough, nor did they all own before 1789 a mine, a factory or an iron mill that was abandoned during the Revolution. But altogether, there were probably several hundred former gentry who were personally or financially participating in the industrial development of their country while a larger number of others tried hard to modernise another crucial sector: agriculture.

Between 1815 and 1848, the nobility took out at least 360 patents of the 23 000 patents granted by the government, or 1.5 per cent of the total.[11] This figure may seem very low even if one considers that the nobility represented no more than 1 per cent of the population on the eve of the Revolution (200 000 individuals) or some 15 000–20 000 families in the nineteenth century.[12] By comparison, the 23 000 patents should be compared to the 100 000 *notables* who formed the élite of the First Empire and the Restoration, the 200 000–300 000 enfranchised voters of the July Monarchy who paid a tax of 200 francs, or the

160000 *grands notables* who paid taxes over 1000 francs in 1840. It should nevertheless be pointed out that the 23 000 patents consisted of four types: new patents, patents for imports, additions or improvements to old patents and expired patents. For instance, during the years 1831 to 1840, the new patents (4442) represented only 58 per cent of the total of 7394. At that time, noblemen took out a total of 203 patents (2.5 per cent), that is 160 new patents (3.6 per cent), 108 additions (5 per cent) and 35 renewals (8.6 per cent). These approximate figures show that the noble inventor was not representative of the nobility as a whole and that the bourgeoisie was far more involved in the process of invention. Yet, the important question is not to decide if the nobility was more or less industrious than the bourgeoisie but if the noble inventor can be identified as a distinct figure among the nobility.

Even if the logarithmic scale graph shown in Figure 13.1 compares dozens and thousands, the similarities of the two curves of patents taken out during the July Monarchy by the bourgeois and the nobles gives the impression that the noble inventor existed more as an inventor than as a former noble.

This view is confirmed by the analysis of the individual noble patentees. Altogether the 363 patents were taken out by only 202 nobles. This figure is not so small if one considers that according to Isabelle Brelot, one single province of France, the Franche-Comté containing three *départements*, had no more than 500 families – or 2500 individuals – in 1789 and fewer than 450 lineages in 1814. It also suggests that the business of inventing was not always an isolated activity amidst more

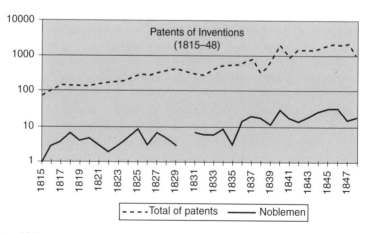

Figure 13.1

traditional noble duties. Nearly half of the noble inventors took out at least two patents and 21 more than five patents. Furthermore, the noble inventors were not newcomers. They were mostly heirs of families which could trace back their noble origins to the sixteenth century and even before.[13] Among these inventors, only 20 had received titles from the Empire, or were ennobled by the Restoration.

A brief survey of nobles' patents finally reveals that the inventions of the nobility were mainly in the key sectors of the Industrial Revolution – textiles (30), iron and steel (27), mines (5), chemistry (24), steam engines (18), transport (35) – alongside agriculture (29), paper (17), gas (9), sugar (7), hydraulic machines (10), clothing (9), the timber industry (6) and earthenware (9). As a consequence, the 200 nobles who took out at least one patent between 1815 and 1848 seem to be fairly representative of the inventor in general, and of the process of industrialisation in France at the time. In that sense, they provide a good starting point to investigate the relationship between the nobility and the modernisation of France and also the broader historical question of the impact of inventions on economic growth and the relations of both these aspects to political attitudes.[14]

Why did noblemen invent? Obviously because some of them were educated professional scientists. François Ajasson de Grandsaigne (1802–45), who took out five patents, was known as a distinguished Latinist and Hellenist scholar who had developed a speciality in natural sciences. He was a member of the Museum of Natural History, where he worked with Cuvier, and was later appointed a member of the *Académie des inscriptions et belles-lettres*. Ajasson not only took out patents: he also published numerous books, among which was a translation of Pliny's *Natural History*. He also edited a *Bibliothèque populaire, ou l'instruction mise à la portée de toutes les classes et de toutes les intelligences* [Popular Editions or Education made available to all Classes and all Minds] written by the most distinguished scientists of his time.[15] His family provided other scientists such as his brother, François-Claude, who studied at the *Ecole polytechnique*, and his son Stéphane who was science post-graduate. Comte Charles de Laboullaye-Marillac (1771–1824) was also a member of the scientific élite of nineteenth-century France. He was director and professor at the *Ecole de Teinturerie des Gobelins* [the Gobelins School of Dyeing]. It is not by chance that he patented in 1820 new machines for dyeing textiles six years after he had completed a *Mémoire sur les couleurs inaltérables pour la teinture* [Treatise on Fast Colours in Dyeing] at the Institut de France. Other inventors had special scientific knowledge: Scipion Bourguet de Travanet was qualified as a civil engineer or Durand de Monestrol was in 1839 *ingénieur géomètre* [surveyor-engineer] in Brignolles and in 1841 *ingénieur-mécanicien* [mechanical engineer] in Paris. Comte Henri-Catherine-Camille de Ruolz Monchal, who discovered an important technique to galvanize steel and many other metals, was a science graduate, then a chemist.

It has not always been possible to identify the motivation that could have transformed noblemen into inventors, but in 1815 Marquis Claude-François-Dorothée de Jouffroy d'Abbans (1751–1832) was still known as the first man who had propelled a steam boat, the *Peryscaphe*, on the river Saône in 1783.[16] If the experiments of Jouffroy d'Abbans and his difficulties in finding investors were partly to ruin him, one of his sons, Achille-François-Léonor (1785–1859), kept up technical interests in the family. Between 1836 and 1843, he took out five patents for several new machines that he sold in Paris where he was established in 1829 as a trader. Army officers, especially artillery officers, also had the scientific knowledge to develop new technologies. Among others, Comte Barrès du Molard was distinguished for his contribution to the building of long bridges. Most of the noble inventors also developed scientific interests because they owned factories and paper mills such as Henri-Charles-Louis, Comte de Beurges, at Ville-sur-Sceaux, or Auguste-Louis de Maupeou, the latter establishing one of the biggest and most modern paper factories near Paris. Chastellux, Brassier de Buros, Didelot and the Maury de Lapeyrouse brothers were directors of spinning mills, while others were iron masters. Jaquot d'Andelarre had an iron foundry and the marquise de Raincourt owned the Fallon iron foundry. Comte Jules de Castellane (1782–1861) who invented a ventilation system for mines in 1816 had an interest in coal mining and had obtained two concessions, the first in 1824 for the working of a 62 square kilometre coalfield at La Cadière in the Var.

These examples show that the noble inventors were usually well placed to develop new technologies. Marquis Charles de Forbin-Janson was one of the largest sugar producers of the nineteenth century, and had a special interest in improving that industry. Comte Etienne Bernard de Sassenay (1760–1840) was, with other members of the *ancien-régime* nobility, among the most successful entrepreneurs of the Restoration and the July Monarchy. He strove to supply crude zinc for his zinc sheet and roofing material factories in Thierceville-près-Gisors. In 1840, Sassenay contracted a lease with Barthold Suermondt, a German banker and philanthropist, to work an establishment in Stolberg, near Aachen, and transform calamine deposits into a marketable commodity, which he successfully accomplished. The Saint-Cricq Casaux family, whose young members had become bankers during the Revolution, invested their money in a ceramic factory at Creil. After having bought up all of their competitors' mills, especially a large factory at Montereau, the Saint-Cricq Company became the largest producer of ceramic and china.[17]

Not all noble inventors were as successful as these men were. But in many cases, the noble inventor was often an entrepreneur or potential manufacturer. The question of the commercial involvement of the nobility and the commercialisation of inventions is illustrated by the statistics of patents taken out by nobles. In the 1830s, noble inventors took out 3 per cent of the new patents but also bought, sold or were financially involved in 6 per cent of all the patents lapsing. A good example of the entrepreneurial activity of the nobility can be found in the case of Baron Alviset de Maisières who had invented an atmospheric machine. With his friend the Baron Roujoux de Buxeuil, he bought the patent from Jalabert, an engineer in Paris, that they commercialised jointly. In 1835, Comte de La Garde-Messence established a company with Liénard, a Parisian merchant, in order to manufacture New Zealand linen known as *phormium tenax* for which he had taken a patent of importation. Comte de Beaurepaire, who developed an interest in baking, set up with two other inventors, Delacroix and Detrimont, a commercial company De Beaurepaire & Co., whose aim was to establish a mechanised bakery in Paris. Among others, Vicomte de Barrès du Molard, who has already been mentioned, sold his concession to build a bridge in Valence to the famous Jules Seguin, one of the great entrepreneurs of the nineteenth century. But Barrès did not abandon his project to build an underground aqueduct to provide Marseilles with water. To this end, he founded a commercial company, Barrès & Co., and obtained credit of 20 million francs from the Parisian bankers Martin, Didier & Co.

Ancien régime nobles would sometimes combine their technical skills, their fortunes and their occupation to manufacture their inventions. Baron de Bourgoing, son of an ambassador and *Baron de l'Empire,* was an ambassador, *Pair de France* and *Sénateur de l'Empire*. He invented a new technique, still known as *litophanie*, which made it possible to print designs on earthenware. His associate was Baron du Tremblay, grandson of a Parisian magistrate at the *Chambre des Comptes* and son of a director of the *Caisse d'amortissement* who received the title of *Baron de l'Empire* and of the Restoration. Du Tremblay carved out a career as an *inspecteur des finances* and was elected mayor of Rubelles, the old family fief. There, near Melun, Bourgoing received financial help from the wealthy du Tremblay to manufacture his invention. Bourgoing also took full advantage of his successive diplomatic posts to sell his patent in various European countries, especially in Germany where his invention was manufactured and his products became fashionable. After several years, both du Tremblay and Bourgoing experienced technical difficulties in further developing their products. They decided to seek a scientist who would have the necessary scientific knowledge they lacked. With the help of their new associate, Tirlat, a student of the *Ecole centrale*, they went on to make new discoveries and to take out new patents. The success of such efforts which symbolised the fusion between two members of an old élite and the talents of a bourgeois engineer educated in a prestigious and competitive scientific school was highly praised in the *Journal des usines*: 'thanks to perseverance and outstanding effort for the cause of industry which cannot be praised highly enough...the factory has become very important, its products intended for a wide range of uses are increasingly sought after and are among the most distinguished products of national industry'.[18]

This industrial achievement shows that noble inventors had the will to profit as much as possible from their inventions. Thomas de la Marche de Manneville was such a man. In 1831, the *Société d'encouragement pour l'industrie nationale* awarded him a prize of 4000 francs and a golden medal worth 1000 francs for his new barrel-making machines. He then established a factory in Paris, at the *rue des Amendiers-Popincourt*. After such efforts, Manneville would not accept any form of illegal competition or imitation. He went to court against David, another inventor, who had patented a system of mechanic cooperage for Manneville and 'considered himself the one and only inventor of the operating technique'. Philippe de Girard offers the most striking example of the desire of the nobility to claim the honour and the financial rights of their ability to invent new techniques. His story began in 1810 when Napoleon decided by a decree (7 June 1810) to offer a million francs to the inventor who could build a machine to spin linen. Philippe de Girard eventually devised the new technology, but the political events of 1814 forced him to flee to Austria and to settle later in Poland where he established a factory. At the same time, his associates left France for England where they sold Philippe de Girard's invention. His widow, Marie-Louise de Romagnat, successfully fought a long battle well into the nineteenth century to obtain international recognition for her husband as the inventor of the linen-spinning machine. One of his sons, Jean-Frédéric-Henri de Girard, an army officer living in Warsaw, continued his father's interest. He established textile factories in Poland and took out two patents (in 1832 and 1843) for the importation to France of new machines designed to spin wool. These examples show that the nobility played a small but significant part in the modernisation and economic development of France.

Noble inventors did not even hesitate to operate in the English market. An index of patentees of inventions for the period 1617 to 1851[19] contains for instance the names of several noble inventors such as Jean-Frédéric, Marquis de Chabannes (six patents for different machines between 1799 and 1821), Hyppolite, Comte de Crouy with two patents in 1838 and 1843, the latter for a rotary pump and a rotary steam engine, Comte de Douhet (1850), Comte de Colombier (1844), Comte de Fontainemoreau (51 patents), Comte de La Garde-Messence with two patents (1825 and 1827), baron Heurteloup (1834, 1839, 1841), Louis-Nicolas de Meckenheim, a *maître de forges* in Champagne with two patents, marquis de Bouffet-Montauban, with two patents in 1838, Comte de Prédaval with a patent in 1833 for an engine producing motive-power, and so on. By comparison, the English aristocracy seems to have taken out very few patents at home and almost none in France. The only exceptions were two members of the Cochrane family who took out 28 patents and, of course, the famous scientist-earl, Charles Stanhope.

Many other indicators would show that part of the French nobility was involved in the general process of modernisation of their country. The membership of the *Société d'encouragement pour l'industrie nationale* mixed distinguished members of *ancien régime* families such as the Duc de Mirepoix, Comte de Lasteyrie (member of the *Société royale d'agriculture*), Baron de Montmorency, Baron Séguier (member of the *Académie des sciences* and the *Comité consultatif des arts et métiers*), Comte de Gasparin (member of the *Académie des sciences*), all noblemen who did not seek to sit with the new élite of scientists such as Baron Thénard, Vicomte Héricart de Thury or Baron Delessert. The *Bulletins* testify to their interest and their role in the development of new techniques. Apart from technical notices or descriptions of industrial achievements, the *Bulletins de la Société* also quoted the donations of less prominent noble families who nevertheless wanted to encourage the aims of the Society. Among many other gifts, the marquis d'Argenteuil bequeathed, for instance, the huge sum of 40 000 francs to reward every six years the most useful discovery. In 1829, the Comtesse Jollivet left 80 000 francs to the Society. General d'Aboville, who had lost an arm at Wagram, bequeathed 1000 francs per annum for ten years to reward a manufacturer who was employing men, women or children who were blind or had undergone any sort of amputation.[20]

This last case highlights another aspect of invention. If inventors were obviously committed to business, how far is it possible to link this interest with a form of political modernity? For inventors were not always, or only, industrialists seeking profit. For instance, the aim of the Chastellux family in establishing textile mills in Alsace was to give work to the poor.[21] Ajasson de Grandsagne was also a philanthropist interested in social reform. His new method of teaching people to write was part of his broader commitment to develop education in France. Baron Bourgnon de Layre, Judge at the Royal Court of Poitiers, was especially interested in the improvement of public health. He established new machines to steam-wash clothes on the model of Chaptal in Poitiers hospitals. He was eventually so successful that his steam laundries were adopted by many hospitals and schools in the department of the Vienne, in Tours, Orléans and many other cities. In the case of Bernard de Sassenay, the zinc manufacturer, his industrial activities were most likely part of his political commitment to the Saint-Simonian Utopia.

There is little doubt that the modern nobleman was more likely to be found among inventors who had received a scientific education. For instance, Honoré d'Albert de Luynes was a moderate republican. He began his career in the King's Guards. He resigned in 1825 to take up the position of deputy director of the *Musée des antiquités grecques et égyptiennes*. Luynes, who owned ironworks, also had an interest in metallurgy and took out a patent in 1833. His technical discoveries gained him several awards at various national exhibitions of industry. As a *conseiller général* for Seine-et-Oise he developed social reforming views and made it a law for public works entrepreneurs to create insurance funds for the salaries of their workers. In fact, Luynes was an aristocrat who had a huge fortune and could be a patron as well as a philanthropist, scientist, scholar and politician, altogether one of the *grands notables*. Comte de Castellane was another of those aristocrats whose fortunes survived the Revolution and who accepted with impunity the meritocratic values of the new society. As he had inherited part of the Crozat and Béthune-Sully fortune, he could afford almost anything and indulge in all his fantasies, such as building a private theatre in the garden of his hotel in Paris, and developing an interest in industry. Comte de Forbin-Janson was also able to mix the superfluous and the essential. The superfluous was his membership of the Academy of Marseilles. The essential was the produce of his estates and his intervention, as a deputy, in the political debates about the laws on sugar.

In general, the commitment of nobles to inventions had no real influence on their political ideas, for noble inventors can be split into three categories at the beginning of the Restoration. The first category of inventors included such men as Jouffroy d'Abbans, Comte de Beust or the Dietrich family who had already developed a scientific activity before the French Revolution, sometimes linked with industrial production. The second group of nobles contained individuals who might well have been ready to enter the process of industrialisation in 1789, and who were propelled forward during the French Revolution. This is the case for instance of Bernard de Sassenay and his associate Prevost d'Arlincourt who were anxious to develop their factories. Others, such as Bourguet de Travanet took the opportunity to buy church land to establish a textile factory in the Royaumont abbey. In both cases, the commitment to business remained in the family whose members became active industrialists. In the nineteenth century, the Bourguet de Travanet families were to be found among inventors, directors of iron mills and textile manufacturers. The last group was formed by *emigrés*, or sons of *emigrés*, who experienced a difficult life in foreign climes and developed their skills, taking advantage of the opportunities that were offered to entrepreneurial minds.

This last group of noble inventors came back to France during the Consulate or the Restoration. They often remained attached to the Bourbons and to legitimism, but nevertheless contributed to the economic development of their country. Among these inventors were members of prestigious families known for their opposition to the Revolution, for instance the La Rochejacquelein or the Bouillé families. Guillaume-Ferdinand de Douhet offers a good example of legitimacy and business. As a page to Charles X, Douhet had little alternative but to resign in 1830 and retire to his castle at Sarlan, in the Puy-de-Dôme. There he developed an interest in natural sciences and agricultural chemistry inventing new fertilisers for which he took out five new patents and seven additions between 1843 and 1846, as well as a patent in England in 1850. It is probably he, under the name of Baron de Cussac, who in 1838 bought half of the royalties in the exploitation of Comte Vandermeere's patent for his cars called *l'aérienne* [the airborne]. He also published two plans to build a railway to make the coalfield of Brassac accessible; this was subsequently developed using his plans. These commitments to developing agriculture and the natural wealth of his region did not change his strong political feelings against the Republic. He remained a firm legitimist and sat three times with the extreme Right, in 1849, 1871 and in 1875 when he was elected Senator. His political views did not change his interest in the economic development of his country. In 1872, he published an *Appel aux amis de l'industrie et de l'invention* [Appeal to Friends of Industry and Invention] aimed at reforming the legislation of patents of inventions, and in 1873 promoted the idea of creating a *Grand prix à décerner aux inventeurs de la solution de deux problèmes essentiellement importants pour l'agriculture et l'industrie* [Major Prize to be awarded to the inventor of a solution to two problems critical for Agriculture and Industry].

This link between agriculture and industry is vital in the history of French modernisation. The classical opposition between a traditional rural world and progressive bourgeois cities is not fully valid for France which experienced, at least until the late 1840s, the coexistence of old and new forms of industrial production, as in the competition between coal and charcoal. But the production of silk, straw, sugar beet or leather also accounts for the existence of strong links between the land and manufacturing. For instance in 1846 Gabriel-Henry Hue de Carpinet, Marquis de Bougy, bought Bareg's patent to make paper out of straw and rape. Finally, the progress of agriculture was intrinsic to the growth of the French economy. The noble estates with their experimental farms and agricultural societies played a vital role in the modernisation of agriculture. So, while some members of a family were more interested in industrial developments, others remained on the family estate and tried to improve its productivity. This was the case with the Ruolz family. Both the Vicomte and the Marquis de Ruoltz received the Legion of Honour, the former because he was in the first rank of scientists and industrialists, the latter for his model farm on his estate of Alleret.[22] Members of the Bouillé family also had pursued various activities. François-Marie-Michel, Comte de Bouillé (1779–1853) was the preceptor of the Duc de Bordeaux. Charles, Comte de Bouillé (1816–89) had a major interest in agriculture, and was vice-president of the *Société des agriculteurs de France*. Claude-François-René-Amour-Albert, Vicomte de Bouillé, took out three patents in 1846 and 1847 for devices aimed at preventing derailments, and was director of the *Société de desséchement et de colonisation de la Basse-Camargue*.

This chapter shows that there is no obvious link between a modern economic attitude and a modern political ideology, a link which is part of the myth of the modern successful industrialist freeing the country from the politically and socially conservative landlord. A recent article published by Ludmila Pimenova, seems to confirm this argument. Her study of 168 registers of grievances of the nobility reaches the same conclusion:

...the paragraphs relating to aristocratic businessmen reveal the changes occurring in traditional gentry values. Indeed there is evidence that trade was an honourable profession and a legitimate method for nobles to re-establish or increase their fortunes. Certain registers suggest the ennobling of merchants. Moreover, it was not for the purpose of serving the King or the court that the nobility was permitted to trade, but to ensure its own enrichment and prosperity.[23]

However, it is important to remember that the nobility was a very diverse social group before 1789 and did not conform to a single model. If some nobles considered industry as a way to increase or maintain their wealth, others saw more noble aims in such activities. Baron de Gerando made this clear in his funeral oration for the Duc de Praslin who had been one of the first students to enter the *Ecole polytechnique*:

There is a noble and salutary ambition, that is to be useful to men; there is an honour above all honours, that is to succeed in being useful to them. The Duc de Praslin had that ambition and no other... research was in his opinion the most fruitful of all work... His whole life is like a mirror in which a fine sentiment was reflected, namely that all the wealth of the world and the highest ranks in society can only be considered by those who have access to them as a mission entrusted to them by providence to serve the interests of humanity more efficiently.[24]

For men such as the Duc de Praslin, the commitment to the modernisation of their country was not only a response to Sieyès. It was also a moral and economic answer to the social and political issues of the French Revolution.

Notes

1 David Higgs, *Nobles in Nineteenth-Century France. The Practice of Inegalitarianism* (London, The Johns Hopkins University Press, 1987), p. xii.
2 Claude-Isabelle Brelot, *La Noblesse réinventée. Nobles de Franche-Comté de 1814 à 1870* (2 vols, Paris, Annales littéraires de l'Université de Besançon, 1992), vol. 2, p. 897.

3   Maurice Block, *Statistique de la France comparée avec les Etats d'Europe* (Paris, 1860, 2 vols), vol. 2, p. 109.

4   The 'portable water roller skates' had nevertheless the honour of a technical description in the very serious *Bulletin de la Société de l'encouragment pour l'industrie nationale.*

5   On the statistics of patents in England see B.R. Mitchell and P. Deane, *Abstract of British Historical Statistics* (Cambridge, 1962), pp. 268–9 and Maurice Block, *Statistique de la France comparée avec les Etats d'Europe* (Paris, 1860, 2 vols), vol. 2, p. 109.

6   This figure shows the total of new patents and imports of foreign patents taken out in 1840. If one adds patents for improvements taken out that year for older inventions, the total for 1840 would reach 1932.

7   *Bulletin de la Société d'encouragement pour l'industrie nationale* (1841), p. 217.

8   'Compte-rendu des travaux du comité de l'union des constructeurs de machines', *Journal des économistes*, VIII, December 1843–May 1844, p. 106.

9   Claude-Isabelle Brelot, *La Noblesse*, vol. 1, p. 360.

10 Jean-Marc Cenini, Sociétés industrielles et commerciales de 1830 à 1850 dans le département de la Côte d'Or', *Annales de Bourgogne*, 1975, January–March, pp. 5–31.

11 These results are part of earlier research on the involvement of the nobility in the industrialisation of France between 1815 and 1848. Patents of inventions were published in the *Bulletin des lois*. The identification of nobles is of course a very difficult task for the particle 'de' was never a synonym for nobility. Furthermore, inventors who took out several patents appear sometimes under different names, their patronymic name or the name of their estate. For instance, Comte Dufaure de Montmirail appears in the *Bulletin des lois* as Dufaure, Montmirail, Dufaure de Montmirail. In 1841, 68 inventors had a name with a particle. Among them, only 48 can be attached to an *ancien-régime* noble family. For obvious reasons, I also considered individuals whose family was given a title by the Empire, the Restoration and the July Monarchy.

12 The number of nobles is not precisely known. On the number of nobles in 1789 see Guy Chaussinand-Nogaret, *The French Nobility in the Eighteenth Century: from Feudalism to Enlightenment* (Cambridge, 1985). David Higgs, *Nobles*, p. 28, has produced a table summing up different evaluations for the nineteenth century. These evaluations give 45 000 families in 1820, 17 000 in 1830 and only 15 246 in 1840.

13 7 'chevaliers', 34 'barons', 20 'vicomtes', 64 'comtes' and 37 'marquis'.

14 It is generally assumed that there is a relationship between technical progress and economic growth. However, economists and economic historians have expressed different views on the nature of this relationship. These views have been discussed by François Caron, 'Pour une économie de l'innovation', in *Les Brevets. Leur utilisation en histoire des techniques et de l'économie', Table ronde, CNRS, Château du CNRS à Gif-sur-Yvette, 6 et 7 décembre 1984*, Paris, IHMC, 1985, pp. 7–18,

15 The information on the inventors is taken from various sources: dictionaries, *Catalogue des livres imprimés de la Bibliothèque nationale* and various newspapers such as the *Journal des usines* and the *Bulletins de la Société d'encouragement pour l'industrie nationale.*

16 On Jouffroy d'Abbans see Félix Rivet, *La Navigation à vapeur sur la Saône et le Rhône (1783–1863)* (Paris, Presses Universitaires de France, 1962).

17 On the Saint-Cricq Cazaux family and their manufactures see Maddy Aries, *La Manufacture de Creil, 1797–1895* (Fontenay-le-Comte, Librairie Guenegaud, 1974).

18 *Bulletin de la Société d'encouragement pour l'industrie nationale* (1843), p. 443.

19 Bennett Woodcroft, *Alphabetical Index of Patentees of Inventions from 2 March 1617 to October 1851* (first published London, 1854, facsimile edition, London, Evelyn, Adams and MacKay, 1969).

20 *Bulletin de la Société d'encouragement pour l'industrie nationale* (1841), pp. 325–6, 1843, p. 353.

21 See Michel Hau, *L'Industrialisation de l'Alsace : 1803–1939* (Strasbourg, Association des publications auprès des universités de Strasbourg, 1987).

22 Archives nationales, F^{12} 5263.

23 Ludmila Pimenova, 'Analyse de cahiers de doléances : l'exemple des cahiers de la noblesse', *Mélanges de l'Ecole française de Rome, Italie et Méditerranée* 103 (1991–2), pp. 85–101.

24 *Notice sur le duc de Praslin, par M. le baron de Gerando* (Société d'encouragement pour l'industrie nationale, August 1841).

14

Inaugural Acts, Prefatory Texts: Paratextual Strategies for Restoring the Monarchy and a Theatre

Barbara T. Cooper

On 26 December 1814, some seven months after Louis XVIII returned to France to reclaim the throne of his forebears, the *Théâtre de la Porte Saint-Martin* reopened its doors and once again began offering Parisian theatregoers a variety of popular entertainments.[1] While the connection between Louis' return from exile and the resumption of dramatic performances at the *Porte Saint-Martin* theatre might not be immediately apparent, the two events were nonetheless intimately related. Indeed, had it not been for the King and for his first Interior minister, the Abbé de Montesquiou, the playhouse, closed by Napoleon some two years earlier, might well have remained darkened and deserted. By agreeing to the resumption of stage shows at the theatre, the monarch and his minister quite likely hoped to score a propaganda coup. Such a gesture would not only erase a visible sign of the former Emperor's control over the performing arts, but would also highlight the peace and prosperity expected to follow the restoration of the Bourbon régime. After all, as supporters of the Restoration were quick to proclaim, human and economic resources, no longer required for foreign wars or domestic defence, could now be used to revitalise the arts, commerce, and industry.[2] This chapter suggests, however, that timing and political expediency are not the only things that link the reopening of the *Porte Saint-Martin* theatre and Louis XVIII's return to power. Careful examination of the preamble to the constitutional charter (*La Charte*) granted by the King in 1814 and the text of *Le Boulevard Saint-Martin*, a one-act prologue written for the reopening of the theatre, reveals yet another connection between the two events. Using similar techniques of audience manipulation and self-fashioning, both of these paratextual documents seek to persuade the public of the benefits that will accrue from the revival of an abandoned institution (the Bourbon monarchy, a Boulevard play-house).

Normally, one would not think of comparing the preamble to a con-stitutional document with a prologue marking the opening of a theatre. If, however, we set aside our usual preoccupation with disciplinary boundaries, we are more likely to observe the functional similarities between these two Restoration texts. It is, after all, just such a focus on function that has led scholars like Gérard Genette to consider more fully the role played by prologues, prefaces, and other introductory materials in our apprehension of the works they precede. Such prefatory materials, as Genette has shown, serve as a space of transition between the world of the reader and the world of the text and are the site of a transaction or negotiation between the audience and the author of the paratext which we would do well to keep in mind in the analysis that follows.[3]

The first, and no doubt most pertinent, observation that can be made with regard to Désaugier and Brazier's *Le Boulevard Saint-Martin* is that it owes its composition to circumstance.[4] It is not surprising, therefore, that the most significant threads running through this one-act *prologue d'inauguration mêlé de vaudevilles* [inaugural prologue interspersed with vaudeville acts] are firstly an attempt to entice potential 'customers' to 'purchase' the 'wares' now 'for sale' in the newly reopened theatre, and secondly the need to acknowledge and express gratitude to the King whose return and licence-granting authority have made the resumption of performances there possible. This combination of a marketing strat-egy coupled with a political strategy gives the prologue its distinctive character.

As the title of the drama suggests, the setting for Désaugier and Bra-zier's piece is a street scene on the Boulevard Saint-Martin. Initially, the audience sees the exterior façade of the *Porte Saint-Martin* theatre and the doors to the restaurant and café that adjoin it. Baskets of oysters and an oyster shucker's chair are set up outside the restaurant. Opposite the theatre is the home of Saint-Albin, the new director-manager of the playhouse. It is there in the street that a chorus of female merchants and the Muse of the Boulevards take turns singing the stanzas of the opening musical passage or *vaudeville* in Scene i.

Using the *poissard* speech patterns that popular dramatists typically assign to members of the merchant class, the streetsellers sing the lines: 'Ach'tez, belles,/Ach'tez nous,/J'ons des marchandis' nouvelles;/Ach'tez, Messieurs, ach'tez nous,/J'ons d'quoi servir tous les goûts' [Buy my pretty ones,/Buy our wares/Let's enjoy the new products/Buy sirs, Buy our wares/There's something for everyone] (i, 3).[5] This patter, designed to attract the attention of men and women of all tastes and classes to the goods the women purvey, is repeated at intervals three more times. While clearly meant to reproduce a spectacle seen and heard daily on Parisian boulevards, the words sung by the street vendors might just as easily apply to the plays and the actors that the theatre administration is hoping to 'sell' as to the oysters, cakes, and other products the characters are hawking on stage.

In between the vendors' repeated calls to buy their merchandise, the Muse of the Boulevards sings about her role as provider of popular amusements. She first declares: '...Aux jeux de Momus,/L'olivier qui nous courrone/Permet qu'enfin je donne/Un temple de plus' [To Momus' games/The crowning olive branch/Allows me to garnish one more tribute] (i, 3). Calling upon the theatre to awaken from its slumber, the Muse proclaims: 'Quand un doux avenir/Nous réchauffe de ses flammes,/Tu dois, comme nos âmes,/T'ouvrir au plaisir' [When a sweet memory/Warms us with its flames/You must let yourself/Be opened up to pleasure/As our souls are] (i, 4). Both of these statements explicitly connect the reopening of the theatre to the restoration of peace and the bright future that is sure to follow the Bourbons' return to power. Later, after listening to Javotte, the oyster shucker complains about the hard times she continues to endure, the Muse exclaims, 'Ah! que votre plainte est injuste!/Quoi! vous ne gagnez pas assez,/Quand par le coeur d'un prince auguste/Tous vos malheurs sont effacés?/Lorsque la paix, son digne ouvrage,/Dans vos fils vous rend un appui...' [Ah! but your complaint is unfair/That you don't earn enough/Even though through the auspices of an august prince/All your misfortunes are wiped away/When peace, his worthy work/Gives you support in your sons] (i, 4). Urging Javotte not to give up hope for better days, the Muse announces that; 'Ce théâtre (bis)/Dont Paris fut idolâtre,/Ce théâtre/.../Bientôt ressuscitera' [This theatre (repeat)/Whose idol was Paris/This theatre/.../Will soon revive] (i, 5). After this exchange, which once again links the return of peace and the reopening of the *Porte Saint-Martin* theatre to the restoration of Louis XVIII, the Muse and the chorus together sing about the promise of the future.

Peace, prosperity, and the restoration of the Bourbon monarchy are not the only conditions essential to the success of the newly reopened theatre, however. The audience must be convinced that the spectacles performed at the *Porte Saint-Martin* will be of a kind and quality guaranteed to assure their satisfaction. The business of 'selling' the management, cast, and repertoire of the playhouse will thus soon replace the paean to the King as the primary focus of the prologue's remaining scenes. First, however,

Nigaudin, transporting a number of backdrops and stage machines on his back and in his pockets, appears on the Boulevard Saint-Martin. After he announces to Javotte and the cake seller that his master, Saint-Albin, has been granted permission to reopen the theatre (Scene ii), the new manager, accompanied by shopkeepers, street merchants, and others living in the neighbourhood, arrives as well. Saint-Albin's first words, spoken after a musical exchange with the shopkeepers and area vendors, once again sound the theme of gratitude for peace and hope for collective prosperity that comes with the return of the King.

> SAINT-ALBIN. How wonderful my friends, everyone share my joy and congratulate me for the happy privilege which will give hope to a hundred families, revive our trade and double the value of your property. A BOURGEOIS. We have been waiting for such a long time. SAINT-ALBIN. We needed nothing less than the return of peace and the prince who grants it to us but that is not all.
>
> (iii, 8–9).

So that all hearts will have reason to rejoice at the King's return, Saint-Albin tells his listeners, the monarch has generously granted him the right to produce a variety of spectacles: comedy, pantomime, melodrama, and vaudeville. This, as Nigaudin observes, means that there will be speaking, singing, dancing, and mimed actions – in short, something for everyone – at the reopened theatre. Before the merchants return to their daily business, Saint-Albin addresses them once more. He tells them: 'Come my friends, go and spread the good news to all your neighbours and tell them that this is a doubly precious privilege because I will be able to serve both their interests and pleasures.'(iii, 9). His words are ripe with an implied parallel between the theatre manager and the King, whom Saint-Albin has previously described as eager to guarantee the prosperity and the pleasures of his people. Both men, it would seem, share a sense of responsibility for and feelings of (paternal) benevolence toward those whose fate and happiness depend on the success of their (political or theatrical) enterprise.

Left alone in the street, Nigaudin wonders just how well the reopened theatre will fare. Imagining what it will be like on the opening night, he conjures up an image not only of the audience (a great number of beautiful women and handsome men will fill the house), but also of the inaugural prologue and its reception. 'La toile s'lève et l'on commence/Par un prologue d'circonstance;/On applaudit du bas en haut,/ Oh! oh! (bis)/On rit par ci, l'on claq' par là!/Oh! oh! (bis)/Jarni! (bis) l'beau jour qu'ça f'ra!/Il m'semb'déjà qu'j'entends tout ça. (4 fois)/Bis par ci,/Bis par là/ Bon! c'est ça,/V'là qu'ça va' [The curtain rises/And they begin/With an appropriate prologue/They clap from the floor to the rafters/ Oh! Oh! (repeat)/Laughing here, clapping there/ Oh! Oh! (repeat)/Jarni! (repeat) it will be a great day!/I can just picture it already (4 times)/Encore here, Encore there/Good that's great/It will all be fine (iv, 10). This vision, while only partly prophetic – a journalist for the *Gazette de France* writes that the theatre boxes had been booked at least a month in advance of the première and that Désaugiers and Brazier were well known for their wit and gaiety[6] – is, of course, designed both to flatter and to manipulate the audience. It is, in fact, quite likely that the line 'I can just picture it already', which Nigaudin repeats four times, probably with broadly comic gestures and emphases, provoked the very laughter and applause of which the valet speaks. Given that Nigaudin's imagined first-night vision is preceded by his wishful thinking about future box office receipts, it is also clear that these lines and the scenes that follow are intended to make the much-desired and fervently anticipated economic well-being of the theatre a reality.

In order to persuade audience members to return regularly to the *Porte Saint-Martin*, Désaugiers and Brazier devote Scenes v to xiv of the prologue to the introduction of those actors whose performance skills will be crucial to the success of the newly reopened theatre. Individually or in pairs, each of the company's players thus arrives on stage to 'audition' for his or her part in the (re)nascent theatrical enterprise. Some of the individuals 'hired' to join the troupe appear to be 'ordinary folk' whose 'real-life' character and talents make them ideally suited for traditional dramatic *emplois* or lines of business (*cf.* Scenes v and vi). Others are experienced 'actors' who have so well mastered their roles that they are able to pass in 'real life' for the kinds of characters they customarily portray (*cf.* Scene ix and the beginning of Scene x). In every case, there is a deliberate, and intentionally comic, confusion between reality and appearance as actors and actresses superimpose one layer of performance upon another while they execute their conventionally prescribed and pre-scripted parts. In addition to displaying the talents of the troupe, most of whose members were already familiar to Parisian audiences from their successes at other theatrical venues in the French capital,[7] this parade of characters also provides one more opportunity to (quite literally) sing the praises of Louis XVIII. Thus, when asked to try her hand at singing a *chanson poissarde*, Javotte, the oyster shucker, chooses a tune '[...] qui est dans toutes les rues et dans toutes les bouches. C'est c't'elle-là qu'les dames d'la Halle ont été chanter à not' bon Roi, l'jour d'son r'tour dans sa bonne ville d'Paris' [Which you can hear on every street corner from everyone. That is what the Halles market women went to sing to our good King the day he came back to his fair city of Paris] (x, 22).

While there is a temptation to quote all three stanzas of the song Javotte sings, the last one is particularly well suited to the purpose of this chapter and must serve to represent the tenor of the whole.[8] It reads: 'C'Prince, l'meilleur des meilleurs,/N'connoît ni hain', ni vengeance,/ Quand j'lons abreuvé d'douleurs;/C'est lui qui finit nos pleurs/Et nos malheurs./Pour not' rébellion,/Il nous rapporte en France,/La joie et l'union;/C'est ben un' punition/A la Bourbon,/A, à, à la Bourbon' [This prince, the best of the best/Knows neither hatred nor vengeance/When we are overcome with pain/He will stop our tears/And our woes/For our rebellion/He brings back to France for us/Joy and unity/It's really our punishment/In the Bourbon style/In the, in the Bourbon style] (x, 22). As we shall see in a moment, some of this language echoes that used in the preamble to the *Charte* and in other works of Bourbon propaganda. It also secures a job for Javotte as a member of the troupe. Not surprisingly, the role she will 'play' on stage coincides with the one she already holds in 'life': that of a *poissarde* [fishwife].

After all the personnel required for the successful operation of the theatre have been hired, Nigaudin wonders what kinds of plays his master is likely to produce (Scene xv). Upon a sign from the Muse of the Boulevards, who has overheard his question, the set shifts and a magnificent temple is revealed. Scenes xvi to xviii bring actors incarnating the allegorical figures of Melodrama, Pantomime, and Vaudeville on to the stage one after the other.[9] Each performs an abbreviated and thoroughly conventional sample of the kind of play he or she represents. In the final song of Scene xviii, with Vaudeville, 'the enfans de Momus', and the other actors on stage, the troupe proclaims its desire to please the public and to work harder than rival companies to achieve that end. The nineteenth and last scene in the play shows Love presiding over the theatre as the players, addressing the audience, sing: 'Soyez pour nous ce que vient d'être/Un prince que nous adorons,/Par lui nous venons de renaître,/Mais c'est par vous que nous vivrons' [Be for us what has just been shown/A prince that we adore/We have come back to life through him/But it is through you that we shall live] (xix, 40). The very last lines of the play are again directed to the audience members and designed to dictate both their immediate response and their future actions: 'Dites sans cesse: *"Nous reviendrons"'* [Say over and over again: *"We shall return"*] (xix, 40; emphasis in original). This closing scene thus once again highlights the intimate relationship between the political and the economic motives that underlie the entire prologue. Looking back over the text of the prologue, it is clear that Désaugier's and Brazier's brief drama seeks to communicate certain political ideas to the audience and to shape the public's response to the new administration and the new acting company setting up for business at the *Porte Saint-Martin* theatre. To that end, the play uses flattery and scenes that intentionally seek to blur the difference between reality and representation. The lines of demarcation between actors and characters and between the actual and the painted scene of the action are purposely obscured. What may be just as important as this game of illusions, however, are the characteristics ascribed to the *Porte Saint-Martin*'s new manager, Saint-Albin.

If we look closely at the portrait of the manager-director described in Désaugier's and Brazier's play, we shall discover a character who is intimately involved in the operation of his theatre and who has carefully selected the personnel best suited to carry out his projects. An engaged and active leader, Saint-Albin is also shown to be judicious, generous, and caring. He is concerned both with providing quality entertainment for his audience and with improving the lot of his neighbours whose future success is tied directly to his own. Whether this representation of M. Saint-Romain, the actual licence-holder of the *Porte Saint-Martin*, was accurate or not is rather beside the point. What is important is that the authors of the prologue chose to represent him in such a manner. As we shall see, a similar image of administrative competence and reasoned benevolence can also be found in the preamble to the constitutional charter Louis XVIII bestowed upon his countrymen after returning to France.

Improbable as it may seem, the *Charte* of 1814, like *Le Boulevard Saint-Martin*, was a work whose composition was dictated by circumstance. 'In 1814', writes constitutional historian Pierre Rosanvallon, 'it was more a matter of dressing the wounds of history than simply organising public powers. The question of the Revolution and the means to end it still overweigh French constitutional history.'[10] What is true of the overall document is especially true of its preamble.[11] Drafted at the last moment by one of the King's closest advisors, Count Jean-Claude Beugnot, the prefatory text was read to the assembled members of the *Chambre des députés* [the lower house] and the *Chambre des pairs* [the upper house] on 4 June without Louis XVIII previously having seen it.

Just as *Le Boulevard Saint-Martin* attempts to 'sell' a newly reopened theatre to the public and to foster a positive image of its personnel and its repertoire, so does the Preamble to the *Charte* of 1814 seek to 'market' a newly restored government and to promote a particular view of the Head of State. The 'audience' for Louis' prefatory remarks was, as we have seen, initially made up of the members of the two legislative branches of government. Beyond that immediate public, however, the King was no doubt conscious of the fact that his text would reach the men and women of France and the rulers of those allied nations (Russia, Prussia, England, and Austria) whose military forces had brought an end to Napoleon's reign. Thus, the image of the monarch and the monarchy found in the preamble is perhaps just as important as the articles of law and procedure it introduces.

A salutation, included at the beginning of the preamble when it was first published in 1814, but omitted from more recent printings of the text, reads: 'Louis, by the grace of God, King of France and Navarre, to all those here present, greetings!'[12] When considered together with the opening words of the preamble ('Divine Providence, having recalled us to our Estates after a long absence [...]') and the concluding formula, also absent from recent printings of the document ('Decreed in Paris in the year of our Lord and in the nineteenth year of our reign'),[13] it is clear that the King wished to put forward the idea that his authority and legitimacy came from God. Such a vision would not only justify the restoration of Bourbon rule, but would also counter the impression that Louis' return to power had been imposed by the forces successfully allied against Napoleon. It is also apparent that, by claiming the title of 'King of France and Navarre' and by declaring 1814 to be the nineteenth year of his reign, Louis was attempting both to attach his regime to those of his Bourbon ancestors and to erase the Revolution, the Directory, the Consulate, and the Empire from the official annals of French history.[14]

It would, however, be a mistake to view the preamble as nothing more than an attempt to put forward *ancien-régime* views of the monarch and the monarchy. While that prefatory text does indeed endeavour to reauthorise certain royal powers and prerogatives, it also recognises that events of the past half-century have made changes in governmental operations necessary. To make those changes appear to be the consequence of the King's wisdom and beneficence rather than the result of historical and political pressures imposed upon him, the preamble declares the concession of limited forms of power-sharing to be a long-standing royal tradition in France. 'Nous avons considéré que, bien que l'autorité tout entière résidât en France dans la personne du roi, ses prédécesseurs n'avaient point hésité à en modifier l'exercice, suivant la différence des temps... [We consider that authority in France rests wholly with the King although our predecessors did not hesitate to modify its exercise according to changing circumstances] (p. 9).[15] Having concluded that the time for change has once again arrived, Louis claims that he is ready to grant his people's request for a constitutional charter. Nonetheless, he insists, '... en cédant à ce voeu, nous avons pris toutes les précautions pour que cette Charte fût digne de nous et du peuple auquel nous sommes fiers de commander' [by granting this wish we have taken every precaution to ensure that this Charter is worthy of us and of the people we are proud to command] (p. 10).

The portrait of the King that emerges from these passages of the preamble is one of a wise and prudent monarch who is not only conscious of his rights and mindful of the institutional traditions that have best served his country, but who is also aware of the changed circumstances under which he must now exercise his authority. Affirming his own supreme power ('commander') and his willingness to listen to the legitimate supplications ('voeu') of those over whom he exercises a God-given control, Louis wishes to 'lier tous les souvenirs à toutes les espérances' [relate all the memories to all the hopes] (p. 11). At once caring and cautious ('précautions', 'digne de nous et du peuple'), he will agree to forge a new relationship with his subjects provided that it connects the present to the past and guarantees the security and stability of both the country and the monarchy ('renouer la chaîne des tems que de funestes écarts avaient interrompue') [renew the chain of time that ill-considered behaviour had broken] (p. 12).

It is not merely the broken links in the chain of history that Louis wishes to repair, however. Without claiming for himself the thaumaturgic powers traditionally ascribed to the Kings of France, Louis does assert his wish to bring a form of healing to his people:

> ...Nous avons effacé de notre souvenir, comme nous voudrions qu'on pût les effacer de l'histoire, tous les maux qui ont affligé la patrie durant notre absence. Heureux de nous retrouver au sein de la grande famille, nous n'avons su répondre à l'amour dont nous recevons tant de témoignages, qu'en prononçant des paroles de paix et de consolation. Le voeu le plus cher à notre coeur, c'est que tous les Français vivent en frères, et que jamais aucun souvenir amer ne trouble la sécurité qui doit suivre l'acte solennel que nous leur accordons aujourd'hui. [We have erased from our memory what we would like to erase from history, all the misfortunes which have afflicted the country during our absence. Happy to find ourselves back in the heart of a great family, we have only been able to respond lovingly to all the manifestations of love by making speeches of peace and comfort. Our

most heartfelt wish is for all Frenchmen to live as brothers and that no
bitter memory should trouble security which should ensue from the
solemn act which we grant them today]

(p. 12)

The royal voice heard in these lines takes on a distinctly paternal tone.
Instead of describing the French as a people long divided by political
factions and ideological differences, Louis represents them as a *grande
famille* racked by flawed judgements and ill-considered behaviours that
took place at a time when they were deprived of his fatherly wisdom and
guidance. The disagreements of the past ought now to be set aside and
forgotten, the King asserts. Stimulated by his words of peace and con-
solation, the French should once more endeavour to see themselves as
brothers united by a common bond of love for their sovereign and a
shared desire for security. (Needless to say, this type of fraternity has
nothing whatsoever to do with that espoused by the proponents of the
Revolution.)

There is, of course, nothing terribly original about the role the preamble ascribes to the King. The image of the monarch as a wise and
generous father who is the architect of domestic peace and unity and the
guarantor of national security was as conventional and as clichéd as any
of the jobs depicted in *Le Boulevard Saint-Martin*. However, in striking
such a conciliatory and paternal pose, the King may have hoped to allay
the fears of those who worried that his return would cause them to lose
some of their recent social, political, or economic gains. By holding out
the promise of unity and oblivion – the former notion embodied in such
terms as 'family' and 'brothers' and the latter contained in the phrase
'erase from memory' – Louis may also have been seeking to soften the
more assertive, less tractable side of the royal persona that the preamble
also sets forth. If that were the intention, however, it does not appear to
have had the desired effect.

In the final lines of the preamble, the King declares: ' . . . Nous avons
volontairement, et par le libre exercice de notre autorité Royale, accordé
et accordons, fait concession et octroi à nos sujets, tant pour nous que
pour nos prédécesseurs [sic for successeurs], et à toujours de la Charte
constitutionnelle qui suit' [We have willingly and by the free exercise of
our Royal authority, granted and do grant as a concession and bestowal
to our subjects, as much for us as for our predecessors [*sic* for successors]
and for all time the constitutional Charter below] (p. 12). The word *octroi*
[a grant or bestowal] struck some opponents of the Restoration as representing an unacceptable return to the vocabulary and the posture of

France's pre-Revolutionary rulers. Rather than acceding to a modification in the relationship between the monarch and his people, by this word, Louis makes it clear that he has favoured his subjects with his generous concession. Former deputy Jacques-Charles Bailleul, looking back at the text of the preamble in 1819, also objected to the reference to past ills needing to be erased from memory.

Effacer le *souvenir des maux qui ont affligé la patrie,* était sans doute un but digne d'une ame généreuse; mais il semble qu'on remontait un peu haut; il ne fallait pas laisser à des esprits déjà tourmentés, la chance de croire, au moins, d'après le vague de l'expression, car je suis convaincu de la pureté des intentions, que l'on avait voulu confondre avec des maux trop réels, des principes devenus depuis longtemps les lois fondamentales de l'état... Il ne fallait pas oublier l'époque où ces principes avaient été reconnus et consacrés, et moins encore la défense du sol de la patrie, de son indépendance et de ses droits... [To wipe out the *memory of the misfortunes which had afflicted the country* was no doubt a generous act worthy of a generous soul; but it seemed to go a bit far; it would have been better to have been less ambiguous rather than let the tormented minds think there was hope because I am convinced the intentions were honourable that the real misfortunes were confused with what have long become fundamental principles of state... It was better not to forget the moment when these principles had been recognised and sanctified, and even more important the defence of the country, its independence and its rights...][16]

Both of the paratexts examined here – the preamble to the *Charte* of 1814 and *Le Boulevard Saint-Martin* – were put forward as the 'inaugural' acts of a revived (political or cultural) institution. While neither text truly constitutes the first public display of the operational practices and administrative intentions that would guide the workings of the monarchy or the theatre, both documents do offer their audience an official image of the way those organisations wished to be perceived.[17] For all their similarities, however, there are some fundamental differences between these two prefatory texts.

As seen earlier, both the preamble and the prologue recognise and acknowledge the legitimating authority that serves as the guarantor of a restored institution's rights and privileges (God or Providence, in the case of the Bourbon monarchy; Louis XVIII, in the case of the *Porte Saint-Martin* theatre). Both texts also seemingly admit that the public (comprising the King's subjects and the legislative bodies that represent them, the theatre's audiences) has a role in determining the future success of the re-established enterprise. What distinguishes one document from the other, though, is the nature of the relationship that it suggests exists between each institution and its constituents.

Whereas *Le Boulevard Saint-Martin* emphasises the reopened theatre's total dependence on the public's satisfaction with its future undertakings 'Soyez pour nous ce que vient d'être/Un prince que nous adorons,/Par lui nous venons de renaître,/Mais c'est par vous que nous vivrons' [Be for us our restoration/A prince whom we idolise/Through him we have just come back to life/But through you we shall live] (xix, 40), the preamble to the *Charte* suggests that the restored monarch is much less dependent on the approval of his people. It is as a result of his magnanimity, wisdom, and sense of dynastic tradition that Louis agrees to grant ('fai[re] concession et octroi à') his subjects some of the changes they had solicited. They depend on his heartfelt concern for their welfare and his sense of duty to God and country. He may look to them for their continued expressions of love, but insists that they respect his authority.

These differences in the rapport between the theatre and its public and the monarch and his people are not entirely surprising. After all, as an economic entity, the *Porte Saint-Martin* theatre had to contend with such market forces as freedom of choice (in the use of one's disposable income) and competition among similarly positioned playhouses (similar not only by virtue of their geographic location on the Parisian boulevards, but also as a result of their repertoire and pricing structure). Despite the historic experience of Revolution, however, in France in 1814, the free consent of the governed was not a prerequisite for political legitimacy and authority. Whatever currents of liberalism may have been abroad in the country – and these were by no means negligible during the Restoration – they do not seem to have wielded the same power as the market economy to effect change. Still, the language of the preamble notwithstanding, Louis XVIII understood that the age of absolute monarchy had passed.[18] That his brother and successor, Charles X, understood that lesson less well was clearly part of what would bring about his overthrow in 1830.

Notes

1   The *Porte Saint-Martin* theatre was authorised to perform melodramas, panto-mimes, and *vaudevilles* (comedies with musical couplets generally sung to familiar tunes). The playbill on opening night featured an inaugural prologue by M.-A.-M. Désaugiers and N. Brazier, *Le Boulevard Saint-Martin, ou Nous y voilà!* (Paris, Barba, 1815) and a three-act melodrama by J.-G.-A. Cuvelier de Trie, *Le Vieux de la montagne, ou les Arabes du Liban* (Paris, Barba, 1815). One of the final pieces of the inaugural twelve-month period was Delestre-Poirson [pseud., Ch.-G. Poirson] and Eug. Scribe's one-act vaudeville, *Encore une nuit de la Garde nationale, ou le Poste de barrière* (Paris, Fages, 1815).

2   A. Hus, a Bourbon apologist, makes this point explicitly in his brief pamphlet, *Le 25 août 1819, ou la Fête de S[a] M[ajesté] Louis XVIII, des beaux-arts et de l'industrie française* (Paris, Rougeron, 1819), p. 2: 'The era of the *royal Charters* has arrived, the words *history, posterity* resound in the ears of princes, and a sound liberty has just tied the sacred knots which link kings to their people for the happiness of nations and for the glorious immortality of Kings. [...] The *Odéon* [a Parisian theatre] rises from its ruins. Melpomène and Thalie [the Muses of tragedy and comedy] will soon have two temples worthy of it [the Odéon and the Théâtre-Français], of France and of the Minister of the Interior, to whom all noble, useful *brilliant ideas* henceforth belong.' [emphases in the original] See, too, a proclamation, signed by Count Roger de Damas and published under the rubric 'Intérieur' in the *Moniteur officiel*, 165 (14 June 1814), 654, which likewise claims that resources once squandered on war will now be used to restore agriculture, industry, and so on.

3   Gérard Genette's *Seuils* (Paris, Seuil, 1987) has been followed by many other studies on paratexts.

4   The practice of composing a 'prologue d'ouverture' for the (re)opening of a theatre was, of course, always circumstantial and always designed to promote a new troupe or theatre. Consider, for example, A. Martainville's *Le Mariage du Mélodrame et de la Gaîeté, scène d'inauguration* (Paris, Barba, 1808), first performed at the Théâtre de la Gaîeté on 26 March 1808, or *Le Panorama de Momus, prologue d'inauguration* (Paris, Barba, 1807) by M.-A.-M. Désaugiers, *et al.*, first performed at the Théâtre des Variétés on 24 June 1807. Other examples of this type include C.-F. Moreau [de Commagny], Scribe and Mélesville's *Le Boulevard Bonne-Nouvelle* (Paris, Fages, 1820), a prologue written for the inauguration of the Gymnase dramatique on 23 December 1820, and P.-F.-A. Carmouche and M.-N. Balisson de Rougemont's *Monsieur Boulevard* (Paris, E. Buissot, 1821), first presented on 14 April 1821 for the opening of the Panorama dramatique. On this phenomenon, see B.T. Cooper, 'Stimulating the Theatre Public in Early Nineteenth-Century French Dramatised Prologues', *Romance Notes*, 30 (1989), 149–59.

5   In order to eliminate unnecessary footnotes, this and all future references to the prologue by Désaugier and Brazier will be made parenthetically, in the text, by scene and page number.

6   'France. Paris, 26 décembre.' *Gazette de France*, 361 (27 décembre 1814), 2: 'The prettiest women of Paris seem to have descended on this theatre [le Porte Saint-Martin]; all the boxes had been booked for a month. The inaugural prologue was a runaway success. It displayed all the wit and humour of Messrs. Désau-

giers and Brazier.' The theatre's audience was also composed of men and women of lesser means than those who rented the boxes. For a general description of those who filled the rest of the house, see p. 2 in C., 'Théâtre de la Porte Saint-Martin. Pour l'ouverture de la salle...', *Journal des Débats* (28 décembre 1814), pp. 1–4, *feuilleton*. See, also, p. 2 in A. Martainville, 'Théâtre de la Porte Saint-Martin. *Ouverture.*' *Journal de Paris*, 361 (27 décembre 1814), 1–3, *feuilleton*: 'This ingenious prologue which has initiated or renewed the acquaintance of the actors with the Parisian public, has provoked applause and mirth. This popularity and gaiety comes as no surprise when we learn that the Director had made Messrs. Désaugiers et Brazier responsible for the prologue.'

7   Several of the drama critics reviewing the play mention this recognition factor while noting that these particular players had never before performed together in the same troupe. See, for example, the descriptions in D.C.y., 'Théâtre de la Porte Saint-Martin (pour l'ouverture)', p. 2; *La Quotidienne*, 213 (30 décembre 1814), 2–3, *feuilleton*, and in Martainville, 'Théâtre', p. 2.

8   Sung to the tune of a song entitled '*A la Papa*', each stanza concludes with the same refrain: 'A la Bourbon,/A, à, à la Bourbon.' It would be surprising if the audience did not sing these words along with the actress by the time she reached the second and third stanzas. According to the critic for the *Journal des Débats*, 'The ease, the popular reception for the way in which the most august name was inserted into the chorus of a fishwife's vaudeville song especially delighted the audience and roused lively applause' (C., 'Théâtre de la Porte Saint-Martin,' pp. 2–3). It is also likely that the tune to which this praise of Louis XVIII is sung was chosen precisely because the original text, '*A la Papa*' further underscores the message of paternal benevolence attached to the new words. On this and other dimensions of reused melodies, see B.T. Cooper, 'Playing It Again: a Study of *Vaudeville* and the Aesthetics of Incorporation in Restoration France,' *Nineteenth-Century Contexts*, 13. 2 (1989), pp. 197–210.

9   For a rapid review of the history of Boulevard theatres in this period, see Marvin Carlson, *The French Stage in the Nineteenth Century* (Mitten, NJ, Scarecrow Press, 1972), pp. 41–53.

10   Pierre Rosanvallon, *La Monarchie impossible. Les Chartes de 1814 et 1830* (Paris, Fayard, 1994), p. 15. See also Rosanvallon's observation that 'Even the fact that it [the *Charte*] had been written so speedily and with so little attention by Louis XVIII is significant. It is not based on any set of well-thought-out principles because it was considered to be simply a document for that moment...' (p. 61).

11   In fact, according to another constitutional specialist, Jacques Godechot, 'The preamble... is the section of the text which bears the strongest hallmark of the Restoration', in Jacques Godechot (ed.), *Les Constitutions de la France depuis 1789* (Paris, GF-Flammarion, 1979; rev. edn. 1993), p. 214.

12   *Charte constitutionnelle* (Paris, Hacquart, impr. de la Chambre des Députés, [1814]), p. 9. The preamble and charter may also be found in Godechot, pp. 217–19, and in Rosanvallon, pp. 250–51.

13   *Charte*, pp. 9 and 30, respectively. In order to eliminate unnecessary footnotes, all future quotations from the preamble should be understood to refer to the 1814 text and will be made parenthetically in this chapter.

14   Louis XVIII is thus presented as having acceded to the throne of his ancestors upon the death of Louis XVII, the son of Louis XVI who had died in the Temple prison 19 years earlier. In his analysis of *Les vrais principes de l'église gallicane* (Paris, impr. A. Le Clere, 1818), p. 149, Bishop Denis-Luc Frayssinous would later explain that 'It was important for the triumph of legitimacy that the successor of so many kings should not date his reign from the day he first entered the capital.' I wish again to make clear that in ascribing the authorship and apparent purposes of the preamble to the King, I am using a type of shorthand since that text was not actually written by Louis.

15   See Munro Price's chapter on the Bishop of Pamiers for other allusions to this 'antique constitution' in this volume.

16   Jacques-Charles Bailleul, *Situation de la France considérée sous les rapports politiques, religieux, administratifs, financiers, commerciaux, etc.* (Paris, Ant. Bailleul, December 1819), p. 33 (emphasis in the original).

17   Fr.-D. de Reynaud, Comte de Montlosier, *De la monarchie française* (Paris, Nicolle *et al.*, 1814), p. 397, makes an interesting observation on a related point: 'Here, something of primary significance must be pointed out, that to constitute is not to create. Thus, as the word itself indicates it is to establish. After having sought in existing relationships the rule which governs these relationships one must then reveal this rule and declare it to be the law.'

18   For additional background on the life of Louis XVIII, see also Jacques Bonin and Paul Didier, *Louis XVIII, roi de deux peuples: 1814–1816* (Paris, Albatros, 1978), Philip Mansel, *Louis XVIII* (London, Blond and Briggs, 1981), and Evelyne Lever, *Louis XVIII* (Paris, Fayard, 1988).

Index